Isaac Newton
and the Temple
of Solomon

Isaac Newton and the Temple of Solomon

An Analysis of the Description and Drawings and a Reconstructed Model

TESSA MORRISON

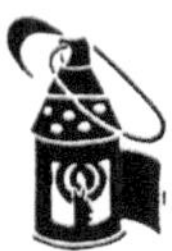

McFarland & Company, Inc., Publishers

Jefferson, North Carolina

Unless otherwise indicated, photographs are by the author.

Library of Congress Cataloguing-in-Publication Data

Names: Morrison, Tessa, 1954– author.
Title: Isaac Newton and the Temple of Solomon : an analysis of the description and drawings and a reconstructed model / Tessa Morrison.
Description: Jefferson, North Carolina : McFarland & Company, Inc., Publishers, 2016 | Includes bibliographical references and index.
Identifiers: LCCN 2016019642 | ISBN 9781476665542 (softcover : acid free paper) ∞
Subjects: LCSH: Temple of Jerusalem (Jerusalem)—Design and construction—Early works to 1800. | Newton, Isaac, 1642–1727—Knowledge—Architecture. | Temple of Jerusalem (Jerusalem)—In art. | Jerusalem—Buildings, structures, etc.
Classification: LCC NA243 .M67 2016 | DDC 726/.30933442—dc23
LC record available at https://lccn.loc.gov/2016019642

British Library cataloguing data are available

ISBN (print) 978-1-4766-6554-2
ISBN (ebook) 978-1-4766-2513-3

On the cover: Sir Isaac Newton © 2016 duncan1890/iStock; The Temple Precinct drawn by Newton Ms 434 (courtesy of the Huntington Library)

Printed in the United States of America

McFarland & Company, Inc., Publishers
Box 611, Jefferson, North Carolina 28640
www.mcfarlandpub.com

Acknowledgments

In this project I have used a wide range of Newton's unpublished manuscripts which have been generously made available by many libraries. I would particularly like to thank the Huntington Library for making public an excellent reproduction of Babson MS 434 which is the main manuscript this book is based on. I am grateful to the Newton Project at the University of Sussex for making many manuscripts public that would have been formally unobtainable. I would also like to thank the staff of the Rare Books and Manuscript Rooms of the British Library who have been of great assistance in obtaining much of this material and a big thank you to the interlibrary loans staff at the University of Newcastle for their continued support in locating sources that sometimes appeared to be impossible to locate. Furthermore, I would like to thank my husband John for his continuous invaluable support and assistance.

Table of Contents

Preface

Isaac Newton had an interest in the Temple of Solomon that lasted more than fifty years, and culminated in his writing a manuscript that reconstructed the Temple precinct in words and six diagrams. He examined the Biblical measurements of the Temple by studying the length of the sacred Hebrew cubit. He analyzed the rituals performed in the Temple and the meaning of these rituals. Newton considered the vessels and the instruments used in the Temple. Finally, he examined its architecture, and in his unpublished manuscript entitled "A Treatise or Remarks on Solomon's Temple, Introduction to the Lexicon of the Prophets, Part Two: About the Appearance of the Jewish Temple," more commonly known by its call name Babson MS 434, he provided information from which reconstructions could be based. Newton did not date many of his manuscripts, and they can be notoriously difficult for others to do so because he recycled his papers over many years. However, from the style of the writing, it is thought that Babson MS 434 was written between the mid–1680s and the early 1690s. It is a working document with two reconstructions: the second is a refinement of the first, indicating that it could have been worked on over this period of time.

Babson MS 434 built on some of Newton's other unpublished manuscripts, but it is unique in that it focuses on the reconstruction of the Temple's architecture. Written in Latin, with some Greek and Hebrew expressions, Babson MS 434 uses the Book of Ezekiel as the main source to reconstruct the Temple, but it also supplements gaps of information in Ezekiel by examining and citing a wide range of Biblical texts, as well as the Greek text *Septuaginta*, texts in Hebrew and Vulgate Latin, the Alexandrian Codex, and the Arabian version of the Old Testament. In addition, Newton referred to Flavius Josephus's *Antiquitates Judaicae* (Antiquity of the Jews), *Bellum Judaicum* (The Jewish Wars), and *Contra*

Apionem (Against Apion); Philo's *Upon the Monarchy*; Maimonides's *De Apparatu Templi* (On the Apparatus Temple) and *Tratado sobre el culto divino* (Treatise upon the divine worship); Constantijn L'Empereur's *Talmudis Babylonici Codex Middoth, sive De Mensuris Templi*; Arias Montano's *De mensuris* (On Measurements); Johannes Buxtorf's *Lexicon Talmud*; and Walton's *Bible Polyglotta*. He also mentioned contemporary texts such as *In Ezechielem Explanationes et Apparatus Vrbis Templi Hierosolymitani* by Juan Battista Villalpando and Louis Cappel's commentary on Villalpando in *Trisagion sive Templi delineatio triplex Hierosolimitani* in Brian Walton's *Biblia Sacra Polyglotta*. Cappel and Johnannes Drusius are mentioned together without any reference. Finally, Newton also demonstrated a good knowledge of Vitruvius and his proportions and principles of architecture.

Babson MS 434 is over 80 pages of Newton's minute and tightly written script. The present author translated this manuscript in full, making it possible for her to actually build a reconstruction of the Temple based on Newton's description. This exhibition model was built at the Architecture and Built Environment Workshop at the University of Newcastle, Australia. It was constructed with an architectural modeling laser machine and involved fused deposition modeling—an additive manufacturing technology that is commonly used for modeling, prototyping, and production applications. The materials used include medium-density fiberboard (MDF) and acrylonitrile-butadiene-styrene (ABS) plastic. The model has 1,000 columns and 1,200 window grids, and it took over six months to build. The model was built by Ben Percy, and painted and decorated by the author.

In Babson MS 434, the description in his second reconstruction of the Temple fills in some of the "gray" areas of the first description. The architectural model of Newton's Temple in this book was built to the more complete second description. Most of the plan is clear but there is the occasional contradiction. For example, in the first description, Newton stated that there were twelve chambers in the separate place for the principals of the priests, but in the second description, he claimed there were fifteen. However, these contradictions are minor and concern internal features not shown in the model.

Newton did not mention how to access the upper floors of the Temple. There is no room to add any stairs internally in his plans and no stairs are added externally, since he did not mention any. Nor did he mention the number of floors on the top of the Temple. Newton gave thirty cubits as the interior height of the Temple, but the exterior height is given as 120 cubits. Both measurements are from Biblical sources but, unlike what he did with other anomalies in the Biblical text concerning the architecture of the Temple, Newton does not mention or try to explain the difference. Although this space on the top of the Temple is unexplained, it is a clear part of the architecture that Newton described. The only thing left to the author's invention was the colors of the Temple. Newton stated that the building was made of stone, but he did not state what type of stone was used, so sandstone was chosen. Inside the Temple, Newton described the appearance of the cherubim and how they were arranged facing a palm tree, but he did not indicate their colors. To address this, the typical colors found in the frescos from that region from the tenth century BC were used.

Newton was not the only one interested in the reconstruction of the Temple. In 1604, architect and Jesuit priest Juan Battista Villalpando published *In Ezechielem Explanationes et Apparatus Vreis Templi Hierosolymitani* (Ezekiel's explanation and the preparation of the city and of the Temple of Jerusalem), which contained a reconstruction of the Temple. The work took twenty years to make and the publication was an elaborate one, with forty-two detailed etchings, including some that folded out to over a meter wide. This expressive production could only be achieved with the sponsorship of Phillip II of Spain. Villalpando's reconstruction stimulated a debate on the architecture of the Temple consisting of both support and criticism of his reconstruction. Many other reconstructions were executed over the next 150 years. Most of these reconstructions remained only on paper, but some were built as architectural models. A few of these models were exhibited to the public for a fee and their reputation spread. Two models traveled to England in Newton's lifetime—the Schott model from Hamburg and Rabbi Jacob Judah Leon's model from Amsterdam. It is very likely that Newton was familiar with these models. He does not mention either of them in his manuscripts, but this would not have been unusual since, although Newton wrote a prolific number of manuscripts, he did not keep a diary, or at least none that have survived.

The public exhibitions of these models were very successful and guidebooks were sold that explained the features and the architecture of the models. The guidebooks "walked" the viewer through the model.

Separate images were also sold. Some surviving guidebooks have images of other reconstructions bound up with them, revealing that the viewer was not satisfied with only the one reconstruction. Their amazing popularity was a phenomenon of the time—a time when apocalyptic writing was all too common.

This book considers Newton's model of the Temple in conjunction with the models of the Temple that he possibly knew of and that were exhibited in London. It creates an illustrated guidebook of his reconstruction, using Newton's unpublished manuscripts on the Temple and his studies of the prophets. In addition, it considers why Newton needed to reconstruct the Temple and whether this need went beyond his religious convictions. This book "walks" the reader through the Temple as Newton would have perceived it. To travel though the Temple, its structure, its symmetry, and its proportional elegance is to steal a glimpse into the mind of Isaac Newton.

Introduction

Isaac Newton died on March 20, 1727. In the years after his death, he was immortalized by the English public. Antiquarian William Stukeley referred to Newton in his unpublished manuscripts as "immortal Newton."[1] On May 8, 1727, the *Daily Journal* announced, "On this day is published a poem sacred to the memory of Sir Isaac Newton by James Thompson."[2] The poem has 203 lines and it begins thus:

> Shall the great soul of Newton quit this earth,
> To mingle with his stars; and every muse,
> Astonish'd into silence, shun the weight
> Of honours due to his illustrious name?[3]

In the poem Newton is revered, his name is "illustrious," and he is "O' Britain's boast!"[4] Throughout the poem there is no doubt about his immortality and his place in the heavens, which he had explained in his *Philosophiæ Naturalis Principia Mathematica*, commonly called the *Principia*.

Newspapers published many epitaphs to Newton for many years after his death.[5] The most famous of all is by Alexander Pope:

> Nature and nature's laws lay hid in night;
> God said "Let Newton be" and all was light.[6]

Newton had explained the workings of the heavens. His memory has also been immortalized by painters, sculptors, and architects. However, not all were in praise of Newton. In 1795, William Blake produced a print that depicted Newton holding a compass intent on his measurements while turning his back on the beauty of nature. The image is the embodiment of Blake's prayer in verse, "May God us keep from single vision & Newton's sleep."[7] Blake believed that Newton and his fame had created a false religion of rational materialism, and that humanity was in danger of losing sight of the reality of God.[8] This would have been a horrifying idea to Newton, and his intentions were clearly the converse. For Newton, the purpose of his study of natural philosophy was to praise God and to bring knowledge of God's plan into the public realm. In 1995, artist Eduardo Paolozzi created a bronze sculpture that is a modern adaptation of Blake's image of Newton. Located in the courtyard of the British Library (see Figure 1), it has become a symbol of the world's knowledge. However, Blake's original intention was not to praise Newton but to denigrate his knowledge as being impure.

This image of Newton as an ideal scientist and natural philosopher prevailed for over 200 years. In the paintings, etchings, poetry, and mythology that were built around his image, he was presented as a dreamer who stared into the heavens to discover their meaning. The reality is quite different; only a small percentage of Newton's writings are on mathematics and natural philosophy.[9] It is now well known that Newton dabbled in alchemy, and his religious beliefs at the time would

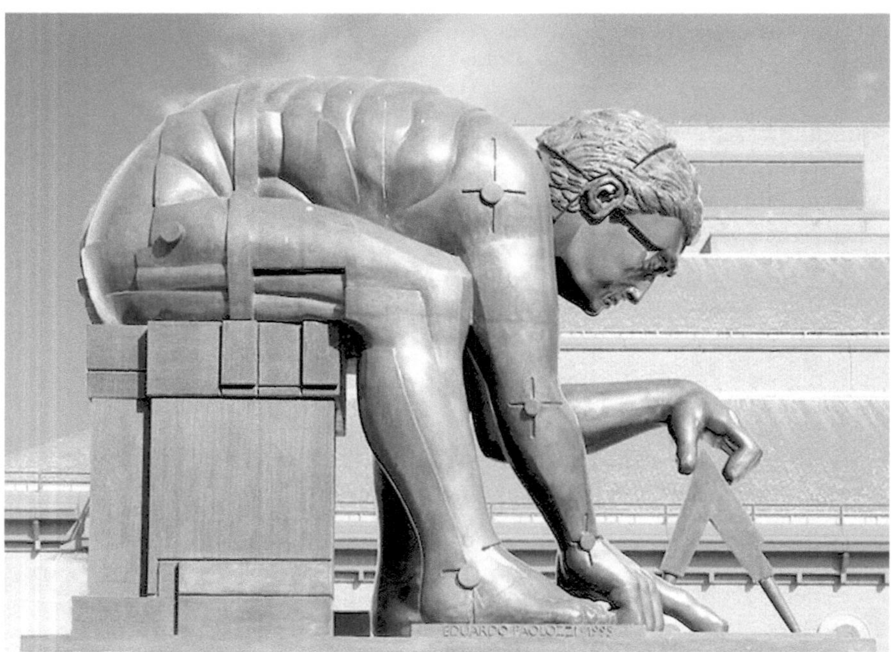

Figure 1. Sculpture entitled *Newton,* **Eduardo Paolozzi, 1995, in the courtyard of the British Library.**

have been considered heretical. Newton published very little in his lifetime and the majority of his work remained in manuscripts. His manuscripts were retained by the family and were held in the Portsmouth Collection until 1936, when they were auctioned and dispersed into collections around the world.

The auction was held in July 1936 at Sotheby's. The manuscripts were divided into 330 lots and sold to thirty-three buyers. It is surprising that these manuscripts were allowed to leave England but the manuscripts were on prophecy, Newton's unorthodox theology, and alchemy, which was an illegal practice at the time, although secretly practiced by many of the members of the main English scientific society, the Royal Society of London.[10] It does appear strange that the works of Britain's greatest scientist were being distributed in this manner all around the world instead of being held in the British Library or Museum. José Faur considered that the reason for this was the somewhat problematic content of the manuscripts. It was "to protect Newton's 'good name' [that] the importance of the manuscripts was denied."[11] However, the auction actually stimulated the interest of the public, libraries, and scholars internationally.

One of the buyers at the auction was the famous economist John Maynard Keynes. What he found in the manuscripts was a true revelation to him. Instead of finding the great immortal and dreaming scientist, Keynes found manuscripts that changed the image of Newton forever. He found manuscripts on alchemy, prophecy, and religious scriptural commentary that revealed that Newton was searching for the secret of the universe, not only in natural philosophy, but also in the secret language of the prophets in the Scriptures. Keynes claimed,

> Newton was not the first of the age of reason. He was the last of the magicians, the last of the Babylonians and Sumerians, the last great mind which looked out on the visible and intellectual world with the same eyes as those who began to build our intellectual inheritance rather less than 10,000 years ago.[12]

This famous quote has become synonymous with Newton. Yet, though nearly 300 years have passed since Newton's death, there is still more to discover about Newton. All of Newton's work was intermeshed, and there are no clear lines dividing his interests. His studies in natural philosophy, alchemy, chronology, and prophecy, and his lesser-known interest in architecture, reveal a man who learned from the past and also saw further into the future than anyone else of his time. However, Newton was a product of the English Age of Reason, and although he did see further than anybody at the time, he was very much a part of that time and his empirical methods of research were promoted by the Royal Society of London.

The Royal Society was founded in 1664 for the improvement of knowledge of the natural philosophies. One of the central aims of the Royal Society was to compile a meticulous and accurate reporting of nature. This aim can be traced back to the Baconian inheritance. Francis Bacon considered natural history the foundation of natural philosophy. William Wotton, a fellow of the Royal Society claimed that the true business of the society was "to collect a perfect history of nature in order to establish thereupon a body of physics."[13] Bacon's Salomon's House, the college in his unfinished utopian work *The New Atlantis* posthumously published in 1627, was dedicated to the study of works and the creation of God, as well the discovery of the true nature of things. By interpreting accurate recordings from observation, it was possible to derive the truth. The new empirical inquiry of natural philosophy was a method that "included experiment but did not consist in experiment. They consisted rather in a continuous progress of interaction between experiment and reason, a true and perfect marriage between the empirical and rational facility."[14]

Early in the 17th century, scientific curiosity was perceived by some as a heresy. German Lutheran pastor Johann Valentin Andreae's *Treatise on the Pestilence of Curiosity* published in 1620 described curiosity as devotion to heresies—particularly mystical spiritualism—and he saw curiosity as including the buying or commissioning of clocks, statues, paintings, and jewelry, fraudulent alchemy, magic and divination, and the search for the secrets of perpetual motion.[15] Curiosity was seen as the original temptation and a sin. Adam's temptation to take the apple in the Garden of Eden was pure curiosity. For Andreae, scientific investigation was instigated, not from idle curiosity, but by the need to understand nature and God—it was a very limited investigation. However, many of the key figures of the Royal Society were puritans, and just as reformist thought rejected traditional Biblical authority and reverted to the individual interpretation of the Bible, so the new science ignored traditional Aristotelian logic and refined the truth of natural philosophy as the result of experimentation and demonstration.[16] Scientific curiosity would lead to the development of the empiricist new philosophies of the Royal Society, which in turn would lead to the understanding of nature, which would, they believed, reveal the true nature of God.

Newton placed emphasis on the authority of the Scriptures and personal holiness, which included industrious guard against pride and self-discipline. His search for the fundamental truth of nature was indivisible from his belief in God. He believed that uncovering the mathematical principles of natural philosophy demonstrated the existence of a designer—God. However, the reality is that only a small percentage of Newton's writings are on mathematics and natural philosophy; the majority of his manuscripts are studies in theology.[17] Newton's time encompassed a mixture of old philosophies and the development of new ones. He had been born during the English Civil War and went to university at the time of the Restoration of King Charles II, and by the time he had completed his great work *Philosophiæ Naturalis Principia Mathematica* in 1687, political and religious turmoil was on the rise.

In the 17th century, the spheres of science and religion generally overlapped; in Bacon's works, he commonly attempted to describe one sphere in terms of the other. He also held that the book of nature was the key to understanding the book of God's written words and that the rise of experimental science was directly sanctioned by God. By the middle of the 17th century in Britain, millenarianism was being preached by the reformists. Preachers drew on imagery of the Apocalypse. In a sermon in 1642, reformist preacher William Sedgwick stated, "The Tabernacle of God, is coming down to dwell with the man.... God will at last establish, and make Jerusalem a praise in the earth."[18] Joseph Mede's influential Latin text *Clavis Apocalyptica*, published in 1627, was reprinted in 1632 and translated into English as *The Keys of Revelation*, published in 1643 and reprinted in 1651. Mede claimed that the Second Coming was imminent and that it was not just the actions of kings that would help this come about but also the actions of normal people.[19] Newton had studied many prophetic texts and commentaries that had proliferated throughout the 17th century, particularly the work of Henry More, who was at Cambridge at the same time as Newton and wrote many prophetic books.[20] However, Newton acknowledged that in his own prophetic studies, "Mr Mede laid the foundation & I have built upon it."[21] It was an era when studying prophecy was promoted in the universities of Cambridge and Oxford[22]; it was considered just as much a science as a natural philosophy, and given the same rational and scientific methodology.

The English Age of Reason brought diverse transformation to British political power, including changes in the parliamentary system, a decline in the power of the monarchy, religious upheaval and a clash of philosophies and ideologies. Reason was used to support the established procedures of Christianity and to confirm Revelation. Enlightened minds no longer believed that religion was a body of commandments that were carved into stone and accepted on faith. "Belief was becoming a matter of private judgement for the individual to adjudicate within the multi-religionism sanctioned by statutory toleration."[23] Society disagreed over how to worship God and to organize the church. However, there was a belief that scientific inquiry would reveal God and nature. Toward the end of the 17th century, curiosity was no longer considered a heresy. The relationship between God and nature was not only a legitimate form of inquiry; it was considered a religious duty for devout Protestants.[24]

Newton's manuscripts reveal this inquiry. The majority of his manuscripts are on theology, in which he attempted to reveal the secret language of the prophets of the Scriptures. He believed this secret language would reveal the truth. One of his studies was of Solomon's Temple. To assist in that study, he reconstructed the Temple in a manuscript through a scriptural commentary on the Book of Ezekiel. Some manuscripts show studies of the Hebrew cubit and others show his examinations of the prophecies of Daniel, Ezekiel, and Revelation of the Temple of Solomon as an important symbol.

It is often said that Newton's work on the Temple of Solomon is the work of his old age or after he had a nervous breakdown in 1693.[25] However, his work on Solomon's Temple spanned over 50 years and many of these manuscripts were written before he had his nervous breakdown. In addition, his breakdown seems to have been very short-lived, because in 1695 Newton was appointed Warden of the Mint, in 1699 he became Master of the Mint overseeing the Great Recoinage of England, and in 1703 he became the president of the Royal Society. The overseeing of the recoinage depended not only on Newton's excellent command of mathematics but also on vast organizational skills that entailed the rationalization of the Mint by establishing country branch mints.[26] Newton's interest in the Temple of Solomon was not due to mental decay, nor was it an isolated interest. In fact, there was a great deal of interest in the Temple, not only from theologians, but also from the public.

Many academics reconstructed the architecture of Solomon's Temple from sources such as the books of Ezekiel and Kings. Many of these reconstructions were published, and there was also an interest in reconstructing architectural models of the Temple. These were displayed as exhibitions to the public. The different sources and ideas on the Temple's appearance produced different styles of architectural models, creating controversy and a great deal of academic and public interest.

The purpose of this book is to put the work of Isaac Newton on Solomon's Temple into perspective with other works on the Temple of the time. Two architectural models were displayed in London when Newton was writing about Solomon's Temple: those of Jacob Judah Leon (Templo) and Gerhard Schott. Public lectures were held in opposition to their designs and other models were also presented; unfortunately, these are not so well documented. These models displayed to the public were part religious instruction and part museum exhibition. Guidebooks were published to "walk" the viewer around the models; these guidebooks were extremely popular and many examples still exist. Public and scientific fascination with Solomon's Temple was widespread at the end of the 17th and in the early 18th century.

Newton's work on the Temple should be examined in context with these models and the attitudes of the time. Although he wrote on the Temple for over 50 years, he produced only one architectural manuscript, "A Treatise or Remarks on Solomon's Temple, Introduction to the Lexicon of the Prophets, Part Two: About the Appearance of the Jewish Temple," now known by its call name Babson MS 434.[27] The dating of this cannot be precise; the Newton Project claims that the date is early 1690 but with no justification. However, many other manuscripts, particularly on the Hebrew cubit, which was essential for its construction,[28] that can be dated and relate directly to this manuscript imply that it was written between mid–1680 and 1690. The handwriting in the manuscript also verifies this date. Babson MS 434 is a commentary on verses in the Book of Ezekiel that relate to the Temple. Newton reconstructed the Temple, described the measurements, and provided its architectural details.

To consider Newton's reconstruction in context, Chapter 1, "Newton's Manuscripts," will examine the manuscripts that relate to his thoughts on the Temple. First, his work on alchemy will be examined; these works demonstrate his strong belief in the purity of ancient knowledge. Second, the chapter examines his study of chronology, and although his book on chronology entitled *The Chronology of Ancient Kingdoms Amended* was posthumously published in 1728,[29] it was in fact one of the first topics that he studied in his early days at Cambridge University in the 1670s. *The Chronology* has a chapter on the Temple of Solomon; however, it has very little resemblance to his early work. Finally, his work on prophecy, the Temple, and the Hebrew cubit is examined.

Chapter 2, "A Brief History of Models up to the 18th Century," is an overview of the development of architectural models and their use, not only for architecture, but also for scientific experimentation and religious contemplation. Chapter 3, "Paper Reconstructions of the Temple of Solomon from the 17th and 18th Centuries," highlights some of the reconstructions from manuscripts and published books. Chapter 4, "Architectural Models of the Temple of Solomon Exhibited in London in the 17th and 18th Centuries," examines two main public exhibitions: the models by Jacob Judah Leon who was commonly called Templo and one commissioned by Gerhard Schott. It also reviews the interest of the public and academics in these models. Chapter 5, "The Model Guidebooks," analyzes the guidebooks that accompanied the Temple model exhibitions and how these guidebooks guided the "mind's eye" around the Temple. Chapter 6, "The Architectural Model of Newton's Temple of Solomon," highlights images of the architectural reconstruction built from Newton's description in Babson MS 434 by the workshop of the School of Architecture and Built Environment at the University of Newcastle, Australia. In Babson MS 434, Newton used Ezekiel's commentary on the Temple, which walks the reader through the Temple. The images correspond with this walk and create a guidebook in the same vein as those of Templo's and Schott's model guidebooks. A conclusion places this guidebook and Newton's work into the context of the time.

Newton's interest in Solomon's Temple is often taken out of perspective, but in the context of his times it was not an unusual interest. His study to reconstruct the Temple was intensive, and it demonstrates access to a large range of sources, both ancient and contemporary. His careful study of measurements and his examination of Ezekiel's text are executed according to the same scientific standard as his work in natural philosophy. Newton assessed the prophetic text of Ezekiel through a historiographical, analytical, and mathematical approach in the tradition of the Royal Society and the English Age of Reason.

1

Newton's Manuscripts

The Newton Project is an organization that publishes Isaac Newton's writings online.[1] They have transcribed and made publicly available over 6.4 million words of text written by Newton. The web site shows the diversity of his work in science, mathematical writing, alchemy, and particularly, religious texts, which make up the bulk of his manuscripts. In this chapter, only manuscripts that are relevant to his study of the Temple of Solomon are examined. Although alchemy has nothing to do with the Biblical texts of Solomon's Temple or architecture, it is important to consider his study of alchemy since it reveals how he revered ancient knowledge.

Alchemy

Newton desired the truth of all things, and of all universal knowledge. For Newton, it was through this true knowledge of the universe and its workings that, in a sense, he found the true knowledge of God. Experimental discovery and religious revelation were products of reason, speculation, and mathematics. To this end, he researched chronology, theology, and particularly, prophecy. Newton organized areas of his study—whether scientific, historic, or theological—with exactly the same approach, and he did not distinguish between them. He perceived that God had designed the universe. However, his Divine Architect was not the medieval image of the Divine Architect, with compass and rule (see Figure 2),[2] but an architect who planned and designed the universe according to strict rules and with scientific rigor. God had encoded the truth into the universe, and this truth was held through prophecy and ancient wisdom. Newton used all the sources that were available to him,

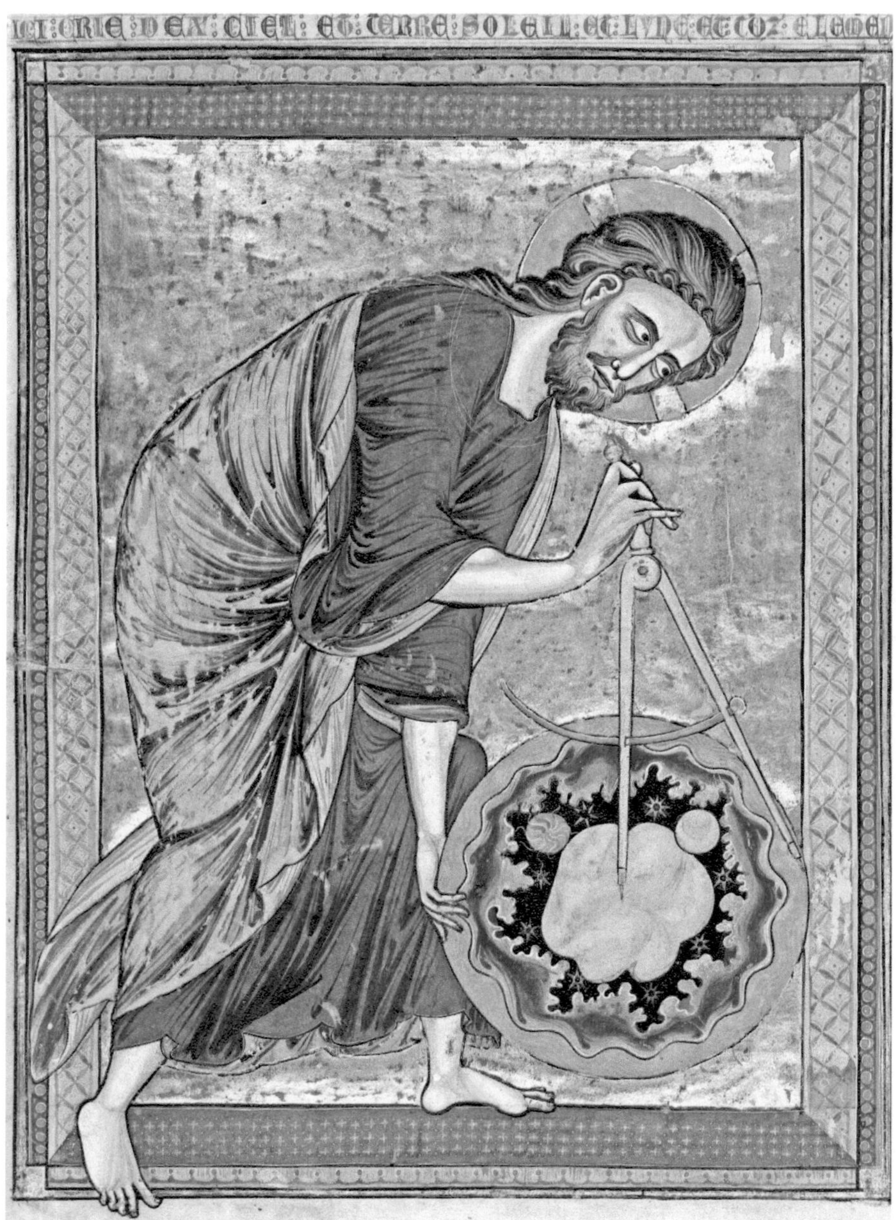

Figure 2. The divine architect, mid–13th century (frontispiece of *Bible Moralisee*; courtesy of the Österreichische Nationalbibliothek).

such as historical records, myths, mathematics, experiments, observation, revelation, reason, classical writings, and the remains of ancient wisdom to uncover this truth. Above all, however, he used the Bible, which he considered the oldest and the most reliable document of all time.[3]

The purity of ancient knowledge was a core belief of Newton's. He was deeply committed to the idea that the art of alchemy extended back into ancient times, and he practiced it, not to change base metal into gold, but to unlock the secrets of nature.

Newton made a study of *Emerald Tablet*[4] and *Seven Chapters*,[5] two alchemical texts that are attributed to Hermes Trismegistus. In the 17th century, Hermes was considered an Egyptian priest who lived before Moses. His works contain expressions such as the "Father" and "Son of God." Therefore, Hermes Trismegistus was perceived to be a significant Gentile prophet who had foreseen the coming of Christianity.[6] However, although tales of Hermes Trismegistus are ancient, the works that are attributed to him are from the second century AD. Newton considered that ancient knowledge such as Hermes Trismegistus's writings encapsulated the mysterious phrases of all the occult ancient wisdom regarding divine actions in the creation of the world. He regarded the practice of alchemy as the pursuit of replicating and uncovering the divine creativity of the universe.[7]

The first of Newton's translations, dated to the early 1680s, was the *Emerald Tablet*. It is one of the best-known alchemical texts in history. In the early 1670s, prior to translating the *Emerald Tablet*, Newton experimented with quicksilver and sulfur. He conducted these experiments over a small furnace, experimenting with the cooling, heating, and mixing of quicksilver and sulfur, and recorded all of his experimentations and observations. In one of his manuscripts, "Of Natures Obvious Laws & Processes in Vegetation,"[8] he claimed that minerals and animals draw from the vegetable spirit the "material soul of all matter." All things are born, live, and die that is the principle of all vegetation.[9] In "Two Incomplete Treatises on the Vegetative Growth of Metals and Minerals," he claimed that metals and vegetables obey the same laws and that all things are corruptible.[10]

Newton translated Hermes's *Emerald Tablet* text thus:

> Tis true without lying, certain & most true.
> That wch is below is like that wch is above & that wch is above is like y^t wch is below to do ye miracles of one only thing.

> And as all things have been & arose from one by ye mediation of one: so all things have their birth from this one thing by adaptation.
>
> The Sun is its father, the moon its mother, the wind hath carried it in its belly, the earth is its nurse. The father of all perfection in ye whole world is here. Its force or power is entire if it be converted into earth.
>
> Separate thou ye earth from ye fire, ye subtle from the gross sweetly wth great industry. It ascends from ye earth to heaven & again it descends to ye earth & receives ye force of things superior & inferior.
>
> By this means you shall have ye glory of ye whole world & thereby all obscurity shall fly from you.
>
> Its force is above all force. For it vanquishes every subtle thing & penetrates every solid thing. So was ye world created.
>
> From this are & do come admirable adaptations whereof ye means (or process) is here in this.
>
> Hence I am called Hermes Trismegist, having the three parts of ye philosophy of ye whole world.
>
> That wch I have said of ye operation of ye Sun is accomplished & ended.[11]

In Newton's commentary on these texts, he claimed that quicksilver and sulfur are united elements; they act on each other and are mutually transmuted into each other to create a nobler offspring:

> And just as all things were created from one Chaos by the design of one God, so in our art all things, that is the four elements, are born from this one thing, which is our Chaos, by the design of the Artificer and the skillful adaptation of things. And this generation is similar to the human, truly from a father and mother, which are the Sun and the Moon. And when the Infant is conceived through the coition of these, he is borne continuously in the belly of the wind until the hour of birth, and after birth he is nourished at the breasts of foliated Earth until he grows up. This wind is the bath of the Sun and the Moon, and Mercurius, and the Dragon, and the Fire that succeeds in the third place as the governor of the work: and the earth is the nurse, Latona washed and cleansed, whom the Egyptians assuredly had for the nurse of Diana and Apollo, that is, the white and red tinctures. This is the source of all the perfection of the whole world.... And just as the world was created from Chaos through the bringing forth of the light and through the separation of the aery firmament and of the waters from the earth, so our work brings forth the beginning out of black Chaos and its first matter through the separation of the elements and the illumination of matter. Whence arise the marvelous adaptations and arrangements in our work, the mode of which here was adumbrated in the creation of the world.[12]

Newton believed in the power of ancient wisdom and that these ancient societies had understood the true system of natural philosophy. However, he strongly believed that this knowledge of the ancients had been lost because of subsequent corruption of the true and original religion. Since Newton considered that the *Emerald Tablet* was a pre–Christian text that was dated before the time of Moses, he believed that it was less corrupt and closer to the perfect knowledge of the original and true religion. Because of this, such texts were of scientific and theological merit.

Science and theology came together because, according to Newton's commentary on the *Emerald Tablet*, in the alchemy of Hermes they have

> three parts of the philosophy of the whole world, since he signifies the Mercury of the philosophers, which is composed from the three strongest substances, and has body, soul, and spirit, and is mineral, vegetable, and animal, and has dominion in the mineral kingdom, vegetable kingdom, and the animal kingdom.[13]

Newton's alchemical experiments revealed support for his belief that the ancients, such as Hermes, had a full and perfect understanding of natural philosophy but this knowledge had been lost because of corruption of the original religion. Newton was committed to the idea that alchemical wisdom extended back to ancient times. Newton believed that in the Hermetic tradition was embedded the body of alchemical knowledge that held knowledge of the universe, therefore, God's creation. His interest in alchemy was very intense for a span of several years. However, he discontinued this interest when he left Cambridge and did not practice alchemy again. This was perhaps because he was dissatisfied with the results; through alchemy, he had not succeeded in defining the laws and processes of vegetation. Whatever the reason for discontinuing alchemy, it was not because he had lost interest in ancient knowledge. On the contrary, he remained interested in what he perceived to be lost ancient knowledge.

Chronology

After Newton's death, John Conduitt edited and published *The Chronology of Ancient Kingdoms Amended*, which Newton had been revising for publication at the time of his death. In the preface to a 1770 edition of *The Chronology*, which is in the form of correspondence between Dr. Thomas Hunt, Hebrew professor at Oxford University, and Rev. Zachary Pearce, the Bishop of Rochester, Hunt claimed that when Newton died he left sixteen drafts of *The Chronology*. The Bishop expressed his concerns about Newton's methods of writing:

It is a pity, that he took so much of the same method in his chronology which he took in his Principia &c: concealing his proofs and leaving it to the sagacity of others to discover them. For want of these, in some instances what he says on chronology does not sufficiently appear at present to rest upon anything but his assertions; … But proofs he may have had, which he chose to conceal, though what now stands in the Margin in those few places may have come from another hand, and may not amount to a full proof, as it pretends to do.[14]

William Whiston, former pupil and successor to Newton as Lucasian Professor at Cambridge, claimed that he wrote out eighteen copies of *The Chronology*, but that they were not very different from each other.[15] Only a couple of the later versions, which Whiston would have known about, still exist. However, Newton's existing works on chronology do demonstrate that his interest in chronology, the Temple of Solomon, and Jewish history was established by the middle to late 1670s.[16] Newton wrote and rewrote *The Chronology* repeatedly from works that stemmed back over fifty years. However, instead of making it better every time or adding in new information, he made it duller and blander, and the published version is exceptionally dull and cannot be considered a success.

Newton used many ancient sources in the development of his chronology of human history, although he was selective in the sources he chose. Newton claimed that "*Greek* Antiquities are full of Poetical Fictions, because the *Greeks* wrote nothing in Prose, before the Conquest of *Asia* by *Cyrus* the *Persian*."[17] He clearly revered Herodotus, calling him the father of history,[18] and he excluded other writers if they contradicted Herodotus. He probed for reports of astrological events, comparing different accounts. He also used myths, for example, to derive some of his dates. Kings had genealogies drawn up for them that linked them to mythical and heroic characters such as Aeneas of Troy. These chronologies established not only their claim to the throne but also their impressive and divine lineage, and Newton drew on these and considered them fact.[19] Following the front matter of *The Chronology* is a chapter called "A Short Chronicle from the first Memory of Things in Europe, to the Conquest of Persia by Alexander the Great," which is essentially a list of dates and events. The "Short Chronicle" highlights Newton's use of Biblical events with Greek mythical events and characters, for example:

1017. *Solomon* by the assistance of the *Tyrians* and *Aradians*, who had mariners among them acquainted with the *Red Sea*, sets out a fleet upon that sea....

> 1015. The Temple of *Solomon* is founded. *Minos* Reigns in *Crete* expelling his
> father *Asterius*, who flees into *Italy*, and becomes the *Saturn* of the
> *Latines*....
>
> 989. *Dædalus* and his nephew *Talus* invent the saw, the turning-lath the wim-
> ble, the chip-ax, and other instruments of Carpenters and Joyners, and
> thereby give a beginning to those Arts in *Europe*. *Dædalus* also invented the
> making of Statues with their feet asunder, as if they walked.
>
> 988. *Minos* makes war upon the *Athenians*, for killing his son *Androgeus*. *Æacus*
> flourishes.
>
> 987. *Dædalus* kills his nephew *Talus*, and flies to *Minos*. A Priestess of *Jupiter
> Ammon*, being brought by *Phœnician* merchants into *Greece*, sets up the
> Oracle of *Jupiter* at *Dodona*. This gives a beginning to Oracles in *Greece*:
> and by their dictates, the Worship of the Dead is everywhere introduced.[20]

The following chapters are divided into kingdoms: Greek, Egyptian, Babylonian, Median, and Persian. However, first, he challenged their
antiquity. In the beginning of the chapter on the Greek kingdom, Newton claimed, "All Nations, before they began to keep exact accounts of
Time, have been prone to raise their antiquities; and this humour has
been promoted, by the Contentions between Nations about their Orig-
inals."[21] He systematically demonstrated that all of the kingdoms exag-
gerated their antiquity, and the Egyptians were the worst:

> The Egyptians anciently boasted of a very great and lasting Empire under their
> Kings *Ammon, Osiris, Bacchus, Sesostris, Hercules, Memnon*, &c. reaching eastward to
> the Indies, and westward to the Atlantic Ocean; and out of vanity they had made
> this monarchy some thousands of years older than the world. Let us now try to
> rectify the Chronology of *Egypt*, by comparing the affairs of *Egypt* with the syn-
> chronizing affairs of the Greeks and Hebrews.[22]

Not only did Newton greatly reduce the antiquity of the Kingdom of
Egypt, he also reduced its power by demonstrating that throughout
most of Egyptian history Egypt was a collection of small kingdoms.
Newton believed that the Kingdom of Israel was the first important
political society that could be truly called a civilization. However, Newton had difficulty justifying this when comparing the accounts in the
Old Testament that he had previously claimed were the oldest existing
records of any civilization in the ancient world. The Book of Exodus
demonstrates that Moses had led the Israelites out of a powerful and
large Egyptian Empire. However, Newton had reduced this empire to
a country of little city kingdoms that was not united and did not become
a great empire until the reigns of Ammon and Sesac.[23] In the *Chronicle*,

Newton dated Ammon 1034 BC[24] and Sesac 1014 BC[25]; both postdate the reigns of David (1059 BC)[26] and Solomon (1019 BC).[27] By establishing these dates as the beginning of the Egyptian Empire, Newton demonstrated that it was not established until after the Kingdom of Israel was founded.

Newton carefully assessed and compared the Greek chronologies and restructured the dates accordingly. He began dating the Greek chronology from two historical events: the first Olympiad, which he dated to 784 BC, and more importantly, the death of King Solomon, which he dated to 982 BC. For example, the reign of *Aristodemus* was "159 years after the death of *Solomon*, and 46 years before the first Olympiad"[28]; "the return of the *Heraclides* into *Peloponnesus* to the *Trojan* War, and the taking of *Troy* will be about 76 years after the death of Solomon"[29]; "in the Reign of *Rehoboam. Dædalus* and his nephew *Talus*, in the latter part of the Reign of Solomon"[30]; "*Theseus*, in the time of the *Argonautic* expedition, was of about 50 years of age, and so was born about the 33rd year of *Solomon*"[31]; and Newton continued in this manner to use Solomon as his main reference point in time.

Newton also attributed the beginning of construction skills and aesthetics to the building of the Temple of Solomon. He claimed to have heard "nothing of the trade of carpenters, or good architecture, before *Solomon* sent to *Hiram* King of *Tyre*, to supply him with such Artificers."[32] Although Hiram supplied Solomon with the skill to build the Temple, the plan of the Temple replicated the plan of the Tabernacle of Moses. The plan of the Tabernacle was given to Moses directly from God.[33] Instead of the portable tent of Moses, Solomon had doubled the size and built a permanent building. This was the beginning of architecture, Newton claimed: "I meet with no mention of sumptuous Temples before the days of Solomon,"[34] and all subsequent temples, he argued, were modeled on it.

In *The Chronology*, Newton mentioned Solomon more than any other ruler in history, and he is presented as being a good, wise, powerful, and civilized ruler. Yet the Kingdom of the Israelites has no chapter in *The Chronology*, although there is a chapter on the Temple of Solomon. This chapter is curiously placed after the Kingdom of Babylon, which destroyed the Temple. He begins the chapter very dismissively: "The Temple of Solomon being destroyed by the *Babylonians*, it may not be amiss here to give a description of that edifice."[35] The chapter has barely 3,000 words and has no interest in the Temple's magnificence. It is a very dull description and gives the impression that Newton is extremely uninterested in the topic of the Temple and that he has no understanding of architectural rules or principles. In fact, it does seem to contradict the importance that Newton gave to the Temple and Solomon in the rest of the book.

The majority of the chapter quotes straight from Ezekiel, with very little added by Newton. The bits that he does add are very strange, for instance, "the cubit was about 21½, or almost 22 inches of the *English* foot."[36] Considering that Newton was one of the greatest mathematicians who ever lived, such imprecision appears to be contrary to his nature. The little architectural detail that he does give does not make much sense. He claimed that

> the Porch of the Temple was 120 cubits high, and its length from south to north equalled the breadth of the House: the House was three stories high, which made the height of the *Holy Place* three times thirty cubits, and that of the *Most Holy* three times twenty: the upper rooms were treasure-chambers.[37]

This strange and confused stepped structure appears to have no precedents, Biblically or otherwise.

Three very detailed plans accompany the chapter, but the detail in the plans is not backed up by description in the chapter. Although expertly drafted, the plans are a mixture of the details of Solomon's Temple and the Second Temple as described in the Bible.[38] The final form of *The Chronology*, in Newton's best handwriting, with hardly any deletions or emendations, can be seen in a manuscript held at Cambridge University Library, Additional MS 3988.[39] However, although the drawing that accompanies the text of this manuscript is also a mixture of the two Temples, it lacks any details. It is the most minimal of plans, with no internal detail (see Figure 3). The outline of the plan is similar to the plan of the Temple precinct in *The Chronology*. The draftsman of the plans in *The Chronology* may have had knowledge of this plan. Yet the three plans in *The Chronology* (see Figures 4, 5, and 6) could not be considered the work of Newton. The details in these three plans are a fabrication from an unknown hand.

Newton had worked on chronology since his earliest days in Cambridge; it was a topic to which he kept returning. The final published version of *The Chronology* was a result of many manuscripts, but instead of improving it, Newton made it blander and blander with each reworking, and his final drafts, which resulted in the published work, had none of

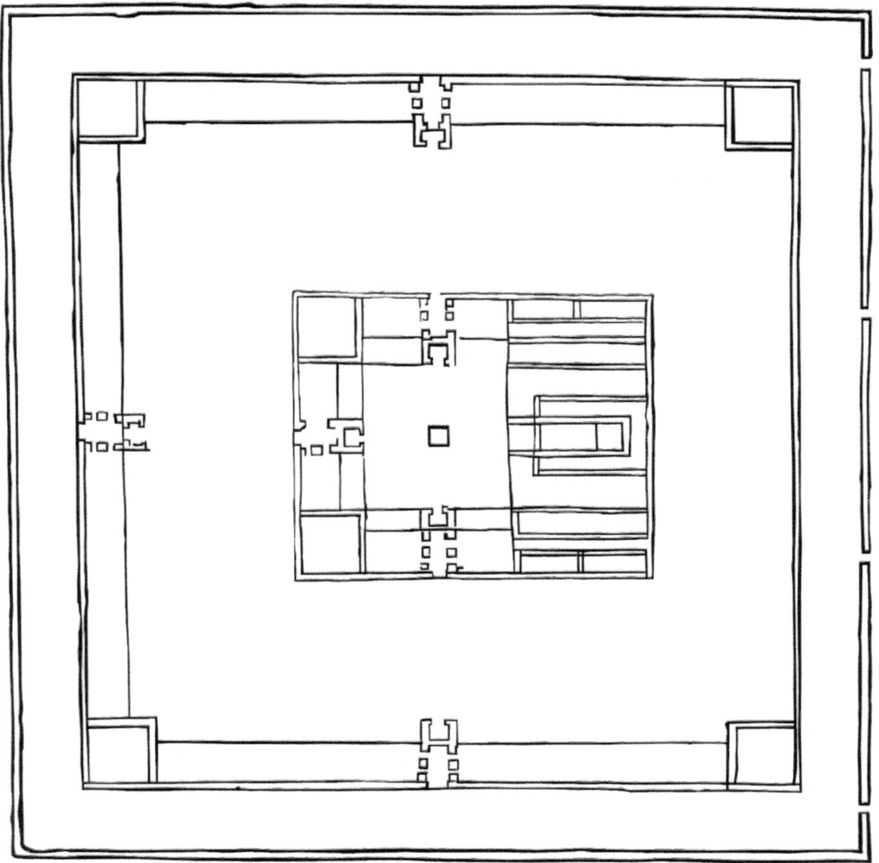

Figure 3. Newton's sketch in the final form in *The Chronology* from Cambridge University Library, Additional Ms 3988 (re-drawn by the author).

the uniqueness of his earlier works. This is particularly demonstrated in his work on the Temple of Solomon.

Prophecy, the Temple of Solomon and the Cubit

It is difficult to establish exactly when Newton's interest in the Temple began. However, his interest appears to have evolved with his

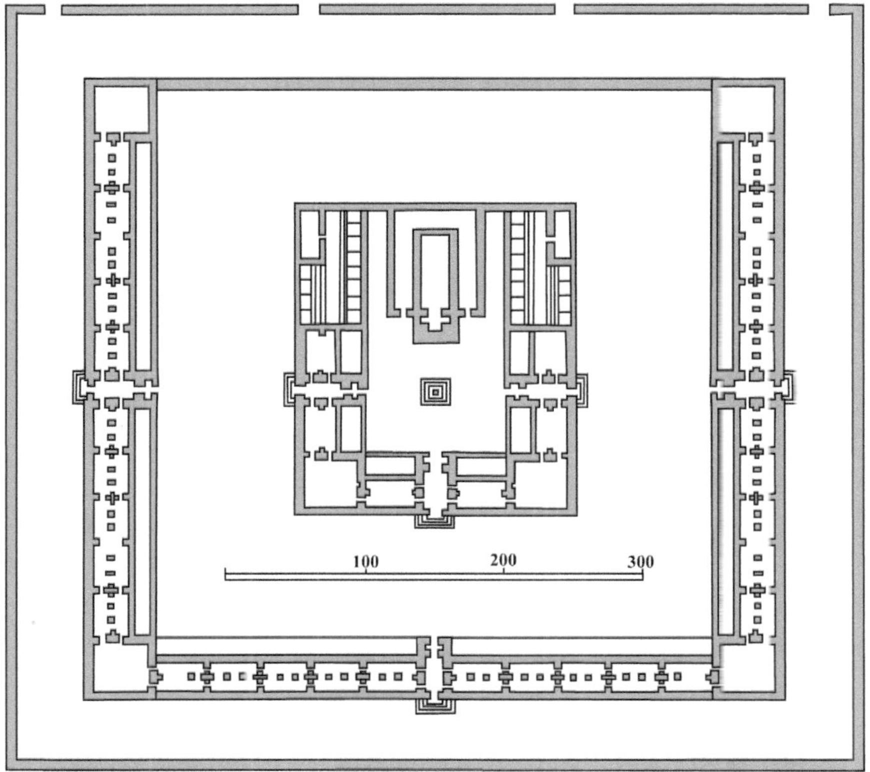

Figure 4. The floor plan of the Temple precinct published in *The Chronology* in 1728 (re-drawn by the author).

studies into prophecy, particularly his studies of Revelation and the Books of Daniel and Ezekiel, in the late 1670s.[40] His more interesting works on the Temple are from that period and up to the early 1690s. This contradicts popular belief in that it is generally thought that Newton's works on the Temple and chronology were the works of an aged and senile Newton.[41] There is no doubt that his "refinements" in the later part of his life were not an improvement, to say the least (as seen in *The Chronology*), but the original works, written in his most productive period, have a freshness and a vitality that were removed in the later reworking.

Newton wrote extensively on the Apocalypse, but this was not unusual for his time. The 17th century had a very rich tradition of

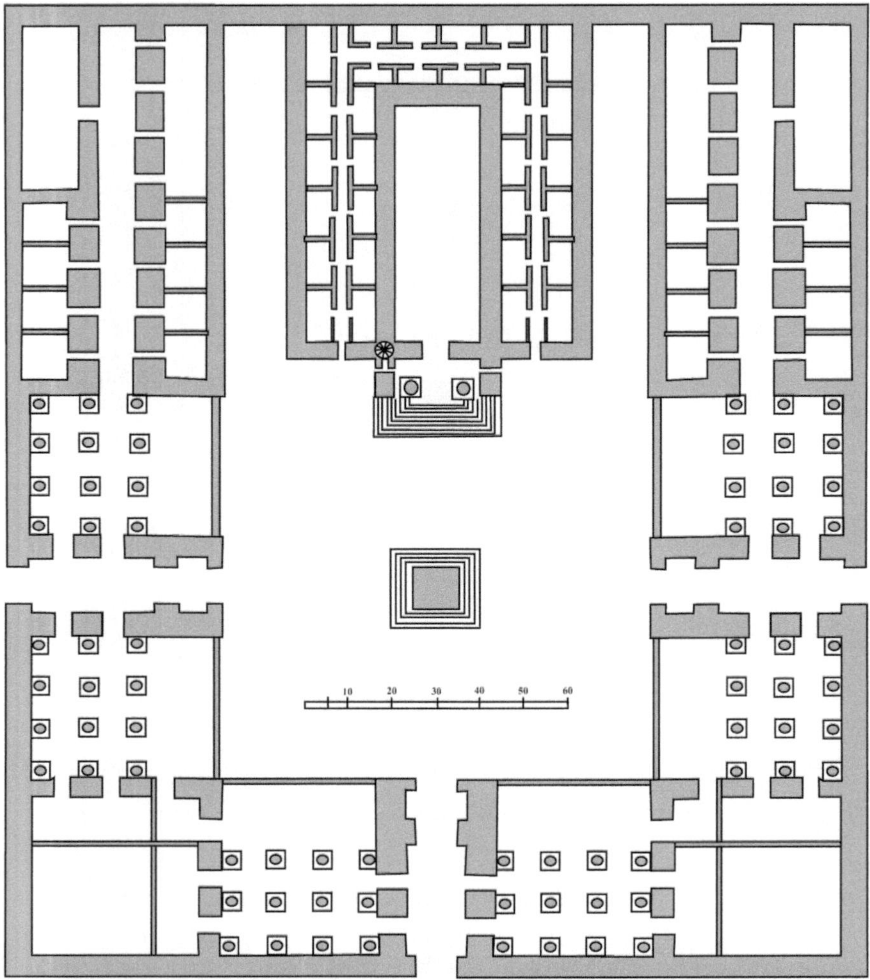

Figure 5. The floor plan of the Temple published in *The Chronology* in 1728 (re-drawn by the author).

apocalyptic and prophetic writings,[42] and given the religious and political events of that century in England, it is not surprising. Newton built on the apocalyptic writings of Joseph Mede and Henry More. He attempted to decode the hieroglyphic language of the prophets that was encoded in the Scriptures. In this hieroglyphic language, there is a correspondence between the symbols of heaven and earth. The earthly

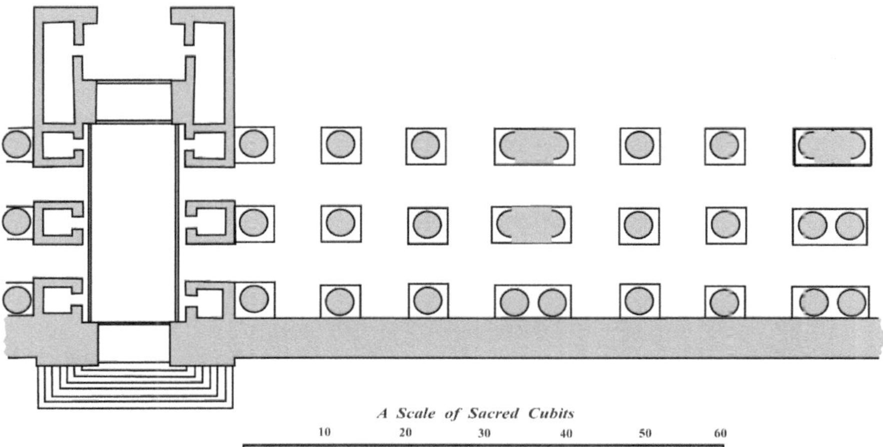

Figure 6. Floor plan of the cloister under the chambers published in *The Chronology* in 1728 (re-drawn by the author).

rituals and parts of the Temple correspond with the celestial city of the future.

Newton owned all of More's published works on Daniel and the Apocalypse, including *A Plain and Continued Exposition of the Several Prophesy or Divine Visions of the Prophet Daniel*, which was a gift to Newton from More and remained in Newton's library for the rest of his life. This book was heavily annotated by Newton with points of his disagreement, and only a few of agreement.[43] Both More and Mede were significant influences on Newton, particularly in the early 1670s. However, Newton's scheme of Biblical hermeneutics goes well beyond More's and Mede's systems. Although Mede and More made mention of the Temple, the Temple was not a central feature in either's work. However, for Newton, the Temple was not only a central feature: "the Temple is the scene of the visions"[44] of the prophets.

According to Newton, the "door of the Kingdom of heaven [is] represented by this Temple or Tabernacle"[45]:

> The Key of the door in heaven so often opened in the following prophesy [Revelation], that is the Key of the Temple or Tabernacle in heaven wherein God has his Throne & worship. For Keys must respect the doors of buildings & there is no other building or door in all this prophesy. Now the door of the Kingdom of heaven represented by this Temple or Tabernacle he had newly opened with these keys by his resurrection from the dead.[46]

Further on in the same manuscript, he noted, "The Tabernacle or Temple is the common scene of all the apocalyptic visions & therefore to be understood as well here [the Apocalypse] as in other places."[47] In Newton's apocalyptical manuscripts, the rituals, the ritual objects, and the building itself are the portals of heaven, and the plan and the architecture of the Temple represent the plan of the earthly universe—it was the microcosm of the macrocosm, meaning that the plan of the Temple of Solomon was based on the plan of the heavens. It was possible to understand the plan of heaven through contemplation of the plan of Solomon's Temple. "In the Apocalypse the world natural is represented by the Temple of Jerusalem & the parts of this world by the analogous parts of the Temple."[48] To understand the architecture of the Temple was to have an insight into the meaning of the prophecies, which was as close to God as was humanly possible. Newton claimed,

Temple the parts hereof have the same signification with the analogous parts of the World, for Temples were anciently contrived to represent the frame of the Universe as the true Temple of the great God. Heaven is represented by the Holy place or main body of the edifice, the highest heaven by the most Holy or Adytum, the throne of God by the Ark, the Sun by the bright flame of the fire of the Altar or by the face of the Son of man shining through this flame like the Sun in his strength, the moon by the burning coals upon the Altar convex above & flat below like an half moon, the stars by the lamps, thunder by the song of the Temple, lightning by the flashing of the fire of the Altar, the Angels or inhabitants of heaven by Cherubim carved round the temple, the Sea by the great brazen laver, the earth by the area of the Courts & the bottomless pit or lower parts of the earth called Hades & Hell by the sink which ran down into the earth from the great Altar & was covered with a stone to open & shut. And all these parts of the Temple have the same signification with the parts of the world which they represent. And in allusion to the River Siloam which ran by the Temple of Jerusalem & flowed thence eastward & was by the Jewish Doctors accounted a type of the spirit, a River of life flowing eastward from the throne of God with trees of life growing on the banks thereof is put for the Law of God going out from the Throne of the kingdom to the Nations, the fruit of the trees & the water of the River being that spiritual meat & drink which Christ has represented by his body & blood & by the bread & wine in the Eucharist; & which were also prefigured by the Manna & rock of water in the wilderness.[49]

The plan of the Temple was the plan of the universe. Clearly, Newton did not perceive the Prytanæum or Temple as a real map of the universe that reflected nature, but rather as a hieroglyph that stood for "ideas" in the knowledge of natural philosophy—the ancient hieroglyph of knowledge of natural philosophy that had been encoded into the plans of the ancient temples and that had been lost over time:

> The placing the fire in the common centre of the Priests Court & of the outward court or court of the people in the Tabernacle & in Solomon's Temple [& the framing the Tabernacle & Temple so as to make it a symbol of the world] is a part also of the religion which the nations received from Noah.... And as the Tabernacle was a symbol of the heavens, so were the Prytanæa amongst the nations. The whole heavens they reckoned to be the true & real Temple of God & therefore that a Prytanæum [the temple] might deserve the name of his Temple they framed it so as in the fittest manner to represent the whole system of the heavens. A point of religion then which nothing can be more rational.[50]

A Temple structure that contained a central fire was to Newton a symbol of the purest form of philosophical wisdom—the heliocentric universe. Therefore, it was essential to understand the building. The best way to understand this building was through its architecture, which was sacred. Moses was given the plan of the Tabernacle—a portable tent used as a sanctuary for the Ark of the Covenant by the Israelites during the Exodus—by God, on Mount Sinai[51]; Solomon copied the plan of the Tabernacle, but he doubled the measurements and made it out of stone, wood, and marble.

This plan of the Temple of Solomon was recorded by the prophets. The Temple of Solomon is discussed in the Bible in twenty-three of the thirty-nine books in the Old Testament and eleven of the twenty-seven books of the New Testament,[52] but only two books describe the buildings of the Temple in any detail: 1 Kings 6–8, and Ezekiel 40–42 and 46. In the Book of Ezekiel, the Temple is seen in a vision of the prophet after the destruction of Solomon's Temple in 586 BC. In the vision of Ezekiel, his spirit is guided by an angel through the Temple, they measuring the height and width of the walls, the courtyards, the altar, and many of the spaces within the Temple precinct as he goes through it, but the prophet does not claim that the temple described is the Temple of Solomon; he only stated that it is a vision of the Temple of Jerusalem. Writers such as Bede in his Biblical exegesis of the Temple used 1 Kings[53] as his source, but Newton chose the more mystical and somewhat darker prophecy of Ezekiel, only using 1 Kings as a support text for Ezekiel. Ezekiel's mysticism was enhanced by his use of language—Ezekiel wrote in the encoded language of the prophets. Newton attempted to decode this language by understanding its measurements and architecture.

One of Newton's unpublished manuscripts, "A Treatise or Remarks on Solomon's Temple Introduction to the Lexicon of the Prophets, Part Two: About the Appearance of the Jewish Temple," more commonly known by its call name Babson MS 434, is a manuscript of more than eighty pages. Despite its name (apart from the first page, which is true to the title), it is an architectural reconstruction of the Temple of Jerusalem by Newton dated circa mid–1680s to the early 1690s. Unlike his small chapter in *The Chronology*, this manuscript demonstrates a good working knowledge of architectural principles, the work of the ancient Roman architectural theorist Vitruvius, and an interest in aesthetics.

In Babson MS 434, Newton twice examined the verses of the Book of Ezekiel that related to the Temple. In his first verse-by-verse examination, he examined the dimensions of the exterior and interior atriums and the gates with their colonnades. He plotted out the floor plan of the Temple, relating it to each verse through three floor plans—two floor plans of the gate and one of the Temple precinct—and he constantly checked all the measurements. In his second verse-by-verse examination, Newton again related the measurements given by Ezekiel to his floor plan with more detail, and he footnoted these with explanations of corruptions in the texts between Hebrew, Greek, Alexandrian, Latin, and Arabian editions, along with traditional Jewish texts. He also expanded some of the details of the text and commented on other contemporary commentators on the Temple such as Juan Bautista Villalpando,[54] and briefly on Louis Cappel, Constantijn L'Empereur, and Benito Arias Montano. However, he also added elements, such as the number of the rooms in a building, as if this number were included in Ezekiel's text.[55] Ezekiel, however, does not mention the number of rooms.

Newton claimed the measurements by Ezekiel were incomplete and that the description of the Temple was open to interpretation. He attempted to rationalize Ezekiel's measurements and to establish the missing measurements from other sources. He examined the architectural features of the Temple through the writings of the ancients, such as Josephus, Hecataeus, Maimonides, Philo, the *Talmud*, and the *Septuaginta*. In his examination of these writers, he was able to highlight the additions and changes made to the design of the Temple through time. Newton also integrated Jewish rituals into the building as another way of justifying the floor plan of the Temple. He looked for confirmation of Ezekiel's description through these ancient writers.

Newton examined the colonnades: the numbers of columns, their height, their thickness, their intervals, and their style. These he discerned to have been constructed according to the proportions of architecture. Newton revealed that he was familiar with the architectural theory of Vitruvius's *De Architectura*, particularly Books III and IV. When Newton derived the width of the inter-columns from the measurement of the column given by Josephus, he paraphrased Vitruvius Book III, Chapter III, "The Proportions of Intercolumniations and of Columns." He claimed that the "intervals of these pedestals, according to the proportions of architecture, should not be less than the pedestals."[56] From Vitruvius, Book IV, Chapter III, and the measurements of Josephus, Newton estimated the height of the columns was "six times the thickness according to the Doric style."[57] In Ezekiel 40:14, the measurement of the height of the doorway was given as twenty cubits; thus, Newton claimed that the "width of the doorway was of ten cubits and the height according to the rules of the architects, should be double the width."[58] For Newton, most of the measurements of the Temple are exactly to the "proportion of architectural demand."[59] Instead of just describing a floor plan (no matter how vague), as he did in *The Chronology*, in Babson MS 434 Newton described the architecture of the entire Temple precinct in enough detail to be able to reconstruct it.[60]

Newton also showed great concern with the measurements. In Ezekiel's vision the Temple is measured. Where Ezekiel gave overall measurements, Newton demonstrated that the collection of buildings described by the ancient writers corresponded with Ezekiel's description and dimensions.[61] His comparison of the measurements through the different stages of the development of the Temple was carefully executed and the inconsistencies were discarded from his floor plan. The measurements are the main feature of the architecture that he gives, and in his description, what is sacred is measured and what is not sacred is not measured. Newton claimed that

the temple with its Court & the holy City is the whole Church & it's here distinguished into two parts; the one (the Temple) measured & not given to the gentiles, & this is therefore the elect part of the Church; the other (the outward Court & holy City) left unmeasured that is neglected, left out of the measure or compass of God's regard, not measured compassed or bounded by God's laws but

> left to transgression, & therefore the reprobate part of the Church. And this is given to the Gentiles to possess, that is to those that should gentilize to be the inhabitants or Citizens which it should contain or consist of: & they tread it under foot, that is, contaminate corrupt & overwhelm the truth of their Christian profession by Gentile practices.[62]

Newton strongly believed in an original religion that had become corrupted by the infusion of "corrupt" philosophies. The act of measuring defined the divisions of the church and distinguished the sacred from the secular and corrupted.

It was not only the art of measuring that defined sacred and secular; the measurements themselves were divided into sacred and secular. Ezekiel distinguished the sacred architectural measurements as being distinct from "common" measurements. The Temple precinct was measured with "a measuring reed of six cubits long by the cubit and an hand breadth."[63] Ezekiel's description of these six sacred cubits that made up a reed is not clear, and to make matters worse he measured in reeds and cubits, leaving it unclear if there were two cubits—one of a forearm and the other a forearm and a hand's width. This leaves the cubit or cubits of the Israelites in debate. What is clear from the Book of Ezekiel is that the ancient Jewish measurements were embodied in the Temple and in the sacred object of the Temple. These measurements were ordained by God and related to the people through prophecy, and thus were an integral part of Newton's examination of the Temple.

Newton made an intensive study of the two Jewish cubits in an appendix entitled "De Magnitudine Cubiti Sacri" in one of his unpublished papers, which is a draft study of Solomon's Temple and the cubit.[64] This was originally written in Latin, but it was translated into English and published in *Miscellaneous Works of Mr. John Greaves, Professor of Astronomy in the University of Oxford* as "A Dissertation upon the Sacred Cubit of the Jews and the Cubits of the Several Nations"[65] in 1737. It is a most intriguing paper, in three respects. First, Newton applied an ingenious system of mathematical limits based on both ancient literary sources and contemporary studies of ancient buildings. Second, Newton created his own Newtonian man, as opposed to the Vitruvian man. Third, the paper highlights the struggle, in the Age of Enlightenment, to fit the literal truth of the Christian Scripture into the science of the day.[66]

Newton compared all of the ancient measurements from ancient texts and, in particular, the ones taken from Greaves's measurements of the Great Pyramid in Egypt, and argued that the common, or what he called the "vulgar," cubit of the Jews was derived from the Memphis cubit dating from the time when the Jews were held captive in Egypt. The vulgar cubit was used for building and daily measurements. Therefore, there was a need for a cubit for profane use and this was provided by the Babylonian cubit of two Roman feet. The proportion of the Babylonian cubit to the Memphis cubit was 6:5.0157 rounded off to 6:5. In Babson MS 434, Newton confirmed that the sacred cubit was six palms[67] and the vulgar cubit was five palms.[68] In the "Dissertation," Newton continued to define his limits using Greaves's measurements and a proposition by French mathematician, Marin Mersennus, which defined the cubit to be 23.25 French inches. He concluded that the sacred cubit was 25.6 *unciæ*.

Newton claimed that the *orgyia* or the fathom of a man—which is the length of the outstretched arms of a man—was supposed to be the same as the height of a man, but in fact is a palm wider.[69] Vitruvius stated in Book III, "For if we measure the distance from the soles of the feet to the top of the head, and then apply that measure to the outstretched arms, the breadth will be found to be the same as the height."[70] The image of the Vitruvian man was famous, even in Newton's time. Since Newton was familiar with Vitruvius's Book III, it was an image he would have recognized. It is odd that Newton moved away from the traditional proportions of Vitruvius, and it creates something of a puzzle. Although Newton insisted on exact architectural proportions, he moved away from the traditional proportions of the Vitruvian man, which had been an important element in other contemporary reconstructions. Newton accepted the Temple's architectural proportions as outlined in Vitruvius's Book III, yet he rejected the human model Vitruvius used as the foundation of these proportions. At the same time, Newton accepted that the human frame was the basis of all ancient measurements, that is, hand, digit, cubit, and *orgyia*, and he attempted to estimate the length of the sacred cubit using the length of the parts of the body and the measurements of the ancient writers, such as Vitruvius. Although it is an interesting puzzle, it is one that cannot be answered.[71]

In the Greaves publication, "Dissertation" is unfortunately presented as a finished paper, which it is not; it is a work in progress. Although Newton repeated a section on Josephus's measurements from

"Dissertation" in Babson MS 434, he never returned to this study. He did not attempt to specify the length of the cubit, except to say that the sacred cubit equals six palms and the vulgar five palms.

Babson MS 434 consists of two scriptural exegeses on the Book of Ezekiel verses 40:5–42:15 and 46:19. These are the verses in Ezekiel's vision of the Temple in which he moved around the Temple measuring it. In both of Newton's exegeses of these verses, he reconstructed the Temple. Babson MS 434 is a working study and the second exegesis is a refinement of the first, and although the second does not have an illustration of the floor plan of the Temple precinct, it is more detailed in its description of the building. The manuscript has been dated to the mid–1680s to 1690.[72] Newton very rarely dated his manuscripts, and he recycled paper for many years, which has left many of Newton's manuscripts undated. However, the date of mid–1680 is strengthened by the annotations in Figure 7, which shows his floor plan of the Temple precinct. His handwriting here still shows the distinctive "y^e," which Newton refrained from using after the 1690s. In addition to the style of writing, the content of Babson MS 434 supports this date: it is the culmination of a series of manuscripts written about the form of the Temple and the length of the cubit from the early 1680s.[73] In Babson MS 434, he brought these papers together to reconstruct the architecture of the Temple. After Babson MS 434, his studies of the Temple were theological rather than architectural.

Although Figure 7 looks similar to Figure 4 in *The Chronology*, there is a great deal of difference. Figure 4 fills in the details that Figure 7 does not have; moreover, this detail is not described in either *The Chronology* or Babson MS 434. However, in the second reconstruction in Babson MS 434 the detail is defined, but the floor plan differs from *The Chronology's* plans. From this description, it is possible to reconstruct Newton's model fully. Figure 8 shows the floor plan of the second reconstruction in Babson MS 434.

An overall similarity in the floor plans remains, but there are significant differences in their details. The floor plan in *The Chronology* has an extra external wall with four gates to the west; this wall belongs, not to the Temple of Solomon, but to the Second Temple. The colonnade of the outer and inner court, which in *The Chronology* Newton called the cloisters, is formed only from the columns that support the rooms above in *The Chronology* plan (see Figure 6), whereas in Babson

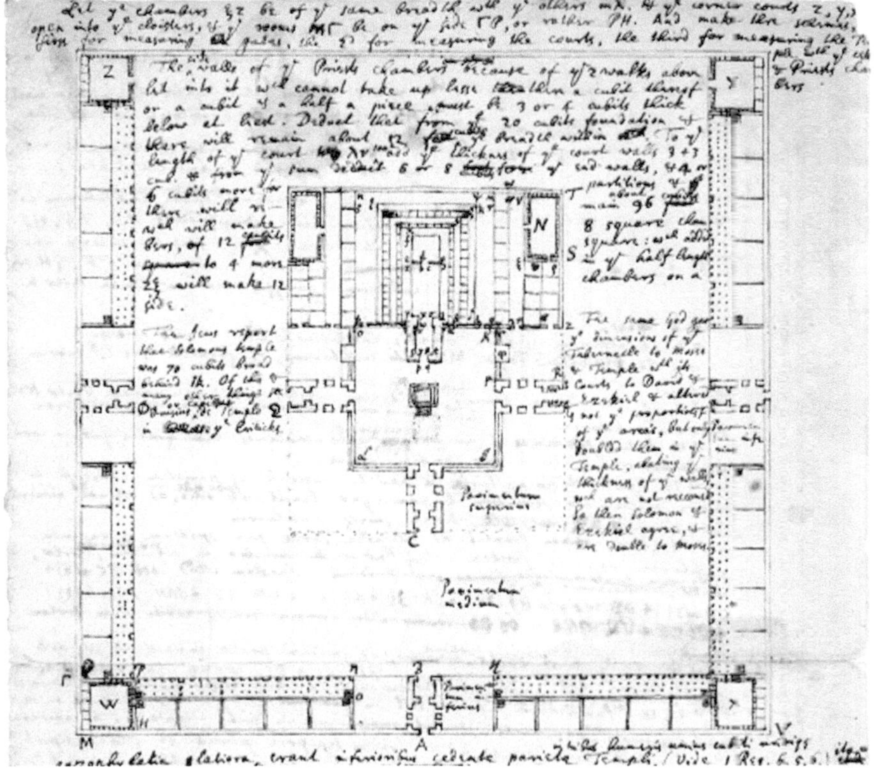

Figure 7. The Temple Precinct drawn by Newton Ms 434 (with kind permission of the Huntington Library).

MS 434 the colonnade extends in front of the building. This is clearly seen in Figure 8 and is described in both reconstructions in Babson MS 434. The thirty rooms around the Temple, the treasury, in *The Chronology* comprise two lots of fifteen rooms facing each other. In Babson MS 434, there are thirty rooms with a storeroom across the hall. There are also differences in the approaches to the Temple by the priests. In *The Chronology* the priest would access the treasury by the front steps of the Temple, whereas in Babson MS 434 there are separate steps on the north and south sides of the Temple. The largest difference is in the inner court in the northeast and southeast corners. In Babson MS 434 these corners are a continuation of the rooms for the priests, with a small staircase in the corner going up to the rooms, whereas in *The*

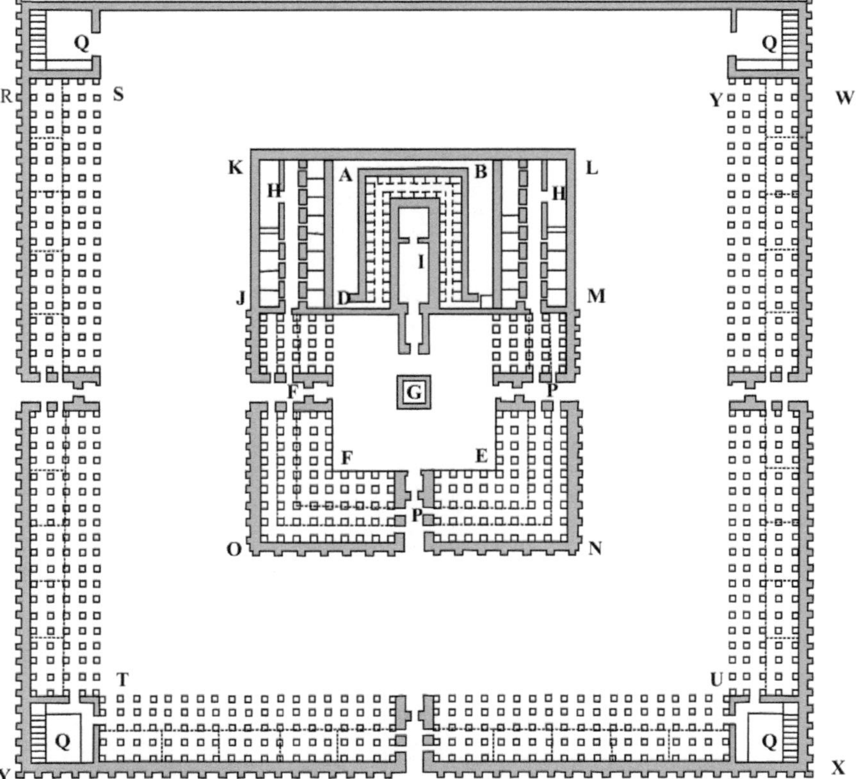

Figure 8. The final floor plan of Babson Ms 434 (re-drawn by the author).

Chronology there are large kitchens, and stairs around the inner wall of the large kitchen. There is no need for these kitchens, since the sacrifices were done and cooked in the great atrium and the priests' kitchens are in the northwest and southwest corners.

The differences are notable in the floor plan, but the difference becomes more acute in the three-dimensional plan. As previously mentioned, in *The Chronology* Newton created a Temple with a strange stepped structure: the porch was 120 cubits high, the holy sanctuary was ninety cubits high, and the holy of holies was sixty cubits high. In Babson MS 434, the porch was the same height as the towers of the great atrium—seventy or seventy-one cubits in height—and the Temple that included the holy sanctuary and the holy of holies were 120 cubits high. This gave the Temple an entirely different shape to the one described in *The Chronology*. However in *The Chronology* apart from the stepped structured Temple no description of the architecture of the Temple precinct was given.

Conclusion

Newton studied the Temple for over fifty years. It was far more to him than just a building described in the Bible or a religious symbol; it was the stage or vision for some of the major events of the Bible, particularly the closing of the seals of the Book of Names in Daniel and the opening of the seals in Revelation—the Apocalypse. To further his understanding of the Temple, he not only examined the prophecies in the Biblical texts, but he also studied chronology, metrology, and architecture.

Newton's library at his death consisted of 2,100 books. In John Harrison's *The Library of Isaac Newton*, published in 1978, he attempted to reconstruct this library. Harrison verified 1,763 surviving books from Newton's library. Many of the sources used in *The Chronology* are present in Harrison's book, and there are thirty-four Bibles in English, Latin, Greek, French, and Hebrew. There are a significant number of books on Jewish rites and customs as well as Jewish sources written in Hebrew.[74] However, many books that he was clearly familiar with in his unpublished papers are not included; either they have not survived or he borrowed a copy. Babson MS 434 and Newton's work on the cubit reveal his knowledge of the architectural principles of Vitruvius. Yet no copy of Vitruvius or any of the commentaries on Vitruvius have survived in his library.

Apart from his work on the Temple, Newton had no other study that would require knowledge of architectural principles, which does suggest that Newton was interested in reconstructing an accurate and realistic recreation of the Temple and not just a prophetic hieroglyph. In his manuscripts on prophecy and the Apocalypse, the reader is "moved" through the rooms and areas of the Temple. Ezekiel was guided by an angel through the Temple as he measured it; since Ezekiel did not see the entire Temple, the Temple was not completely measured. Newton and many others assumed symmetry to complete the design.

Symmetry assists the image of the Temple as microcosm and of the universe as macrocosm; symmetry is harmonious as the universe is harmonious. However, to Newton, it was also a real building that could be reconstructed. By the 17th century, architectural models of existing buildings had begun to be very popular, and they fitted into the Age of Reason and experimentation of which Newton was very much a part.

2

A Brief History of Models up to the 18th Century

At the end of the 17th century and during the 18th century, models were being built as a form of inquiry and to assist experimentation. The National Gallery in London exhibits paintings that demonstrate the fascination with models for experimentation. For example, *An Experiment on a Bird in the Air Pump*, painted in 1768, shows a family standing around a table conducting one of Robert Boyles's air pump experiments and depriving a bird of air in an air bell. The family stands around in fascination and in horror, but at the center of the image is the brightly lit model. After the publication of *Principia*, Newtonian mechanics came to be regarded as the ultimate explanatory science; models of mechanical planetariums and orreries became extremely popular, and many examples, particularly from the 18th century, are displayed in science museums throughout the world. However, the use of models for scientific inquiry was a recent process. This chapter will examine a brief history of models for both architecture and science up to the 18th century.

There is very little evidence that three-dimensional architectural models were used as an aid for building before the Renaissance. While drawings may be copied and archived, and texts published and widely disseminated, the architectural model is difficult to store, move, and maintain. Moreover, few architectural models are intended to last beyond the construction of the particular project they represent. Furthermore, they are generally built of material that has a temporary life span, such as wood. The architectural model will begin to deteriorate during the time that extends from its construction through to the erection of the building it presages. This temporal life span has made the extent of the use of ancient and medieval models difficult to ascertain.

There is some evidence of ancient "architectural" models. The ancient Egyptian architects used small-scale models as part of the design process. For example, a miniature temple portal from Heliopolis, Egypt, now in the Brooklyn Museum, New York, that is carved in sandstone and dated to the nineteenth dynasty reign of King Seti I (ca. 1285 BC) shows the layout and staircases for a temple entranceway. More generally, the Egyptians employed full-scale prototypes to achieve standardization of detail.[1] In one sense, a history of the model could commence with these prototypes even if they served a different purpose than that of the primary categories of architectural models. Small-scale models of people and rooms have also been found in Egyptian burial sites. Such funerary objects can be read to suggest a degree of control; a model of a person's chattels was buried with the person as a sign of the extent of his or her power in the physical world. Alternatively, these models offered a possible way of transcending death; they signified a degree of ongoing support in the afterlife.[2]

Although no ancient Greek scale models survive, their existence is verified by the "term παραδειγμα (a model of a complete building) and τυποε (a wax model of an ornamental detail)."[3] Although the Roman architect and author Marcus Vitruvius Pollio was much enamored of classical Greek architecture, there are few references to the model in his work. In Book One of his *Ten Books on Architecture*, Vitruvius outlined the required education for an architect, acknowledging the need for drawing and related forms of representation, since the architect "must have a knowledge of drawing so that he can readily make sketches to show the appearance of the work which he proposes."[4] However, for Vitruvius, drawing played a relatively minor role in the education of an architect in comparison with knowledge of history, philosophy, and music.

In Book Ten, Vitruvius used the architectural model in a cautionary tale:

> For Diognetus was a Rhodian architect, to whom, as an honour, was granted out of the public treasury a fixed annual payment commensurate with the dignity of his art. At this time an architect from Aradus, Callias by name, coming to Rhodes, gave a public lecture, and showed a model of a wall, over which he set a machine on a revolving crane with which he seized an helepolis [a type of siege engine] as it approached the fortifications, and brought it inside the wall. The Rhodians, when they had seen this model, filled with admiration, took from Diognetus the yearly grant and transferred this honour to Callias.[5]

When the city came under threat, the people appealed to Callias to build his siege engine from the model that he had exhibited to them. Callias stated that it was not possible, since not everything has identical principles when enlarged from a small model. Vitruvius emphatically stated that, although some models might appear practicable on the smallest scale, this does not infer that they are functional on a larger scale.[6] In the end, the people begged Diognetus to protect the town. Initially he refused, but later relented, although the architect did not save the city through architecture or invention, but by cunning. He had the people pour a large volume of water, filth, and excrement outside of the walls of the city overnight so that the enemy's siege engine could not advance on the city. Vitruvius also related a similar instance wherein an architect defeated the enemy, and he concluded that "the freedom of states [has] been preserved by the cunning of the architects."[7] not by machines or, by inference, models. Vitruvius was wary of the seductive power of the model and called instead for architects to rely on their intellects, and not on simulations.

Vitruvius's acknowledgment of models, and his cautionary tales, indicates that the Greek and Roman builders may have used models as a tool. However, it does appear that Vitruvius did not believe that models were useful for structural and engineering problems or architectural problems of the study of space and aesthetics, and they did not seem to have been widely used. Suetonius wrote that Julius Caesar demolished a newly completed house on his estate at Nemi because he disliked its physical appearance.[8] Presumably, this could have been avoided had he seen a model of the building before it was constructed.

The Etruscans' cremation urns were often in the shape of their houses, and later Roman sarcophagi mimic houses with pitched roofs. These "architectural models" were carried on in the Christian tradition. In the medieval period, reliquaries were often built as models of churches. For example, the Shire of the Kings, created by Nicholas of Verdan, ca. 1170–1230, at Cologne Cathedral, is clearly a model of a church; however, the architecture is secondary to the decoration of the figures of the saints. Other examples, such as the Artophorion reliquary of Saint Anastasios of Persia, made in Antioch in ca. 969–70, are a replica of a Byzantine church built of silver and silver gilt.

Miniature churches were also used as votive offerings. In the paintings and mosaics of medieval Europe, donors to churches were depicted holding a model of the church that they helped to raise. A notable example of this is the mosaic showing Theodore Metochites from the Chora Monastery in Constantinople—now Istanbul—presenting a model of the monastery that he paid to have restored in 1316–1321 to the seated Christ. In Gloucester Cathedral, there is a recumbent effigy of a Saxon Abbot, Osric, who is clasping a model to his breast. In Ravenna, a fresco depicts an archbishop who is offering a model of the church of San Vitale to the saint. These architectural models were never used to understand architecture or to assist with designing the building. They are signs of their bearer's achievement as well as symbolic devotional offerings. These are not architectural models, but early forms of the presentation model—a representation of the form of the building that has been constructed to convey a message—and in these cases, the messages signify the role of the creative individual and the power, and supposed divinity, of the patron.

The earliest evidence of three-dimensional models being used for practical purposes rather than devotional purposes is in Giorgio Vasari's *Lives of the Artists*. He related a contemporary account of Lorenzo di Cione Ghiberti seeing a model made by Giotto of the Campanile of the Florence Cathedral. He found it very convincing in that it expressed the design and the invention of the Campanile.[9] The existence of this model has been supported by archival evidence. In contemporaneous accounts, a distinction is made between *modellum seu disegniam*, meaning a three-dimensional model, and *chara pechoris* and *modelli in cartis pecundinis*,[10] meaning plans and elevations. Vasari claimed that Giotto worked on the model himself and it was reported to be in the German style. The model differed from the completed Campanile because it had a spire, rather than a pyramid. Unfortunately, this model no longer exists. From the 14th century onwards, models began to play a greater role in the development of design. For a competition for the two doors of San Giovanni, the Signoria of Florence and the Guild of Merchants required the competitors to produce a specimen scene in bronze. Vasari noted that under the guidance of Bartoluccio, Lorenzo Ghiberti was compelled to create a large number of models to test his design for this competition:

> Lorenzo alone was ever inviting the citizens, and sometimes passing strangers who had some knowledge of the art, to see his work, in order to hear what they thought, and these opinions enabled him to execute a model very well wrought and without one defect.[11]

Between the 15th and 16th centuries, many hundreds of models were made but only thirty or so models still exist from this period.[12] At the beginning of the 15th century, architects and engineers were summoned by the wardens of the works of Santa Maria del Fiore and by the consuls of the Guild of Wool, to discuss the raising of the cupola. Specifically, models were to be produced to demonstrate the method of its construction.[13] The counsel and plan of Filippo Brunelleschi delighted the consuls and the wardens of the works, but they requested that he build a model of the design.[14] However, Brunelleschi feigned a lack of interest, and a public competition to build the cupola took place in 1418 with both plans and models requested. While Brunelleschi was the only expert who was prepared to vault the dome at a reasonable cost, he remained singularly unwilling to present a model that explained the process. According to Vasari, Brunelleschi "could have shown a little model that he had in his possession, but he did not wish to show it, having recognized the small intelligence of the consuls, the envy of the craftsmen, and the instability of the citizens."[15] The consuls, the wardens, and the architects demanded that Brunelleschi

> speak his mind in detail, and to show his model, as they had shown the rs; but this he refused to do, proposing instead to those masters … that whosoever could make an egg stand upright on a flat piece of marble should build the cupola, since thus each man's intellect would be discerned. Taking an egg, therefore, all those masters sought to make it stand upright, but not one could find the way. Whereupon Filippo, being told to make it stand took it graciously, and giving one end of it a blow on the flat piece of marble made it stand upright. The craftsmen protested that they could have done the same; but Filippo answered, laughing, that they could also have raised the cupola, if they had seen the model or the design.[16]

This quote implies that architects of the time made models in secret or with concealed elements, particularly relating to construction of complex structures, such as the cupola, so that the design could not be copied by other architects. Brunelleschi is known to have carved details of buildings, for the workmen to follow, in clay, wax, wood, and even large winter turnips.[17]

Brunelleschi did eventually have a grand model constructed, and this model, preserved to this day in the Museo dell'Opera in Florence, is the oldest architectural model in existence (see Figure 9). The model, constructed by the carpenter Bartolommeo, was required to have "all the exact proportions measured to scale" and all its parts were fabricated, "such as stairs both lighted and dark, and every sort of window, door, tie and buttress, together with a part of the gallery."[18] Such was the importance of this design model that Brunelleschi eventually made his own models of Santo Spirito, the Pazzi Chapel, Palazzo Quaratesi, the Medici Palace, the fortifications of Pesaro and Vicopisano, and the Badia at Fiesole.

Architectural models gained more prominence with the rediscovery

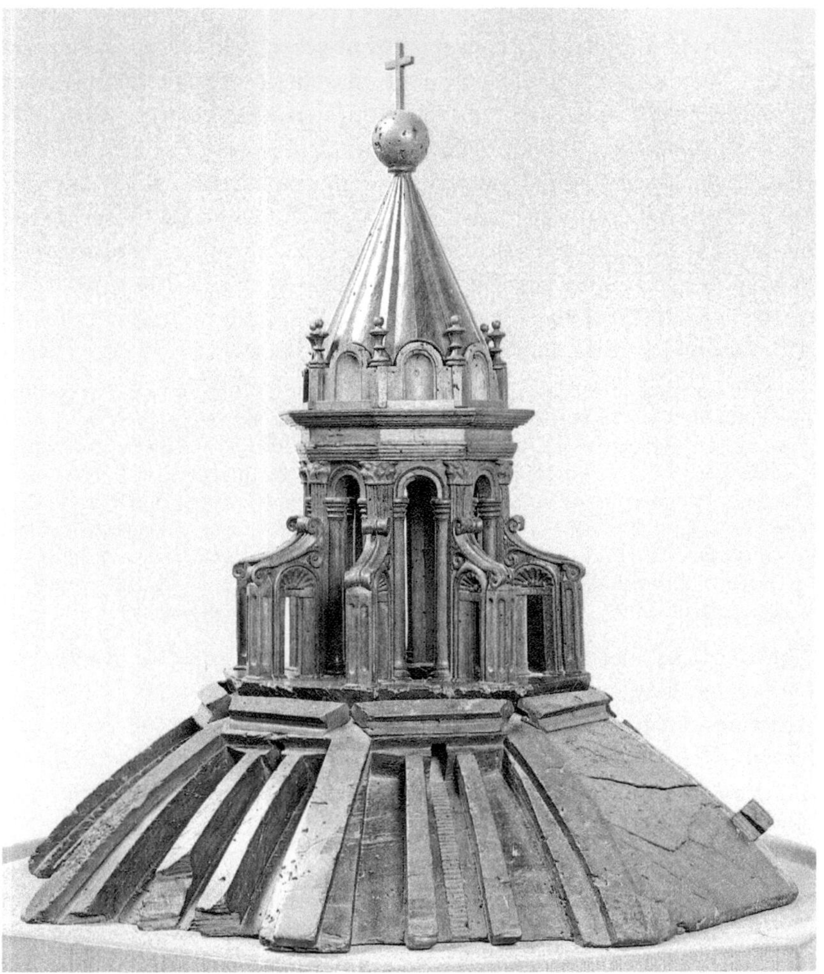

Figure 9. Filippo Brunelleschi's model of the Lantern of Florence Cathedral (copyright Victoria and Albert Museum, London).

of Vitruvius in the 15th century. In *De re Aedificatoria*, published in 1485, Leon Battista Alberti claimed that models were a useful tool for the architect, but at the same time he issued a caution:

> I will commend the time-honored custom, practiced by the best builders, of preparing not only drawings and sketches but also models of wood or any other material. These will enable us to weigh up repeatedly and examine, with the advice of experts, the work of the individual dimensions of all parts, and, before continuing any further, to estimate the likely trouble and expense. Having constructed these models, it will be possible to examine clearly and consider thoroughly the relationship between the site and the surrounding district, the shape of the area the number and order of the parts of the building, the appearance the walls, the strength of the covering, and in short the design and construction of all the elements discussed.... It will also allow one to increase or decrease the size of those elements freely, to exchange them, and to make new proposals and alterations until everything fits together well and meets with approval.... There is a particularly relevant consideration that I feel should be mentioned here: the presentation of models that have been colored and lewdly dressed with the allurement of painting is the mark of no architect intent on conveying the facts; rather it is that of a conceited one striving to attract and seduce the eye of the beholder, and to divert his attention from a proper examination of the parts to be considered, toward admiration of himself. Better then that the models are not accurately finished, refined, and highly decorated, but plain and simple, so that they demonstrate the ingenuity of him who conceived the idea, and not the skill of the one [who] fabricated the model.[19]

Alberti perceived that the model as a tool had a significant role for thinking about designs, for representing these designs for future buildings, and for avoiding errors in design in future buildings. However, he is clear in his caution that to "over-dress" the model might create an illusion that would lead the designer into errors of interpretation. He stressed that the construction of models would allow for the representation of many aspects of the architectural ideas in a sensible form. Although models were no doubt in use for the development of design concepts before the times of Brunelleschi and Alberti, during the Renaissance the model finally began to shift away from being a sign or symbol for a building and took on more practical applications to further the understanding of the construction of the building as well as its aesthetics.

Although the architectural scale model became increasingly used as part of the design process in the late 15th century, it also continued to be constructed for a range of other pragmatic purposes. In particular, by the 16th century, scale models were being used as tactical aids on the battlefield. In 1529, Pope Clement VII was at war against Florence. Wishing to utilize his forces to the best advantage, he ordered that a plan of the city and its surroundings be constructed. Tribola, a Florentine architect, suggested that the plan be constructed in relief, and he set about it with an excessive zeal and diligence, to measure the land in order that an accurate model could be constructed. The model was constructed of cork

> for the sake of lightness, and limited the whole plan to the space of four braccia and measured everything to scale. Having then been finished in this manner, and being made in pieces, that plan was packed up secretly and smuggled out of Florence in some bales of wool that were going to Perugia, being consigned to one who had orders to send it to the Pope, who made use of it continually during the siege of Florence.[20]

However, the most notable models of the Renaissance were architectural, and their creators appear to have taken no notice of Alberti's warning of simplicity, since very extravagant models were produced. Throughout his career, Antonio da Sangallo the younger worked on Saint Peter's Basilica in Rome. At first, he was Donato Bramante's assistant; then, in 1520, he himself became chief architect of Saint Peter's. In 1539, Pope Paul III commissioned Sangallo to build a model of the design for Saint Peter's. It was built by Antonio L'Abacco in wood, and was twenty-two feet long and thirteen feet high. It was reported to have taken seven years to complete, and to have cost 4,184 crowns. L'Abacco finished the model a short time after Sangallo's death. He wished to show, by building the model, "how great was the genius of Sangallo, and to make known to all men the opinion of that architect; for the new plans had been proposed in opposition by Michelangelo Buonarroti."[21] The model was perceived to be in imitation of the style and the manner of the Germans rather than the "good manner of the ancient, which is now followed by the best architects."[22] It is clear that Vasari thought that the model was Sangallo's greatest architectural achievement.

Built to the scale of 1:30, the model is large enough to walk into and was built to show both the external and internal detail. The model "bears traces of a hurried completion," perhaps because of Sangallo's death, and "documents indicate it was built partially by candlelight in the early morning hours."[23] The model remains part of the Vatican collection and is on exhibit at the Vatican Museum.

Michelangelo Buonarroti spent a considerable time constructing his own architectural models.[24] It also appears that the succession of popes for whom Michelangelo worked expected him to make models for them and demanded them at all stages of his projects.[25] Michelangelo rarely produced perspective sketches or completed extensive plans, sections, or elevations, preferring to use models.

This approach to architecture, being sculptural, inevitably was reinforced by special sensitivity to materials and to the effects of light. Michelangelo capitalized upon the structure of the materials because of his desire to achieve a maximum contrast between members used to express force and tension and "neutral" wall surfaces. He invariably minimized the peculiarities of surface materials such as stucco and brick, while he carved and finished the plastic members to evoke—even to exaggerate—the quality and texture of the stone.[26]

By the time Michelangelo worked on the rebuilding of Saint Peter's, he was in his eighties. He wrote to Vasari in 1557, saying, "God give me grace that I may be able to serve him with this my poor person, for my memory and my brain gone to await him elsewhere.'[27] Since there was a delay in raising the cupola, he was urged by his friends to build a model of it. At first, he built a small clay model; from the clay model and from plans and profiles that he drew, it was possible to construct a larger model under Michelangelo's direction. The model is one foot eight inches high by twelve feet eight inches in diameter.

In a letter to Vasari, Michelangelo claimed that he "made an exact model [of the dome] as I do of everything."[28] However, he also continually revised the model while the building was under construction and so his designs were in a "constant state of flux until every detail was ready for carving, a method entirely consistent with his organic approach. His conception of a building literally grew, and a change in any part involved sympathetic changes in other parts."[29] The model represents half of the dome, so that the exterior, the structure, and the inner and outer shells can be viewed. It also still exists, and is located in Saint Peter's Basilica in the Vatican.

In England, the history of the architectural model becomes fraught with linguistic problems. French joiner Adrian Gaunt is reported to have built a model of Longleat House, London, in 1567.[30] However, the term used to refer to the plan can be confused with model. In the language of the era, the word "model" could also be used to refer to a plan, and "platte," "plante," and "platforme" were also used for a plan.[31] This is reflected in *Henry IV, Part II*, written in 1598, when Shakespeare wrote

> When we mean to build,
> we first survey the plot,
> then draw the model.

Similarly, in 1617, Inigo Jones prepared a "modell or platforme for a new star-chamber"; drawn on paper, these are still preserved at Worcester College, Oxford. The Banqueting House in Whitehall, by the same architect, was begun in 1619, "according to a model thereof made"; also drawn on paper, it is now on display in the Chatsworth collection. For these two "modells" he was paid thirty-seven pounds in 1619. In 1618, his "modell" for the new chapel of Lincoln's Inn was approved.[32] These references suggest that Jones's "models" were plans rather than three-dimensional objects.

At around the same time, Henry Wotton's *Elements of Architecture* was published. In his work, Wotton stresses the value of the models in a manner reminiscent of Alberti. Wotton argued,

> Let no man that intendeth to build, settle his fancy upon a draught of the work in paper, how exactly so ever measured, of neatly set perspective; and much less upon a bare plan thereof, as they call the schiographia or ground lines; without a model or type of the whole structure, and of every parcel and partition in pasteboard or wood. Next that the said model be as plain as may be, without colours or other beautifying, lest the pleasure of the eye preoccupies the judgment.[33]

Wotton, like Alberti, strongly advised against the use of "beautifying" techniques that might seduce the eye and distract it from an intellectual rather than a sensual appreciation of the architectural form.

One of the great enigmas of the 17th century was the foundation of the Royal Society of London. As a result of civil war, plague, religious persecution, and destruction, a body of twelve men of science, drawn from different political persuasions, formed the Royal Society. The Society was formally constituted in 1660 and was given a Royal Charter in 1662. Their stated intention was to discuss and resolve "scientific" concerns of the day. Importantly, in the 17th century, the word "scientific" could refer to anything that required a level of problem solving. A common methodological characteristic of the scientific approach of the day was the use of models to demonstrate discoveries. Led by Robert Hooke,[34] who was then curator of experiments for the society,[35] weekly investigations were carried out using a range of models depicting engineering, architectural, scientific, or astronomical problems.[36]

In 1660, the same year that Hooke began to lead the experiments at the Royal Society, architect Roger Pratt advocated the construction of small-scale models as a means of providing a record of the design process.[37] He claimed that "all things both external and internal with all their divisions, connection vanes, ornaments etc., ... there to be seen as exactly, and in their due proportion, as they can afterwards be in the work of which this composed to be the essay."[38] After the fire of London in 1666, Pratt, along with architects Hugh May and Christopher Wren, was appointed to oversee the rebuilding of the city[39]; each presented plans, but Hooke presented a model for rebuilding the city to assembled company of the Royal Society.[40] Unfortunately, none of Hooke's models have survived.

The earliest surviving English architectural model is of a chapel of Pembroke College in Cambridge that was designed by Christopher Wren. Although the model was earlier dated by scholars to 1663,[41] it appears that the model was not delivered to Cambridge until 1667 and the construction of the building did not commence until 1668.[42] Additionally, in 1667, the master of Pembroke College wrote to thank Wren for his "care concerning the model of our chapel,"[43] which undermines the earlier dating of the model from 1663. Wren, one of the founding members of the Royal Society, was described as a gifted model maker, and he used models extensively in both his scientific and his architectural work. Architectural historian Sir John Summerson said of Christopher Wren,

> It seems the enigma of Wren's dual capacity as scientist and architect is not really a very profound one. A young man of exceptional gifts, with natural abilities as a draughtsman and model-maker, was drawn into a circle of men considerably older that himself [the Royal Society]. His remarkably elastic mind enabled him to come abreast with most of them in their own fields when, on nearly every occasion, his propensity for visual expression was made evident.[44]

Wren also built many models for the Royal Society—in his capacity as a professor of astronomy—that predate his surviving architectural miniatures.[45]

Before the Great Fire of London, the Cathedral of Saint Paul was in a poor state of repair and a commission for repairing the cathedral was formed. Five months before the fire, Wren wrote the following recommendation to the commissioners:

> For the encouragement and satisfaction of benefactors that comprehend not designs and drafts on paper as well as for the inferior artificers' clearer intelligence of their business, it will not be amiss that a good and careful large model be made, which will also have the use that if the work should happen to be interrupted or retarded posterity will go on where it was left, pursuing still the same designs.[46]

Early in 1666, Wren clearly thought there were great benefits to building a model.

To support the cathedral, a large wooden scaffold had been built around it. When the fire reached Saint Paul's, the scaffold ignited and assisted in the destruction of the cathedral. Wren produced several plans and drawings for the rebuilding that were "intended to equal, if not exceed the splendor and the magnificence of the old Cathedral"[47] and he presented these to King Charles II. According to a biography written by Wren's son (also called Christopher), "his Majesty well approving one of them, commanded a model to be made therefore in so large and exact manner that it might remain as a perpetual and unchanging rule and direction for the conduct of the whole work."[48] In 1673, Wren commissioned such a model, and after inspecting it, the clergy deemed it too Catholic in design and rejected it. Wren offered a compromise solution; the clergy were "much pleased with the design, and wished to see a model: the surveyor [Wren] complied with their desire as well as his own, and made a very curious large model in wood (see Figure 10)."[49] Despite this, still nothing was resolved, and the chapter and some of the clergy thought the model not Catholic enough in style.[50] Contrary to his earlier proposition, in this specific case Pratt even disputed the need for a model and claimed that Inigo Jones, for example, had done very well without a model.[51] Wren further modified the plan and eventually Charles II approved of it. "From that time [Wren] resolved to make no more models ... which (as he had found by experienced) did but lose time, and subject his business many times to incompetent judges."[52] Wren appears to have kept this promise: he never again made a model of an entire design.[53]

Despite Wren's reluctance to make models, Nicholas Hawksmoor, Wren's personal assistant and clerk of works, continued to produce models of entire designs:

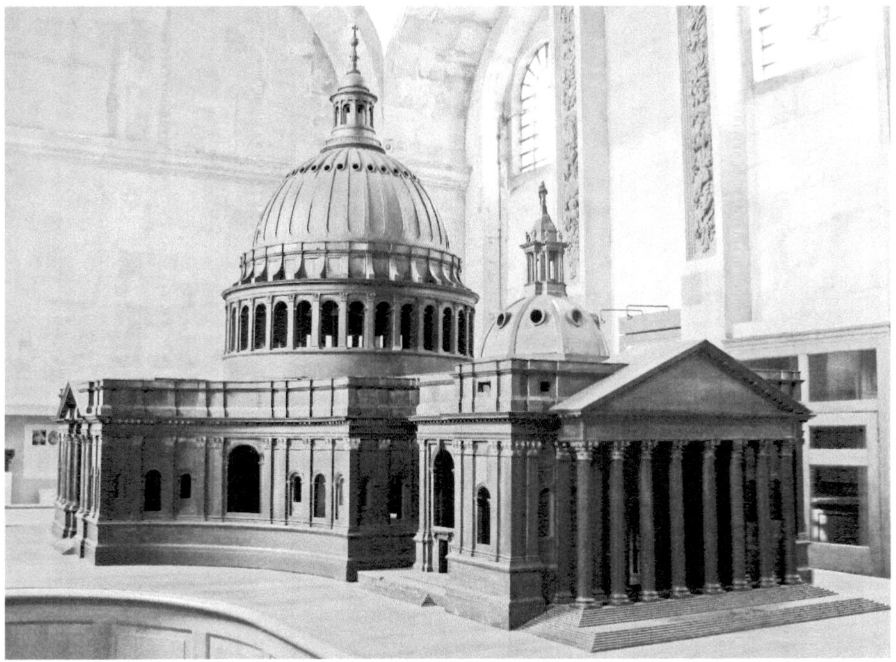

Figure 10. Christopher Wren's model of Saint Paul's (© The Chapter of St Paul's Cathedral).

> [Hawksmoor's] designs involved singular effects of space, texture and lighting which could only have been fully developed through models. ...The comparative simplicity of Hawksmoor's surviving models and various signs of alterations in them suggest that they were in fact used as specialized aids to design beyond a merely explanatory function.[54]

Hawksmoor's surviving models include sections of the Royal Naval Hospital (Greenwich 1699), the model for Easton Neston (Northamptonshire 1690), and the main court at King's College (1713) (see Figure 11).

In the 17th century, architectural models became more commonly used as a tool for visualizing the building at hand and for technical assistance. The vice-president of the Society of the Antiquarian and president of the Royal Society, Martin Folkes, made a fine model out of mahogany of Stonehenge to understand its use as an astronomical measurement and tool.[55] Unfortunately, the model is lost. Similarly, the Royal Society repeatedly used models for experimentation. They were considered practical tools that were embedded into the culture of the

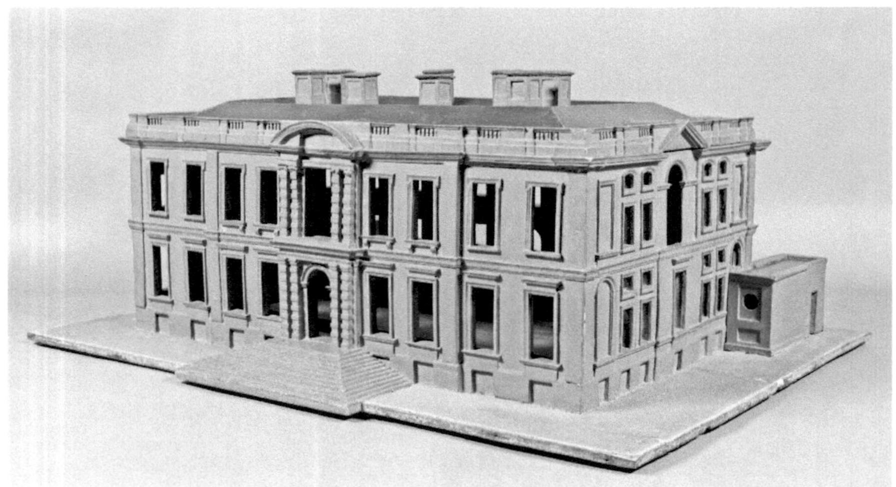

Figure 11. Hawksmoor's surviving model for Easton Neston (courtesy of the Royal Institute of British Architects).

time. This practical tool extended to examining Biblical architecture, to further an understanding of the architecture, its grandeur, and the origin of the architecture.[56]

In the mid–17th century, Solomon's Temple became the center of an exhibition that captured the public's imagination in Europe and in England. Fifty years later, another model of the Temple found public acclaim in London. It is very possible that Isaac Newton visited the exhibition of these models. One exhibition was staged before he wrote his reconstruction in Babson MS 434 and the other was held after. Both of these models approached Solomon's Temple in a scientific manner— a manner that would have appealed to Newton. In his own reconstruction, he approached his model with the same methodology, fusing religion and architecture together in what he thought was a historical reconstruction of the Temple. However, all of these models of Solomon's Temple were not isolated instances of reconstruction; they were developed through a long tradition of paper architecture, of designs that had been created with ground plans—some with sections and elevations and perspectives—but never built.

3

Paper Reconstructions of the Temple of Solomon from the 17th and 18th Centuries

The plan of Solomon's Temple was derived from the plan of the Tabernacle, which God described to Moses on Mount Sinai. The Tabernacle was built as a temporary sanctuary for the Israelites when wandering the desert in exile. The Temple of Solomon was believed to be the first permanent realization of this God-given plan. Between the early 17th and the mid–18th century, there was a proliferation of architectural reconstructions of the Temple of Solomon. However, there had been an interest in the appearance of the Temple before this period. This chapter first considers the background to this proliferation of reconstructions and then the paper reconstructions themselves.

Background

Bede's *De Tabernaculo* and *De Templo* are the two earliest complete and non–Biblical surviving texts on the Tabernacle and the Temple of Solomon. Bede embarked on a full scriptural exegesis in his two books of the Tabernacle and the Temple. In *De Tabernaculo*, Bede gave a verse-by-verse commentary on Exodus 24:12–30:31, and *De Templo* has a verse-by-verse commentary on 1 Kings 5–6. However, Bede also included the description of the Temple from the Books of Paralipomenon and referred to Josephus in the measurements of the Temple. In the entire *De Templo*, Bede only mentioned Ezekiel three times[1] and these references do not relate to the Temple directly. He believed that Ezekiel's text on the Temple was "irreducibly incoherent, literal non-sense, and thus only to be read 'spiritually' and as a metaphor."[2]

For Bede, "the house of God which King Solomon built in Jerusalem was made as a figure for the holy Universal Church."[3] It was in the building of the Tabernacle and the Temple that the Universal Church was signified. According to Bede, the distinctive features of these sanctuaries could be generalized thus:

> The workmanship of the Tabernacle is [of] the time of the synagogue (that is, of the ancient people of God), but the workmanship of the temple signifies the Church (that is that multitude of elect which has come to faith after the Lord's incarnation). For Moses completed the tabernacle with the people of the Hebrews alone, but Solomon finished [building] the temple with a multitude of proselytes gathered together, and also with the help of the king of Tyre and his artisans, who were Jews neither by birth nor by profession.[4]

Bede viewed the building of both sanctuaries as representing different stages of the whole Church, which continued to be built from the beginning of creation to the end of the world. They also depicted "the glory of the life to come."[5]

Bede's selection of verses in *De Tabernaculo* consisted of a detailed description of the plan and of the vessels that were given to Moses directly from God.[6] The entire book is about the plan of the Tabernacle, but he finished *De Tabernaculo* without commenting on the construction of the Tabernacle. Consequently, *De Tabernaculo* does not consider the community for which it was to be built—the divine plan of the Tabernacle was built by the sons of Israel for the Jewish community. This is in contrast to *De Templo*, where the building of the Temple is highly significant. For Bede, the sons of Israel, the proselytes and the Gentiles all worked on the house of the Lord:

> Every kind of person by whom the Church was to be built had already gone before in the building of the Temple. For the Jews and proselytes and gentiles converted to the truth of the Gospel build one and the same Church of Christ whether by upright living or by teaching as well.[7]

Bede built an image of accord and unity in a common purpose in the Universal Church. However, for Bede, this symbolism did not translate to other earthly sanctuaries.

In the *Historia Ecclesiatica,* Bede described the erection and dedication of churches in Saint Albans,[8] Canterbury,[9] York,[10] Lastingham,[11] Lindisfarne,[12] the churches of Jerusalem,[13] and Hexham.[14] While the Tabernacle and the Temple were earthly sanctuaries, they differed from other earthly sanctuaries since their plans were God-given. These other churches were houses of Christian worship built for the glorification of God and directed and planned by man, and for Bede, they were not symbols of the image of God or of the Universal Church.

However, Bede clearly made a distinction between building as a symbol of the Universal Church and the manifestations of churches as places of worship. In his scriptural exegesis, he did not attempt to reconstruct the Tabernacle or the Temple. Bede viewed both sanctuaries as pure metaphor, and their realization in reconstruction or in the form of churches of worship appeared to be irrelevant.

Throughout both the *De Tabernaculo* and *De Templo,* Bede promoted the idea that the Tabernacle and the Temple were allegories of the present and future church respectively. Peter Abelard compared the New Jerusalem, as described in the Revelation of John the Divine, with the Temple precinct of Solomon as God's regal palace. This analogy is found in Wisdom 9:8. The Temple of Solomon was built with the proportions of the celestial harmonies as described in the Book of Kings[15] so that the Temple was permeated by the divine harmony of the celestial spheres. Abelard transposed the heavenly and divine harmonies into the architecture of the Temple,[16] rather than architecture being a vehicle to God and to heaven. Although Philo mentioned the divine harmonies of the Tabernacle,[17] it appears that Abelard was the first medieval writer to suggest that the proportions of the Temple corresponded with the celestial harmonies,[18] making the connection of the Platonic celestial harmony of the spheres,[19] the Temple, and the Christian concept of heaven.

The Gothic cathedral was to be the mystical and liturgical image of heaven and it was to be the vision of the celestial city, as described in the Book of Revelation and the Temple of Solomon, which were both understood as images of heaven. The emphasis was on the architecture and architectural features, such as the stained glass windows, that made a jeweled space within which to remember the heavenly Jerusalem.[20] At Saint Denis, consecrated in 1140 by Abbot Suger in Paris, Suger compared his church to the Temple of Solomon and the choir to the heavenly city of the divine king.[21] Suger had the altar of Saint Denis studded with the twelve gems of the foundations and the pearls of the gates of the New Jerusalem; these gems were the same as those ascribed to the twelve tribes of Israel, which he believed had magical properties.[22] Light filled the upper chapel of the western bays of the cathedral at Saint Denis, and Suger claimed that it was "most beautiful and worthy to be the dwelling of angels."[23] The architecture was an awe-inspiring setting and less earthbound than the buildings it had replaced.

The light that transformed the Gothic cathedral and its stone vaulting gave the church a new style of symbol as the "house of God" and not just a meeting place for the faithful souls. The Gothic cathedral was the "stone from without" that was the meeting point for the "living stones."[24] The two concepts of the Old and New Testament merge in the symbol of the Gothic Universal Church.

This earthly image of heaven in the form of the cathedral was the ritual, spiritual, and economic, as well as the physical, center of the city, and it became both a visible and a spiritual image of heaven. Previously, the source of Christian iconography of the Temple had been within the Jewish tradition. However, in the Christian context, architectural references to the Tabernacle and the Temple as described in the Scriptures were not always considered, and illustrations were often in the contemporary Gothic style.[25] Many of the illustrations of the surviving copies of the commentary on Ezekiel by Richard of Saint Victor (d. 1173), which are dated to the thirteenth century, are Gothic in style, with distinctly Gothic shaped arches[26] (see Figure 12). These illustrations have a similarity to the architecture of contemporaneous depictions of the New Jerusalem.[27] In the illustrations of Nicolaus de Lyra's *Postillae*, the Temple is a medieval building with a Gothic-tower-like crenellated structure with Gothic windows (see Figures 13 and 14).[28] The Temple interior of 1299 in a copy of Petrus Comestor's *Historia Scholastica* has the image of a Gothic choir[29] (see Figure 15). The image of Solomon's Temple as a contemporary medieval cathedral continued into the early 16th century.

The medieval cathedral contains elements of Solomonaic architecture and dimensions. In the Cathedral of Würzburg are two thirteenth-century "oriental-looking" columns with the names "Jachin" and "Boaz" in Hebrew script engraved upon the shafts.[30] In the abbey church of Saint Andrea (1470–1476), the original three bays were

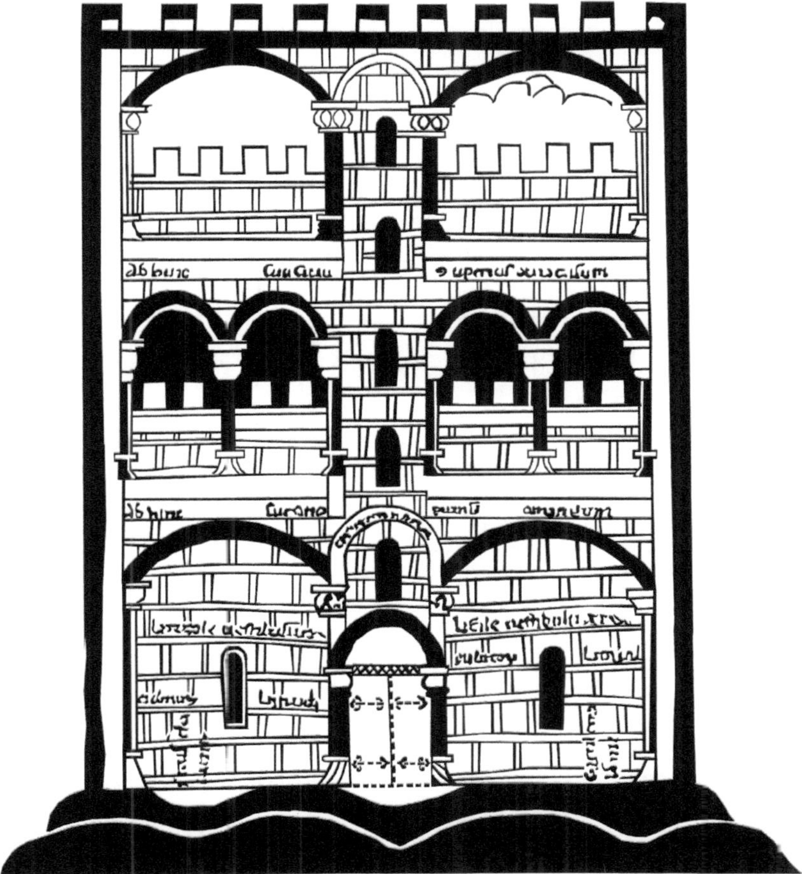

Figure 12. Façade of the eastern gatehouse of Solomon's Temple from Richard of St. Victor in *Ezechielem*, Paris, Bibliothèque Nationale, lat. 14515, fol. 240 (re-drawn by the author).

arranged in the proportion of the sacred sanctuary of the Temple of Solomon.[31] Lorenzo Ghiberti cast a bronze relief panel of the meeting of Solomon and the Queen of Sheba in the "Gates of Paradise" at the Baptistery of San Giovanni in Florence. Sculptures of the Judgment of Solomon appear on the portals of Gothic cathedrals such as Chartres, Amiens, Strasbourg, and Auxerre. It appears that the English coronation throne during the thirteenth century was decorated with the iconography of the throne of Solomon as described in 2 Chronicles 9:17–19.[32]

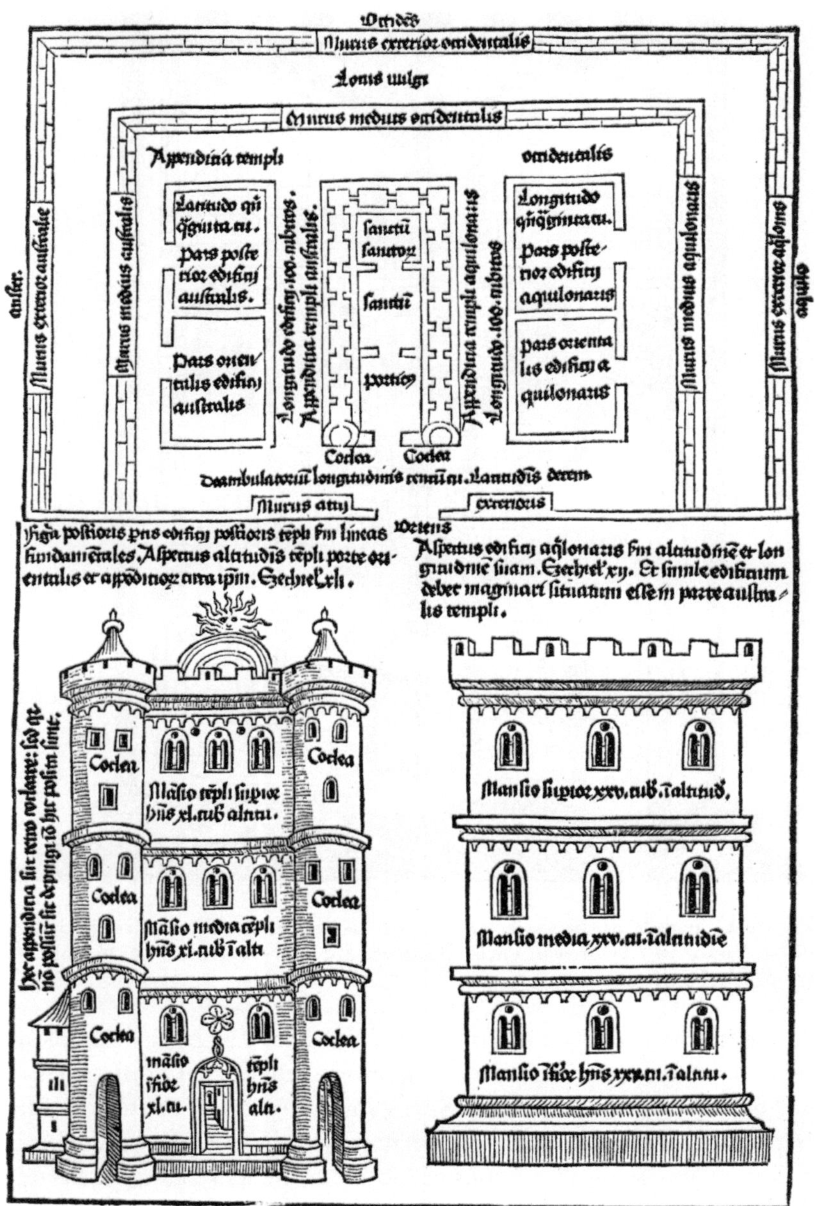

Figure 13. Nicolas de Lyra's plan and elevations of the Temple (re-drawn by the author).

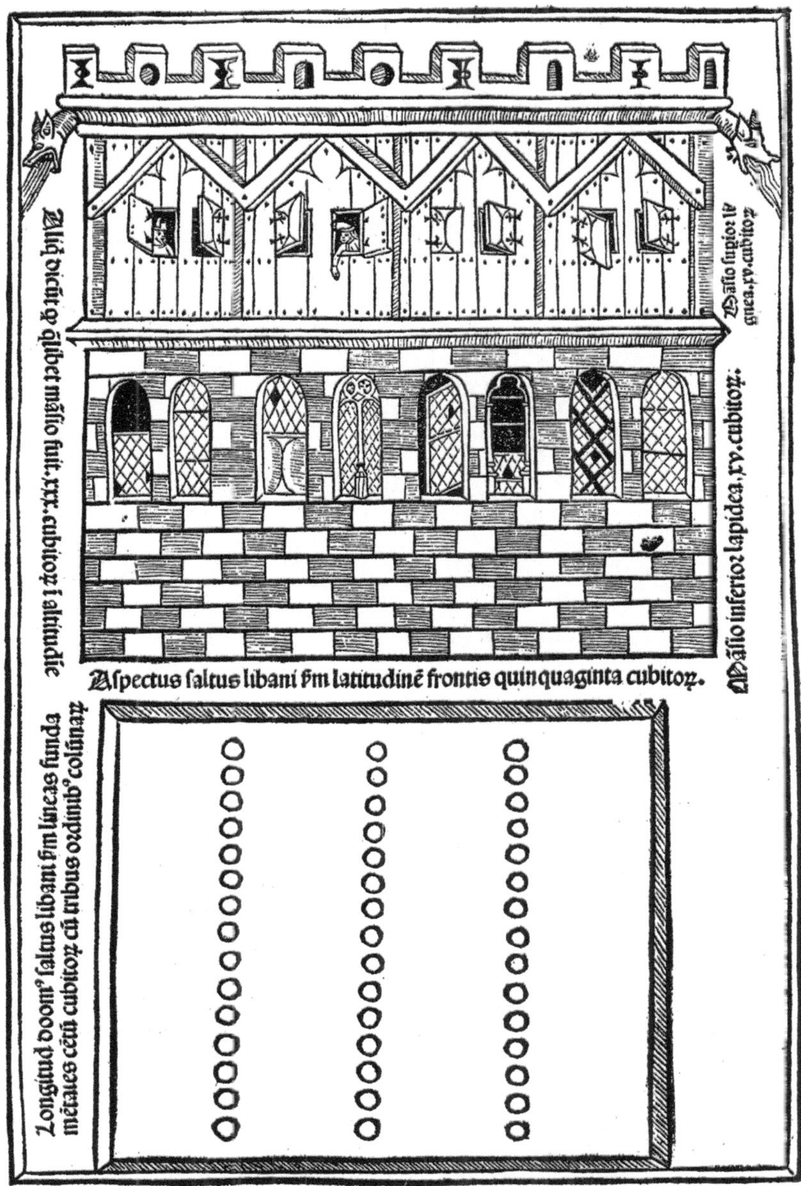

Figure 14. Nicolas de Lyra's plan and elevations of the Temple (re-drawn by the author).

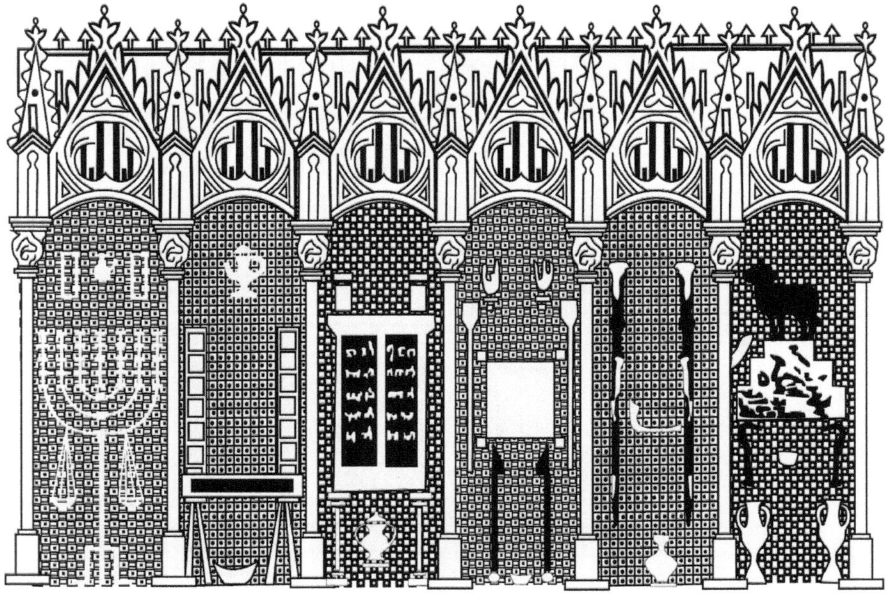

Figure 15. Petrus Comestor's *Historia Scholastica,* Temple interior (re-drawn by the author).

Both the decoration and the structure of churches and cathedrals had Solomonaic elements that became increasingly conspicuous.

Although the connection of Rome with Solomon's Temple dated back to the fourth century, it was in the Renaissance that the idea of Rome as the earthly Jerusalem was strongly established, and a desire to return to the spirit of the first church builder, Constantine, emerged. Rome had not embraced the Gothic style and had continued to build in the traditional Roman style. However, by the early 15th century, the Old Saint Peter's was in decline. Pope Nicholas V planned to rebuild the Basilica; he had studied the plan of the Temple of Solomon in the Scriptures and, according to his biographers,[33] was going to rebuild the Basilica in the style of the classical temples and it would be far superior to Solomon's; yet, at the time of his death, only part of the Basilica had been demolished. Nevertheless, the building project continued along with the Solomonaic connections. The interior of the Sistine Chapel at the Vatican was built to the dimensions of the Temple.[34] The paintings on its walls represent the Moses and Christ cycles expressing the papal claim to universal priesthood, which had been predicted by Moses.[35] In 1507, Aegidius of Viterbo compared the architectural projects of Pope Julius II and Constantine to that of Solomon.[36]

The medieval reconstructions cannot be considered architectural reconstructions of the plan, since they adhered to the descriptions in the Biblical texts, but they did not justify the reconstruction with the rules or principles of architecture or construct any real plan. With the rediscovery of Vitruvius's treatise on architecture in the 15th century, Renaissance theorists such as Leon Battista Alberti (1404–1472), Sebastiano Serlio (1475–1554), Daniel Barbaro (1514–1570), and Andrea Palladio (1508–1580) studied the ancient temples of Rome and based their theories on the principles of Vitruvius. The Christian churches of Renaissance Rome resembled Roman temples, and they used the word "temple" for these churches.[37] Their designs were determined by mathematical relationships between their parts; it was a centralized plan through a system of harmony and proportion that defined Renaissance churches.[38] They were to be the meeting place of man and God. However, unlike the awe-inspiring architecture of the Gothic cathedral, the Renaissance cathedral was built to the very nature of God. It was built to reflect the perfect beauty, harmony, and concord of God and the universe, which are also reflected in the human body. The symmetry of the human body and the Temple reflected the microcosmic order. The glory of the Church was that it was the house of God, defined in terms of nature, which was the microcosm of the invisible architecture of the heavens.

Following the Protestant Reformation, the emphasis shifted to the church of "living stones" of the New Testament. For Luther, the church buildings were secondary considerations to the church of the congregation. However, he did consecrate churches, suited to the new Protestant theology.[39] Calvin acknowledged that pagan temples were places for divine revelation, but these revelations were confined to within the temples. Believers flocked to the temples to see the face of God in the sanctuary:

> Moses speaks of the habitation of God, he at the same time calls it the place of the name of God, the place where he will record his name, thus plainly teaching that no use could be made of it without the doctrine of godliness.[40]

Only in this unity could the face of God be understood. Temples were for removing all superstition; they were Moses's "footstool."

Temples that the "Gentiles built to God with different intention were a mere profanation of his worship—a profanation into which the Jews also fell, though not with equal grossness."[41] The Jews had boasted of their temples and ceremonies—they measured the church by these "external masks"—but the church could exist perfectly without these external masks.[42] Therefore, for Calvin, the Temple of Jerusalem could only be considered in the same light as the pagan temples of the Gentiles, since the building was a church and not the united beliefs of the faithful.

Calvin called the church buildings "temples" and these temples were a public place of common prayer. God only recognized a temple to be a place where his Word was heard and scrupulously observed. If the external masks became the point of worship rather than the work of God, God would abandon it and the place would become profane. For Calvin, the buildings were not the church, for it was wrong to love the walls and it was wrong to venerate the buildings, and the faithful must beware

> of imitating the practice which commenced some centuries ago, of imagining that churches are the proper dwellings of God, where he is more ready to listen to us, or of attaching to them some kind of secret sanctity, which makes prayer there more holy. For seeing we are the true temples of God, we must pray in ourselves if we would invoke God in his holy temple.... Even the Temple was not represented to the Jews as confining the presence of God within its walls, but was meant to train them to contemplate the image of the true temple.[43]

In the dedication to Edward VI in *Commentary on Isaiah*, Calvin defined the state of the Church as being like the ruined temple of God, and Calvin described himself as being one of those who had been selected by God "as architects to promote the work of pure doctrine"[44]; for "God does the honor of appointing us to be sanctuaries and temples.... Each Christian is a temple of the Holy Spirit."[45] The architectural metaphor was embedded into Calvin's rhetoric and into concepts of the Reformation.

In the light of the Reformation, the Roman Catholic Church needed to define its articles of faith and differentiate itself from the doctrines of the Protestants. However, more than just a definition was required; there was a true need and desire for reform.[46] This reform or Counter-Reformation was characterized by three tools: the Council of Trent, which was convened in 1542 and met intermittently until 1563;

the reintroduction of the Inquisition into Italy to root out Protestantism in Southern Europe; and the establishment of the Society of Jesus— the Jesuits.[47]

Paper Reconstructions of the Temple of Solomon in the 17th and 18th Centuries

An important reconstruction of Solomon's Temple was made by the twelfth-century rabbi Moses Maimonides in Book Eight of *The Code of Maimonides (Mishneh Torah)*.[48] Maimonides's measurement for his reconstruction came straight from *Middoth*. The Temple was a square of 500 cubits. There were five gates in the exterior wall, two on the south wall, and one each on the east, north, and west walls. The interior court was 187 cubits long and 135 cubits wide, and had seven gates. The Temple was located in an asymmetrical position within the internal court. Maimonides did not give the exact distances, but the greatest distance was to the south and the least to the west, and the distance to the east was greater than to the north. The length and the width of the Temple were both one hundred cubits. The description of the Temple is very brief, and Maimonides did not justify the plan. His description was basically ignored by Christians until the 17th century, when the Jesuit priest and architect Juan Bautista Villalpando wrote his highly influential book *Ezechielem Explanationes et Apparatus Vrbis Templi Hierosolymitani*, published in 1604. In the 17th century, Maimonides's description became an alternative plan to Villalpando's reconstruction.

Ezechielem Explanationes is in three massive volumes and is the result of over twenty years' work. Initially, it was a collaboration between two Spanish Jesuit priests, Jerome Prado and Juan Bautista Villalpando. However, the premature death of Prado left the entire project to Villalpando, to complete on his own. *Ezechielem Explanationes* is a commentary on the Book of Ezekiel in three volumes. Volume Two contains a lengthy and elaborate reconstruction of Solomon's Temple.

Villalpando's reconstruction presents the Temple of Solomon as the microcosm of the universe; within the architectural plan, he integrated the entire plan of the known cosmos. Villalpando carefully derived all the measurements of the Temple from the sacred texts, but he also drew on support from profane ancient texts such as that of Josephus. He demonstrated that all of the columns of the Temple were in a harmonious ratio to each other as well as to the rest of the building. Villalpando believed that these harmonic proportions were highly appropriate for a building of divine origins, and he strongly inferred the existence of a link between the celestial bodies and harmonic proportions. He believed that the Temple reflected the creation of God, and thus it needed to incorporate itself into the universal harmony according to the movements of the planets and the fixed stars. Villalpando first examined the Tabernacle of Moses, since its plan prefigured that of the Temple, and the camp of the tribes of Israel that surrounded the Tabernacle formed a more primitive plan of the Temple precinct. Villalpando was the first to establish that the proportion of the atrium that surrounded the immediate Temple and the altar was a double square. He then considered the configuration of the camp of the tribes of Israel. The configuration of the camp was highly structured with the Tabernacle placed in the center, fortified by the four Levites' camps: Moses and Aaron, Caathi, Gerson, and Merari. Surrounding them were the twelve tribes of Israel, each tribe camped under a banner that declared its ancient lineage.

The placement and distribution of the tribes within the camp was determined by a perfect plan in which nothing was left to chance, since it reproduced the plan of the Tabernacle but with doubled dimensions. It represented the plan of the microcosm of the universe—the macrocosm. Its ground plan was based on the plan of the heavens. The four Levite tents that surrounded and fortified the Tabernacle in the plan of the Temple corresponded with the four simple elements of the sublunar world, and represented the world of man. These were encircled by the celestial orbits, made up of the seven atriums. The orbits were positioned on the plan as Ptolemy had assigned them in the *Almagest*[49]: "Thus Saturn is situated between Capricorn and Aquarius; Jupiter in Pisces; Mars in Aries; Venus in Libra; Mercury in Virgo; the Sun in Leo and the Moon in Cancer" (see Figure 16).[50] Surrounding the seven courts or celestial orbits were the twelve fortifications or bastions of the Temple precinct perimeter. These fortifications corresponded to the twelve tents of the tribes of Israel that were laid out under the banners or standards that declared their ancient lineage: Judah was represented by the symbol of the Lion, Ruben by the symbol of the Water Bearer, Ephraim by the

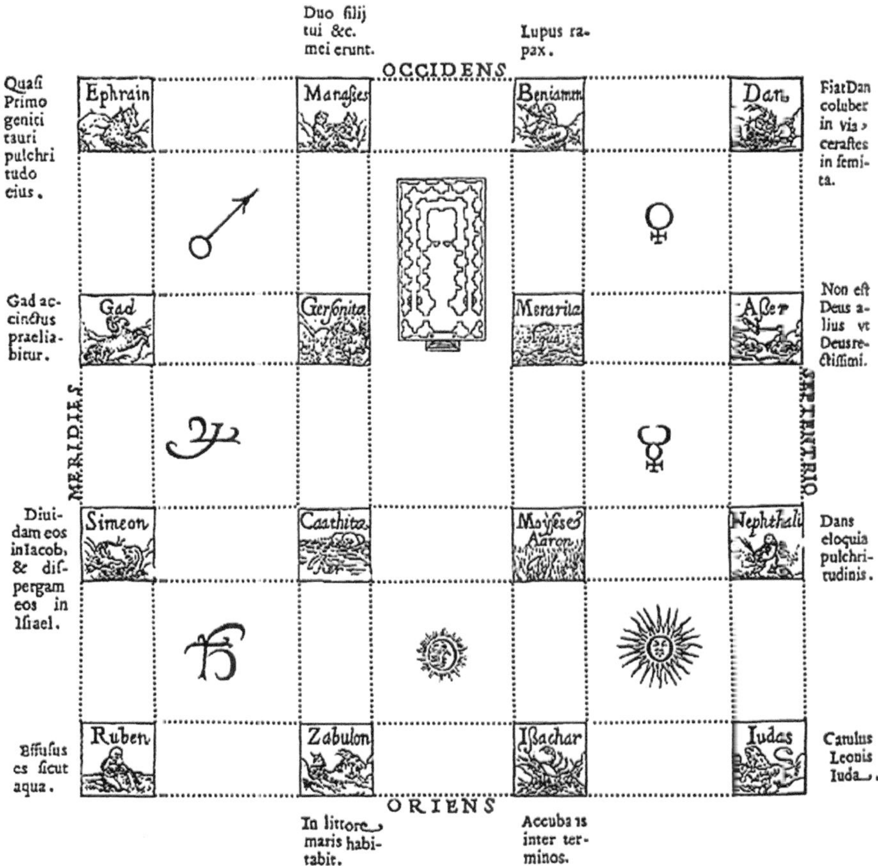

Figure 16. Villalpando's plan for the layout of the tribes of Israel's camp around the Tabernacle (re-drawn by the author).

symbol of the Bull, Dan by the symbol of the Scorpion, and so on, so that the tribes' banners equated to the twelve signs of the zodiac. In the center was the Temple, "dedicated to the profit of man," which represented the "true Sun" of the super-celestial world of the Church. This true Sun is Christ, the "Sun of Justice," whose light is salvation. This light illuminated the seven planets and the twelve constellations, and the centralized earth was illuminated by the planet sun, which is located in Leo (see Figure 17).

The circumference of the heavens was divided into 360 degrees

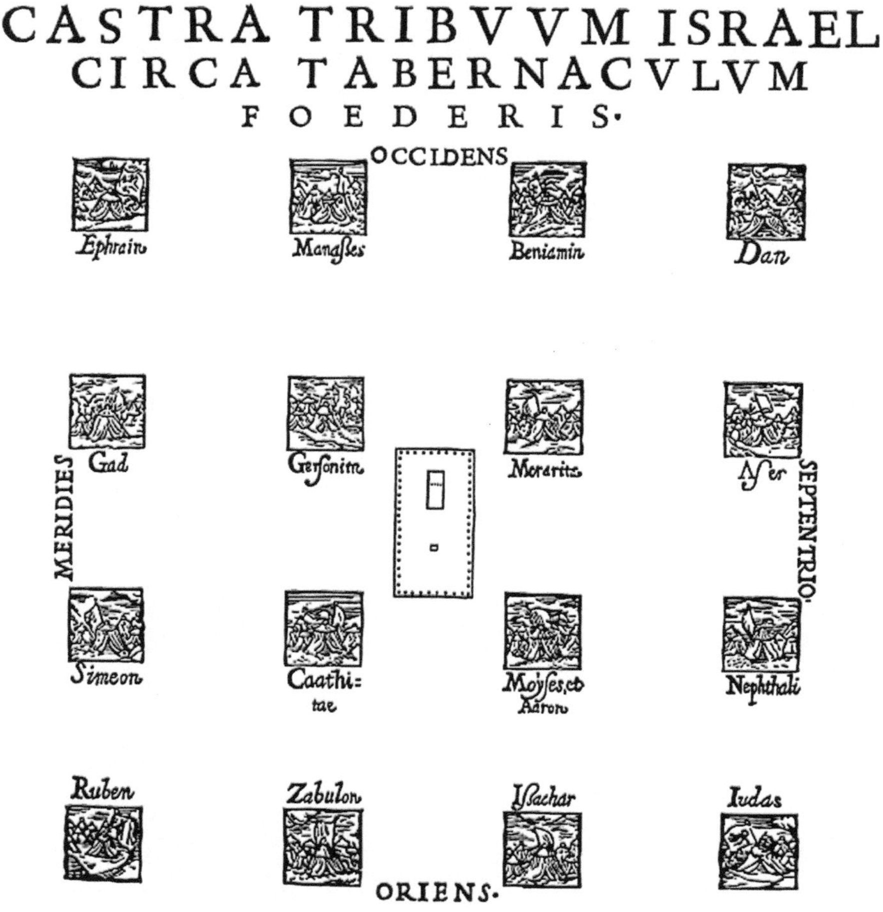

CASTRA TRIBVVM ISRAEL
CIRCA TABERNACVLVM
FOEDERIS·

OCCIDENS

Ephraim   Manaſſes   Beniamin   Dan

MERIDIES

Gad   Gerſonitæ   Merariti   Aſer   SEPTENTRIO·

Simeon   Caathi=tae   Moyſes.et Aaron   Nephthali

Ruben   Zabulon   Iſſachar   Iudas

ORIENS·

Figure 17. Villalpando's astrological arrangement for the plan of Solomon's Temple (re-drawn by the author).

because of the movement of the sun, which returns in a circuit twenty-four hours around the centralized earth. The diameter of the heavens was a third of its circumference. The height of the Temple was 120 cubits, which coincided with the width of the celestial orbit. The atrium, destined to be a residence of the men, was 60 cubits in height, half the circumference of the heavens—that is, man dwells under the heaven of heavens. This perfect plan represented the three worlds of the microcosm and macrocosm: in the center was the super-celestial world of God; this was surrounded by the world of man, and then the celestial world of the seven planets and the fixed stars encircling the earth—Villalpando presented in his description a perfect vision of a geocentric universe.

Villalpando supported the anthropomorphic theories of Vitruvius. He perceived that the humanity assumed by God was mirrored in the geometry and the measurements of the Temple, which prefigured the perfection of the mystical body of the church. The proportions and measurements of the Temple were reflected in the body of man. The measurements of the Tabernacle equated to the ages of man's active military service; the age of twenty was the age to enlist, twenty-five was the age of perfect strength, and fifty was the time of weakening strength. This emphasized the Tabernacle precinct as the camp of the twelve tribes of Israel, and the proportions of the Temple equated to the proportions of man. Man had a height of six feet—this measurement equated to the extension of man's arms—but if the arms were folded in front of the chest, so that the end of the longest finger of the right hand touched the end of the middle finger of the left hand, then the width of man would be one and a half cubits, or three (Roman) feet. The colonnades of the Temple had eight inter-columns, which coincided with the height of the head of man from the chin to the upper part, and were divided into three promenades or galleries that corresponded to the barrel of the chest with the arms. These colonnades corresponded to the proportion of 1:2—not only a double square but also the harmonic ratio of an eighth: an octave (see Figure 18). Here Villalpando portrayed Christ taking the appearance of man as the cosmological man, which emphasized the microcosm-macrocosm analogy, the earthly architectural plan emulating the divine celestial plan.

The gridded floor plan of Villalpando's reconstruction (see Figure 19) corresponded to the plan representing the microcosm of the universe that was crowded with colonnades, and incorporated 1,500 columns. The Temple precinct was 500 by 500 cubits and the exterior boundary was 800 by 800 cubits. The height of the Temple was 120 cubits as prescribed by Ezekiel but in Villalpando's reconstruction of the Temple foundations were 300 cubits and were flanked with elegant and distinct curved buttresses (see Figure 20). The engraving of the sacred sanctuary is the only perspective drawing in his Temple reconstruction (Figure 21).

It is a haunting and mysterious interior of the most sacred part of the Temple, which contained the Ark of the Covenant and the cherubim that guarded it. In his etching the Arc is not depicted to be the same as the biblical dimensions and the cherubim are more human and serene than the biblical four faced guardians. The image adds to the mystery and elegance of the Temple. Every element or part of the Temple was in a harmonious ratio to the entire building. For Villalpando, this was the greatest building ever built and no building could ever surpass it. His was the first full-scale reconstruction of the divine archetype, and it inspired many other commentaries and reconstructions of Solomon's Temple, particularly over the next 150 years.

Ezechielem Explanationes is an extraordinary work; it is very detailed and the illustrations are elaborate. The extremely costly undertaking took twenty years and was financed by Phillip II, King of Spain. Its impact was enormous and impressive. Villalpando's reconstruction stimulated a debate about the plan and architecture of the Temple, and many, very different reconstructions were produced, particularly in the 17th and early 18th centuries.

Benito Arias Montano was a fellow Jesuit who knew of Villalpando's work well before it was

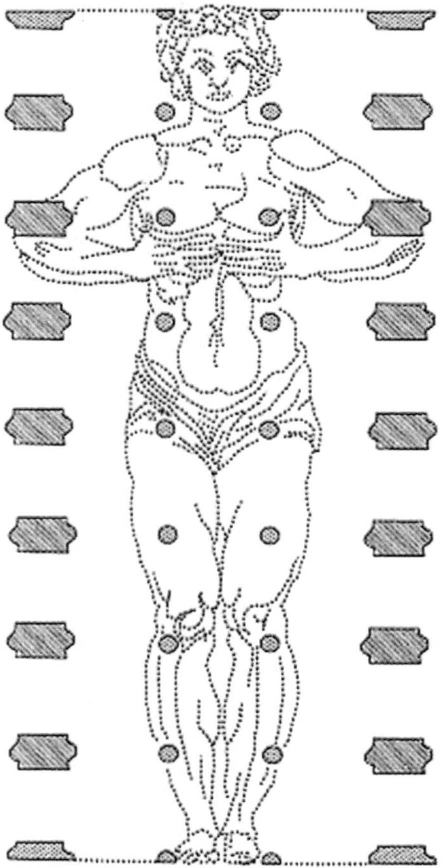

Figure 18. From Villalpando: A single colonnade and the resemblances to the division of the human stature (re-drawn by the author).

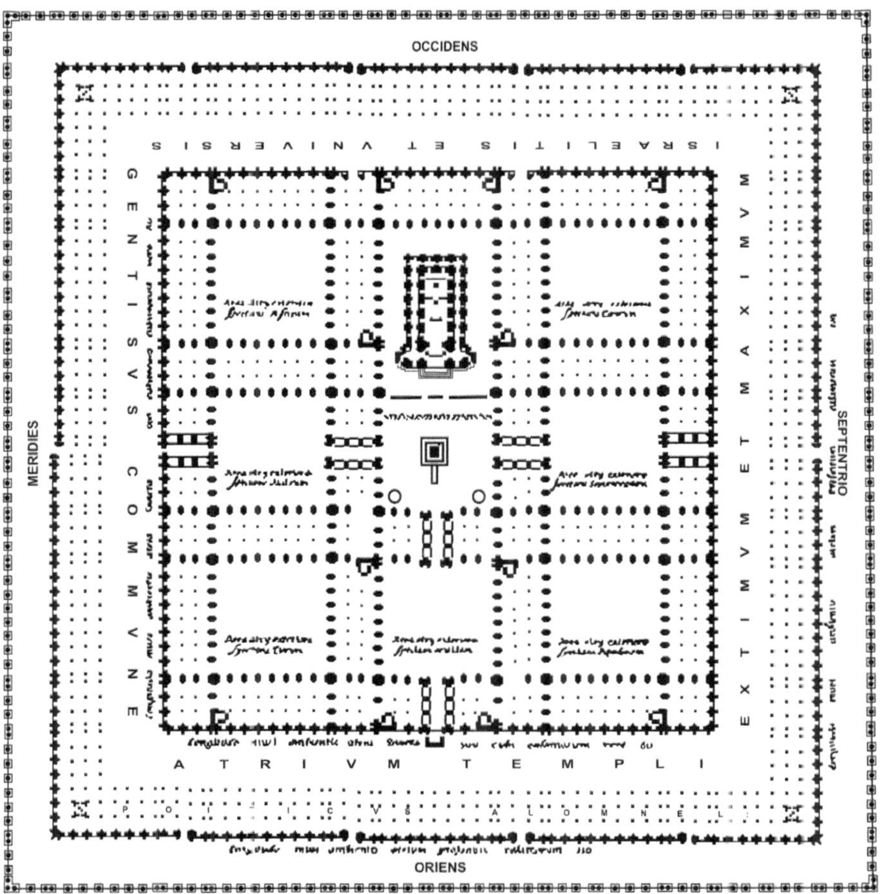

Figure 19. Villalpando's reconstruction of the Temple (re-drawn by the author).

published. He disagreed with Villalpando's design and sources. Montano
edited the final volume of the Polyglot Bible, published in Antwerp in
1571–1572. He included a map of Jerusalem clearly showing the location
of the Temple and a ground plan of the Temple itself. He claimed that
Ezekiel's vision was not the same as Solomon's Temple, and based his
reconstruction primarily upon the Book of Kings (see Figure 22). His
approach was a historical one—he considered that the Temple was not
the perfect work of God, but rather an earthly building that had under-
gone alterations. Although he based his reconstruction on ancient

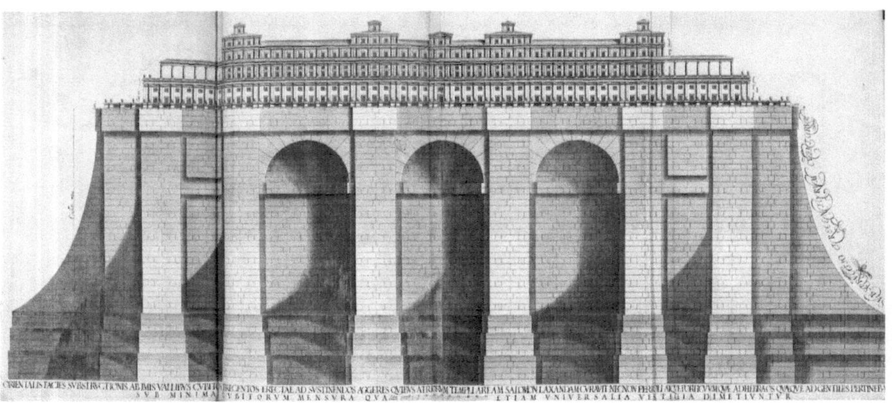

Figure 20. Villalpando estimated the curved foundations of the Temple precinct to be four hundred cubits in height (courtesy British Library [691.k27(2) pl XII]).

sources, he used the technical language and the architectural principles of Vitruvius.

Louis Cappel, in 1613, accepted the chair of Hebrew at Saumur, and in 1633, he became professor of theology. Interested in historical reality, he considered that Villalpando's reconstruction had failed because it had not considered the Jewish tradition. Cappel published a detailed commentary on Villalpando's reconstruction in Brian Walton's great Polyglot Bible in 1657. Cappel's plan was derived exclusively from *Middoth* and Maimonides (see Figure 23).[51]

Claude Perrault, a translator of Vitruvius and architect of the famous eastern colonnade of the Louvre, also illustrated *The Code of Maimonides, the Mishneh Torah*, which had been translated into Latin by Louis Compiègne de Veil in 1678 (see Figure 24).[52] Perrault considered the argument that God had inspired the architect of the Temple with the perfect architectural principles, and that the Greeks had learned and codified them later, as superstitious reverence.[53] Perrault was asked to take his design of the Temple from that of Maimonides, and there is a good deal of similarity to Cappel's reconstruction.[54] In the preface to de Veil's translation, he expressed surprise that Villalpando had spent so much time and effort on an image that did not portray the historical truth. He claimed that the main aim of Villalpando was to establish that the Temple conformed to Vitruvian architectural principles and that the Greeks and Romans had learned the art of building through studying the ancient buildings, particularly Solomon's Temple.[55] Thus, Vitruvius had in fact plagiarized his architectural principles from ancient Jewish architecture.

Nicolaus Goldmann strove for an architectural theory that was a fusion of Christian and pagan ideas based on Vitruvian architectural

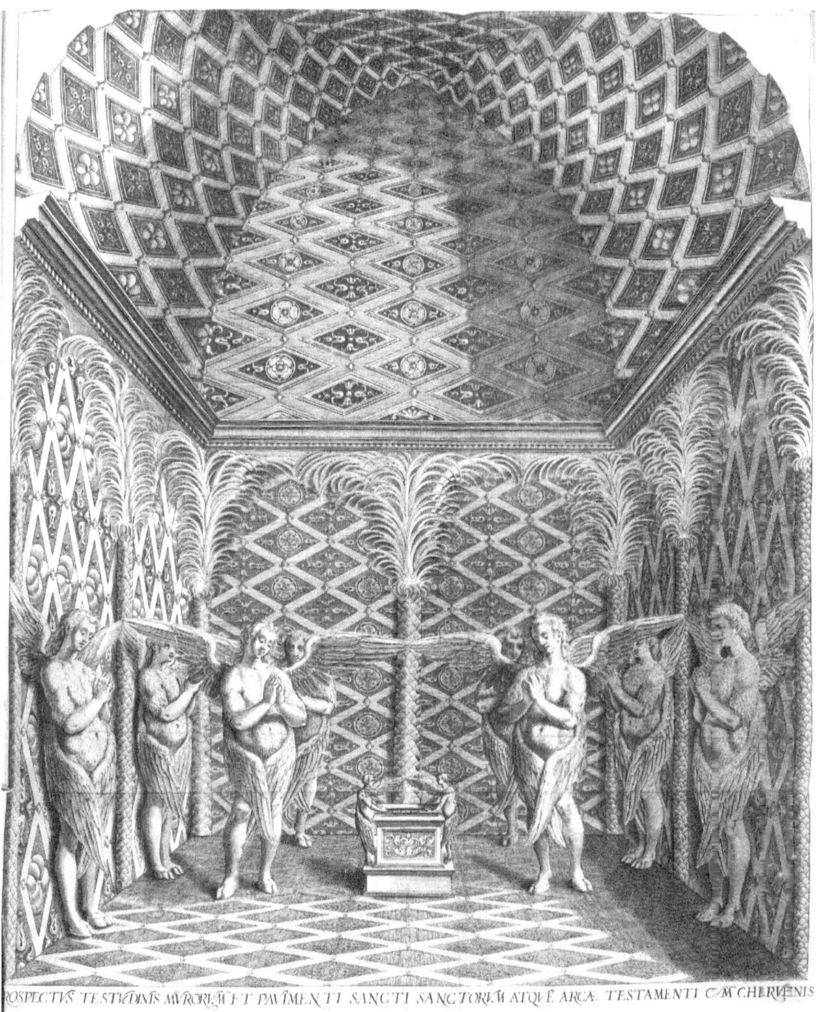

Figure 21. Villalpando's illustration of the Sacred Sanctuary (courtesy British Library [691.k27(2) pl VIII]).

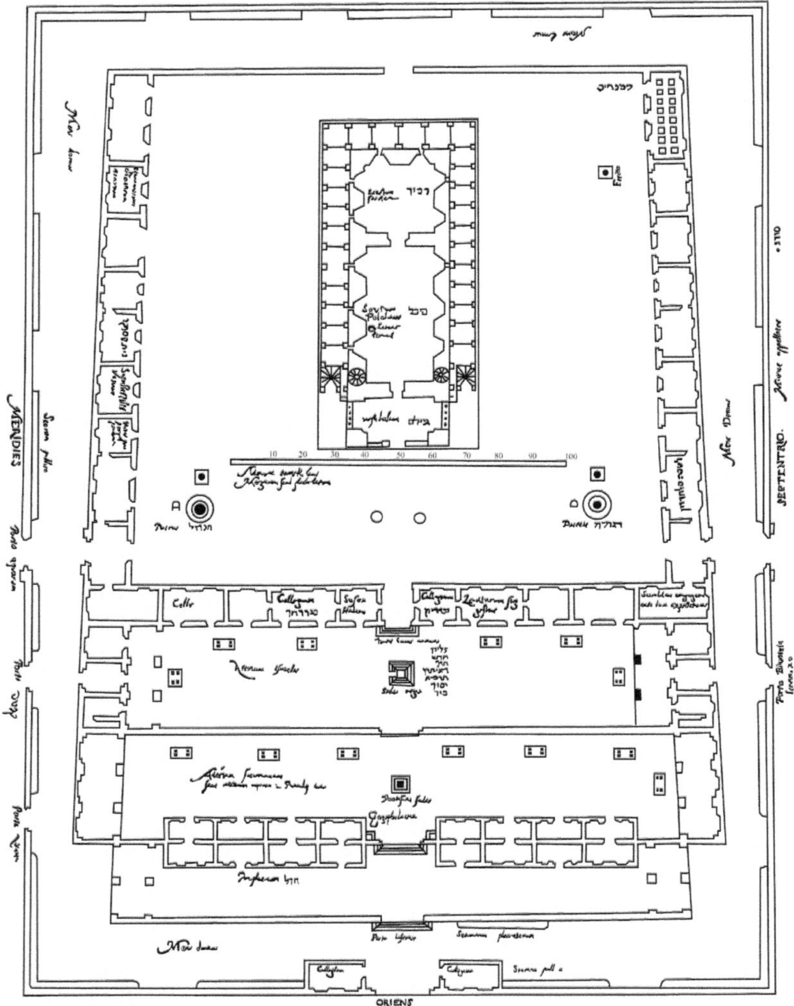

Figure 22. Montano's reconstruction of the Temple of Solomon, from his "Exemplar" in Volume Eight of the Antwerp Polyglot (re-drawn by the author).

principles. Goldmann completed *Die Vollständige Anweisung zu der Civilbaukunst* before his death, and it was subsequently edited by Leonhard Sturm and published in 1698. This book set out to be an entire instruction and theory for civil architecture, and it considered a theory of the orders "according to the 'most excellent rules' of Vitruvius, Vignola,

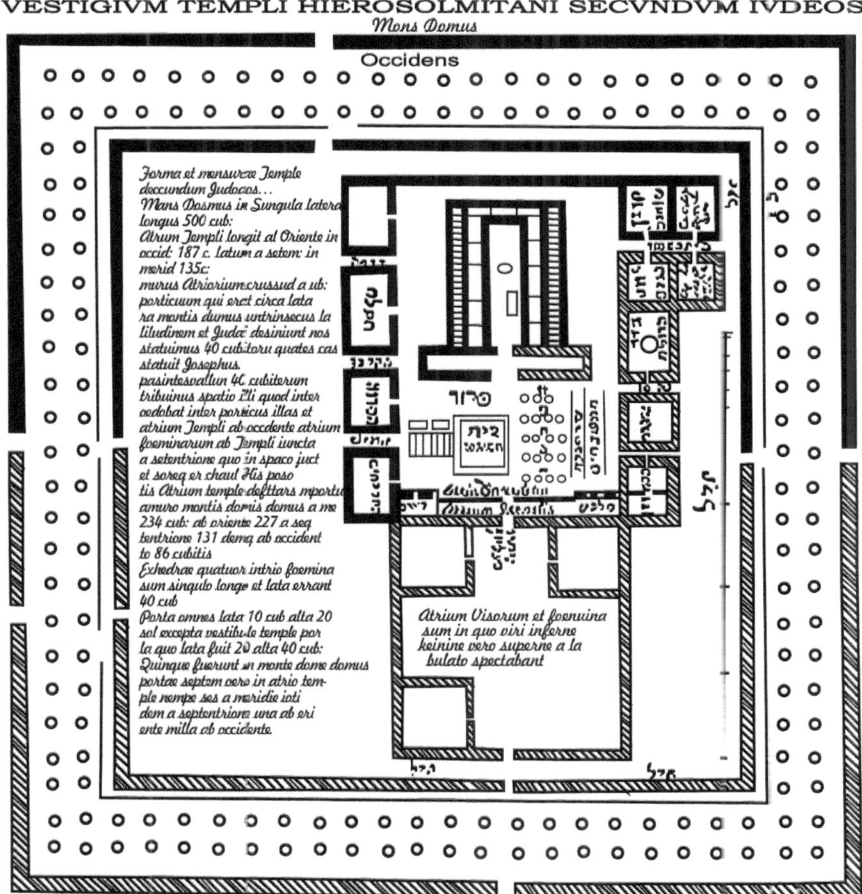

Figure 23. Louis Cappel's reconstruction of the Temple from Brian Walton's Polyglot Bible published in 1657 (re-drawn by the author).

Scamozzi, Palladio, and Villalpando."[56] Goldmann and Sturm discussed Villalpando's reconstruction, emphasizing the important role of Solomon's Temple as the origin of architecture. Although they agreed with Villalpando in almost all aspects, they made "improvement" to the details (see Figure 25).[57]

Constantijn L'Empereur was one of the most important Dutch Hebraists of the 17th century.[58] L'Empereur (1591–1648) was appointed professor of Hebrew at Leiden University in 1627. Unlike the other

PRIMA TABULA

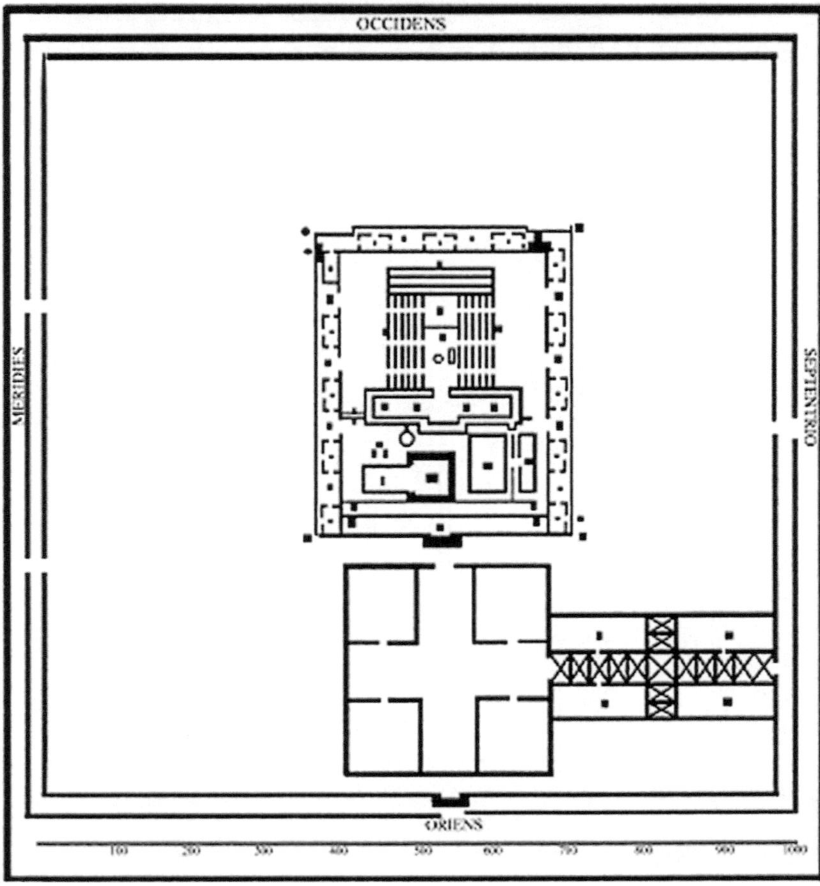

Figure 24. Claude Perrault's floor plan of the Temple for Louis Compiègne de Veil's translation of *The Code of Maimonides, the Mishneh Torah* published in 1678 (re-drawn by the author).

Calvinists of the time, L'Empereur did not believe that Judaism was a threat to Christianity; instead, he viewed it as a monolithic dogmatic doctrine that must be attacked and refuted so that the orthodox doctrine could be vindicated.[59] He gained international recognition through his publications of translations of Mishnaic tractates and other tools for the study of rabbinical literature. L'Empereur became one of the most eminent Christian authorities on Jewish literature and Judaism in the

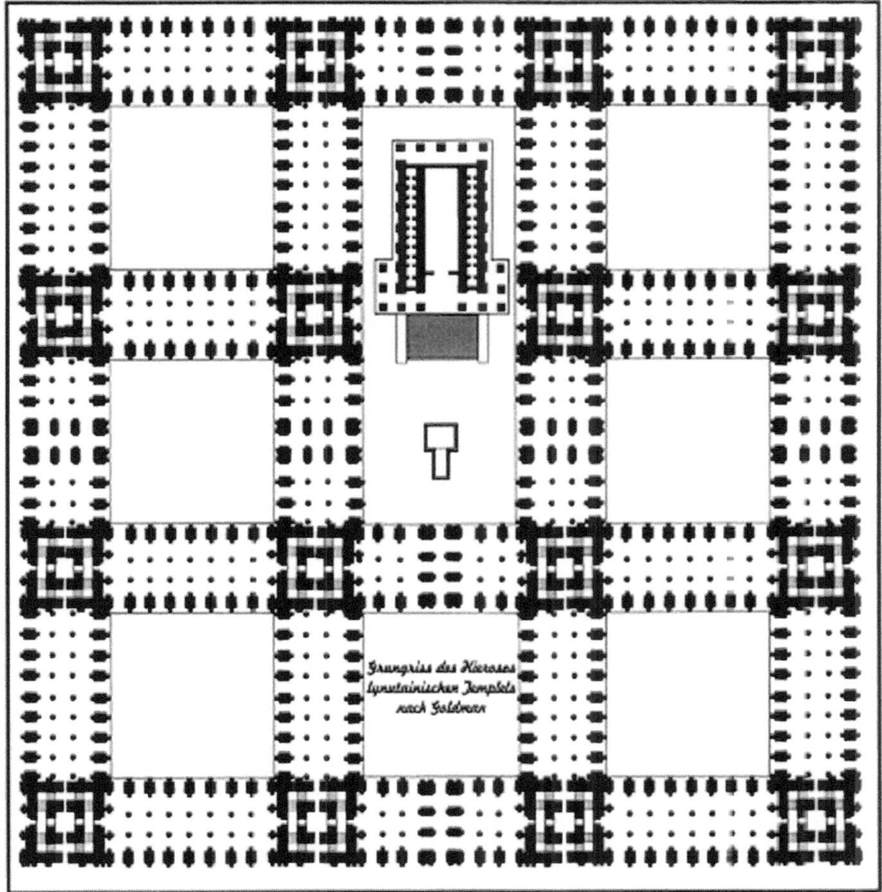

Figure 25. Nicolaus Goldmann's plan of the Temple of Solomon (re-drawn by the author).

Dutch Republic. He was appointed professor of *Controversiarum Judaicarum* in 1633. L'Empereur's reconstruction, with its asymmetrical design, reflects Jewish sources such as the *Mishnah Torah* (see Figure 26).

There were so many commentaries on *Ezechielem Explanationes*, both positive and negative, that Villalpando's work was often known more from the commentaries than from the original work. The plans of Cappel, Perrault, and L'Empereur, derived directly from the Jewish sources, were notably different from those used by Villalpando, and

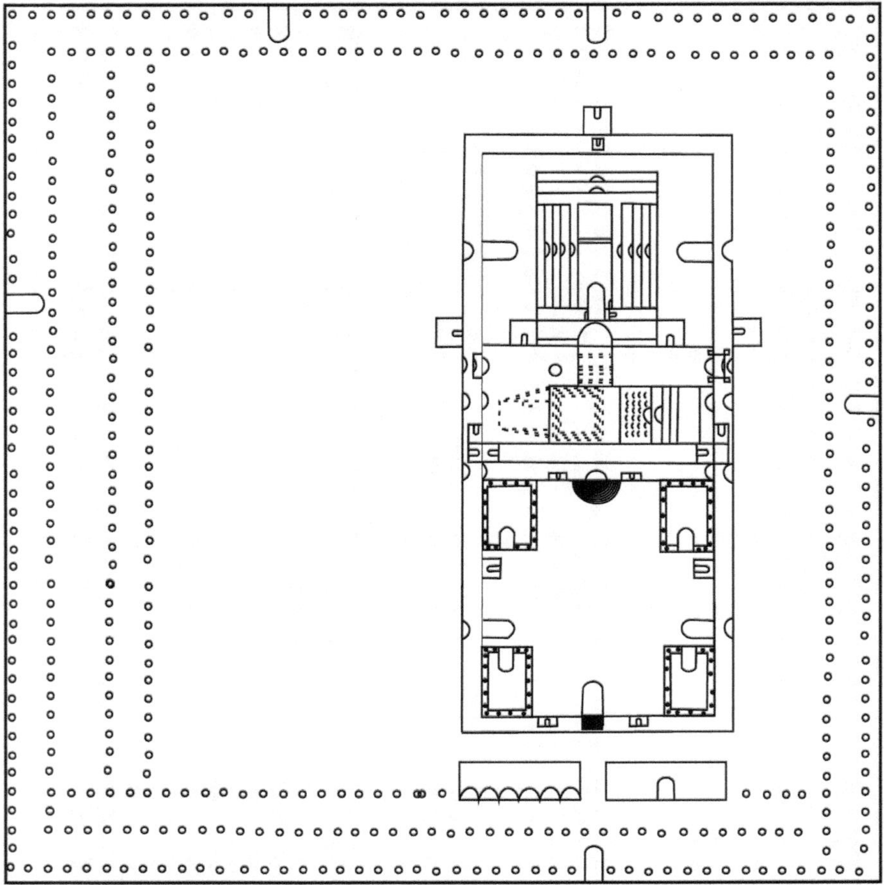

Figure 26. Constantijn L'Empereur's floor plan of the Temple from *Guglielmus Surenbusius; Mishnah sive Legum Mischnicarum liber qui inscribitur Ordo Sacrorum…* (re-drawn by the author).

importantly, the buildings of the Temple were not placed symmetrically within the Temple precinct. These plans would not have been suitable for either Villalpando's image of the Temple as the microcosm of the universe or Newton's frame of the world. In all the criticism of Villalpando, which was extensive,[60] the Temple regarded as the microcosm of the universe was not criticized, and it appears to have been a generally accepted concept.

However, most of this commentary is European,[61] and on the surface there was little English commentary. Samuel Lee was the loudest English critic; he accused both Villalpando and Cappel of using illustrations that were "to be contracted for the beautifying of their preliminary tract, leaving the assertion of the identity of that visionary structure with Solomon's unto others."[62] But while Cappel was much perplexed, according to Lee, by the measurement laid down by Ezekiel, and was over-liberal in his censure of the sacred text, "there was never such a Temple extant, as was described by Villalpando (the most learned and laborious Temple student, that ever proceeded in public light) which hath deduced from the profound and mysterious vision of the Prophet Ezekiel."[63] In Lee's comprehensive treatise he outlined the dimensions and characteristics of Solomon's Temple using Ezekiel as his main

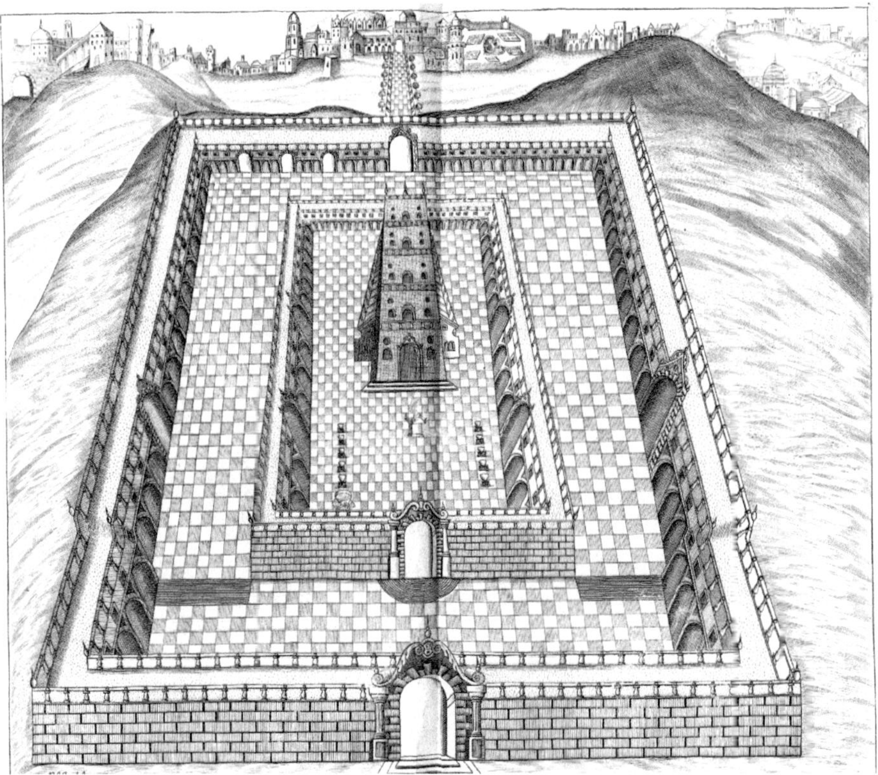

Figure 27. Samuel Lee image of the Temple precinct (copyright © the Library and Museum of Freemasonry; used by permission).

source: the ground plan of the Temple precinct is symmetrical with the Temple centrally placed (see Figure 27).

Christopher Wren was scathing of Villalpando's reconstruction. He stated that great monarchs are ambitious to leave monuments behind them, and with these occasions, great inventions in mechanical arts were developed: "What the Architecture was that Solomon used, we know but little of, though holy Writ hath given us the general Dimensions of the Temple, by which we may, in some measure, collect the Plan, but not of all the Courts." Wren considered Villalpando's reconstruction a fantasy. He claimed that

> Villalpandus hath made a fine romantic Piece, after the Corinthian Order, which, in that Age, was not used by any Nation; for the early Age used much grosser Pillars than the Dorick: in after Times, they began to refine from Dorick, as in the Temple of Diana at Ephesus, (the united Work of all Asia) and at length improved into a slenderer Pillar, & leafy Capital of various Inventions, which was called Corinthian; so that if we run back to the Age of Solomon, we may with Reason believe they used the Tyrian Manner, as gross at least, if not more, that Dorick, and the Corinthian Manner of Villalpandus is mere Fancy.[64]

Wren also called Villalpando's reconstruction "his imaginary scheme of the Temple,"[65] leaving the reader in no doubt that Villalpando's work did not have any architectural merit.

William Stukeley (1687–1765) was a fellow of the Royal Society, a founding member and first secretary of the Society of Antiquaries, and a fellow of the Royal College of Physicians. He was a friend of Newton's, and his first biographer. Like Newton's, Stukeley's reconstruction of the Temple was to be found in unpublished papers. Stukeley was very critical of Villalpando, and claimed that, despite having the purse of the wealthy King Phillip to support his twenty-year project, his design had not "hit the white."[66] Yet Stukeley's design of the Temple precinct used Villalpando's style of precinct and the same foundations (see Figure 28).[67]

In *Memoirs of Sir Isaac Newton's Life*, Stukeley recalled a conversation with Newton at Christmas time in 1725 in which they discussed the Temple of Solomon. Stukeley claimed that, although they did not discuss the details of the Temple, they both agreed that it was not like any other design of the time. Newton claimed, according to Stukeley, that the Temple of Solomon was the oldest temple and the original model for all subsequent temples. He argued that the workmen on the Egyptian temples had generally come from Jerusalem and had imitated the architecture of Solomon's Temple, and that the Greeks had borrowed their style of architecture from the Temple of Solomon. Stukeley claimed that the style of the Temple was Doric and that Newton agreed with him, saying, "the Greeks advanced it (Doric) into the Ionic and the Corinthian, as the Latins into the Composite."[68] However, the Doric order was not mentioned by Newton in any of his manuscripts or *The Chronology*. But Stukeley was always keen to be seen to be in agreement with Newton, whom he called "the immortal Newton."[69]

After the publication of *The Chronology*, John Conduitt sent a copy to Stukeley. In a letter to fellow antiquarian Samuel Gales, Stukeley noted his disappointment with the plan in *The Chronology*; he claimed that Newton "has come pretty near my ground plan of the Temple of Solomon, but he gives no uprights."[70] Stukeley's reconstruction is mainly of the Temple (see Figures 29, 30, and 31) and not the precinct itself, although he does illustrate the precinct (see Figure 28). The architecture, which he claimed not to have discussed, is entirely different from that of Newton, but so is everything else. The plan of the Temple is not very similar; for example, the porch in Newton's plan protrudes from the Temple, whereas in Stukeley's plan it does not. Stukeley has staircases at every corner of the building, whereas Newton has none. Stukeley's precinct is in the style of Villalpando, with which Newton strongly disagreed.

Newton claimed that "Villalpando, although the best [and] the most eminent commentator on Ezekiel's Temple: yet [he is] out in many things."[71] Nevertheless, his comments are a mixture of strong criticism and support. Both Villalpando and Newton strongly believed that the division of Ezekiel of the Temple was the true plan of the Temple of Solomon. In Babson MS 434, Newton studied Ezekiel's vision of the Temple and verified this vision with ancient Greek and Hebrew texts. From this study, Newton reconstructed the building of the Temple and its precinct, which he revealed was mathematically perfect. However, his floor plan and description of the Temple are remarkably different from Villalpando's (compare Figure 8 and Figure 19). Newton stated that the errors in Villalpando's design were primarily derived from his failure to take advantage of Jewish sources, and from his misinterpretation of the Latin texts.[72] Newton pointed out that the Latin text that Villalpando used often differed in its translation from the ancient Hebrew texts. For instance, in the Latin version in Ezekiel 42:3, Villalpando

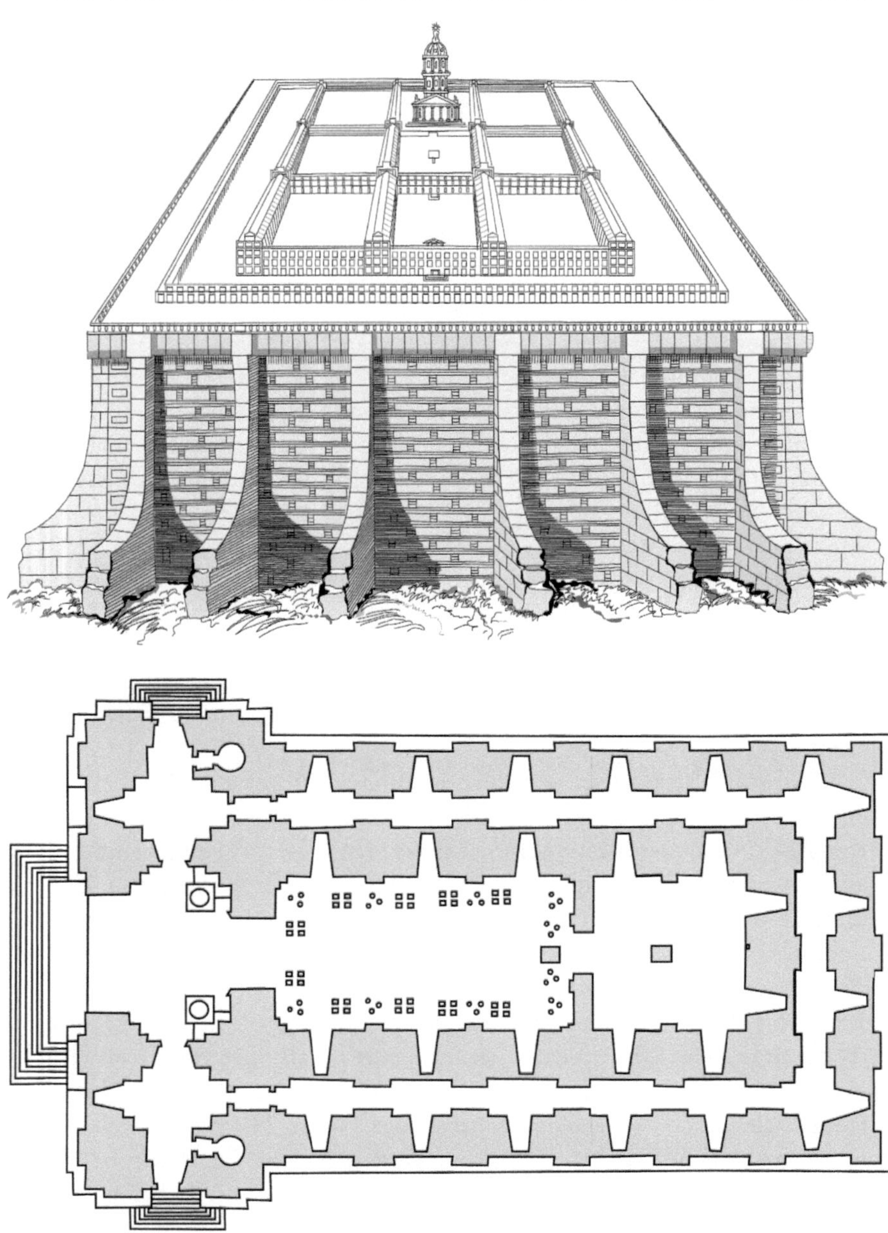

Top: Figure 28. Stukeley's design of the Temple precinct. *Bottom:* Figure 29. Stukeley's ground plan of the Temple (both re-drawn by the author).

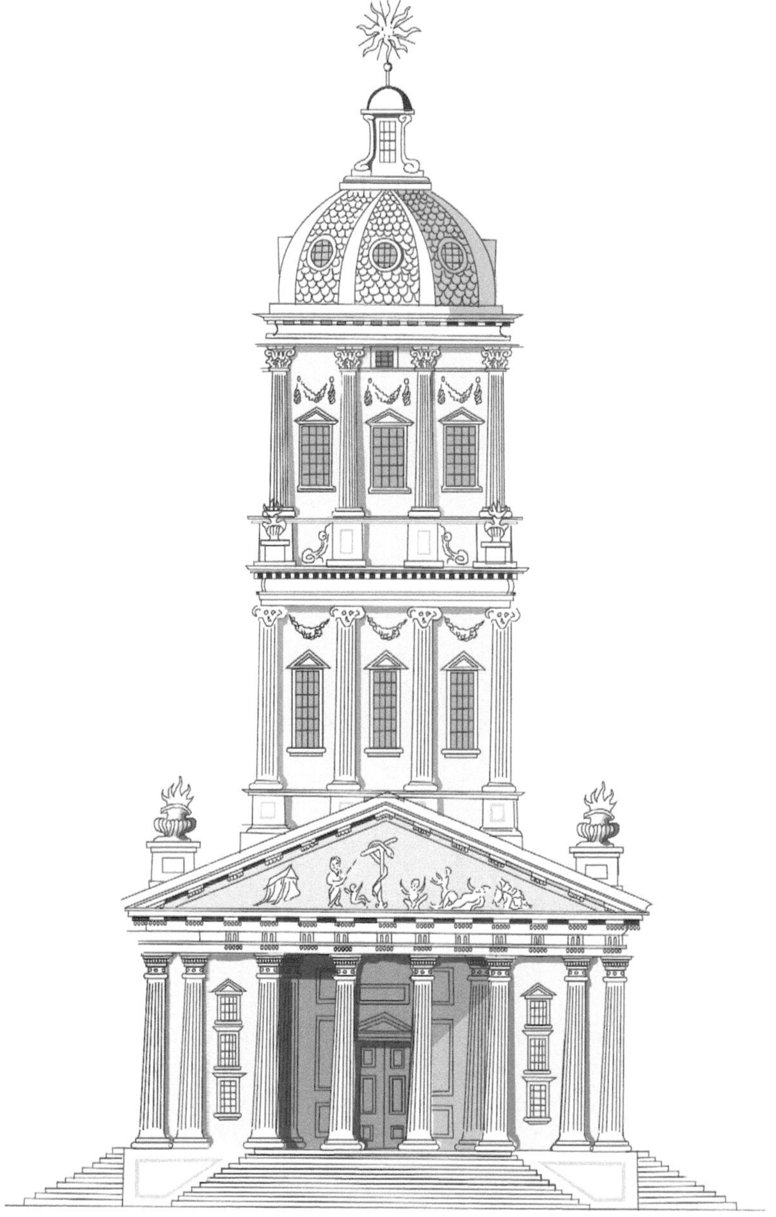

Figure 30. Eastern elevation of Stukeley's Temple of Solomon (re-drawn by the author).

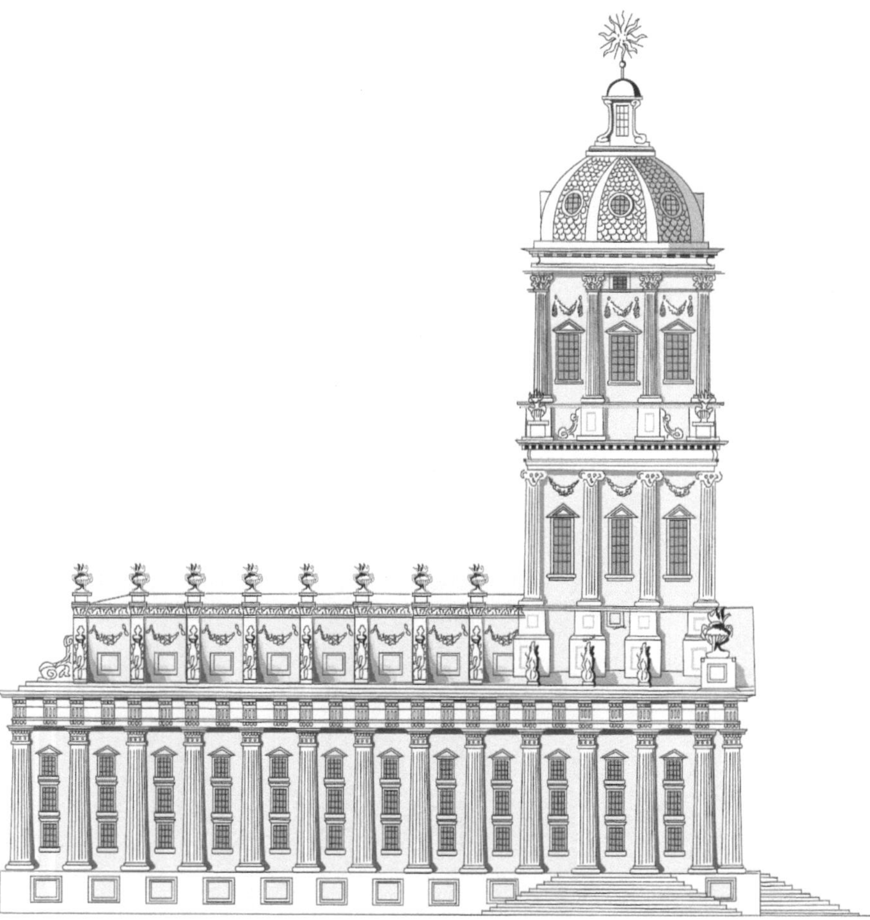

Figure 31. Southern Elevation of Stukeley's Temple of Solomon (re-drawn by the author).

translated "colonnades united" to be a triple colonnade, but according to Newton, in the Hebrew text it translated to "colonnade against colonnade three times," indicating three floors.[73]

Villalpando created a gridded plan of the Temple precinct from what Newton considered an "incorrect translation"; he also considered that Villalpando's plan "has no support and is lacking in reason."[74] Villalpando interpreted Ezekiel 40:19–20 to mean that the length of the atrium from the south to the north was the distance between the gates—

one hundred cubits—and this divided the area of the precinct into small atriums or anterooms, one larger that formed the Temple atrium and seven exterior to it (see Figure 19). These anterooms were divided from each other by triple colonnades of fifty cubits in width. Newton pointed out that not only were these anterooms not mentioned in Ezekiel, but the thirty chambers next to the sides of the gate expressly mentioned by Ezekiel were missing in Villalpando's plan. Unfortunately, Villalpando recognized that in his reconstruction these chambers were impossible if the spaces of the gates were not counted, but this went against the text of Ezekiel. In addition, Newton claimed that the gridded plan of Villalpando could not be accepted unless they wanted to move away from the proportion of Moses's atrium that surrounded the immediate temple and the altar, which was established by Villalpando himself as being a length over double its width.[75]

These criticisms, based on Villalpando's interpretation of the Biblical texts, challenged the very basis of his own reconstruction. The triple colonnades that Newton claimed were a mistranslation were an integral element of Villalpando's plan. First, they portrayed man/Christ as the cosmological man, emphasizing the microcosm-macrocosm analogy. Second, they divided the gridded plan into the seven small anterooms and the Temple atrium that Newton considered "lacking in reason," their creation going against the proportions of the Temple atrium that Villalpando had himself established. These triple-colonnaded atriums not only formed a considerable part of Villalpando's reconstruction; they were also significant for the plan of the three worlds of microcosm-macrocosm. Their removal from his plan changes his reconstruction to an unrecognizable degree. Furthermore, Newton referred to Villalpando's reconstruction as a "fantasy."[76]

Villalpando had changed a theoretical discussion into an architectural one. He had cast God in the light of the Renaissance; following Villalpando's reconstruction, the building of the Temple of Solomon was not only considered a significant Biblical and spiritual event, but it was also the origin of architecture. The divine plan of the macrocosm was perceived in human terms by the microcosm—in the architecture of the Temple. In addition to this blend of science and religion, there was an increased belief that the end of time was approaching and that the rebuilding of the Temple was essential for the Second Coming.

Although only a little amount of commentary on Villalpando

appeared in publications in Britain, there was far more interest in his work than initially appears. It was not only paper architecture that was utilized to refute, criticize, or support Villalpando's reconstruction. Support was at the highest level in England. James I of England was interested in Solomon's Temple and his interest can be dated to 1579,[77] and a copy of *Ezechielem Explanationes* bearing James I's arms on the binding belonged to the royal library.[78]

Conclusion

Villalpando had stimulated debate about the Temple, and this raised questions: What did the Temple look like? What was its design and structure like? The plan of the Temple was of interest to both the Jews and the Christians. For the Christians, the Temple was an important element of the Book of Revelation and the background to the Apocalypse. The colorful images and symbols of Revelation had stimulated the imagination of every era, but particularly that of the 17th and early 18th century. It was important to Christian millenarians, since the Temple was the landscape of the Promised Land and they considered that the end of the world was imminent, whereas for Jewish messianism, the rebuilding of the Temple would see the coming of the Jewish Messiah and the restoration of Israel. The exhibitions of the Leon and Schott models of the Temple were intended to reveal to the public truly divine architecture.

Villalpando was a Jesuit priest and he was strongly influenced by the works and spiritual guidance of the founder of his order, Ignatius of Loyola. Villalpando's main aim was spiritual: by visualizing the Temple and by meditating on that visualization, the reality of the truths within would be revealed. Ignatius of Loyola's *Spiritual Exercise* was a series of meditations that were designed for that purpose.[79] Seeing is the dominant sense; his contemplation exercises begin with "Composition, seeing the place." Ignatius stated that "composition consists in seeing through the gaze of the imagination the material place."[80] In *Ezechielem Explanationes*, Villalpando created an "architecture of theology" by which his fellow theologians would be able to visualize and meditate on the Temple, he would be able to verify its correspondences with sacred texts, and they would be able to verify the truths of the

Catholic Church. However, the impact of *Ezechielem Explanationes* was not what Villalpando intended. A scientific approach to religion was emerging in this extremely troubled time, particularly in England. By applying the principles of architecture to this Biblical building, Villalpando was blending religion and science together. The writings of Villalpando and his critics and commentators were intended for academics and were in Latin, which excluded a large part of the public. Nevertheless, the public showed a great deal of interest when architectural models of the Temple were displayed in exhibitions, which they attended in great numbers.

4

Architectural Models of the Temple of Solomon Exhibited in London in the 17th and 18th Centuries

Architectural models were becoming quite common in the 17th and early 18th century, but these were usually models of existing buildings.[1] However, two architectural models of Solomon's Temple captured the public's imagination in this period—Jacob Judah Leon (Templo)'s model and Gerhard Schott's model. Schott's model was built to Villalpando's plan, whereas the Leon model was built according to the Jewish sacred texts. Newton would have been aware of these two models and more than possibly saw them—at least Schott's model—when he lived in London, although he does not mention either of them in any of his unpublished manuscripts. In fact, it would have been very difficult for Newton to avoid seeing Schott's model since it was constantly in the press and was discussed widely.

Gerhard Schott's Model

Schott's model (see Figure 32) arrived in London in August 1724 to great acclaim by the press:

> A few days ago arrived here from Hamburg, an ingenious mechanic a native of that City, with the finest model of the Temple of Solomon that has been, made by himself, and composed of materials and ornaments so rich that the whole work is valued at 20,000. The extraordinary curiosity was immediately shown to the King, who was so well pleased with it, that it is said his majesty will be the purchaser.[2]

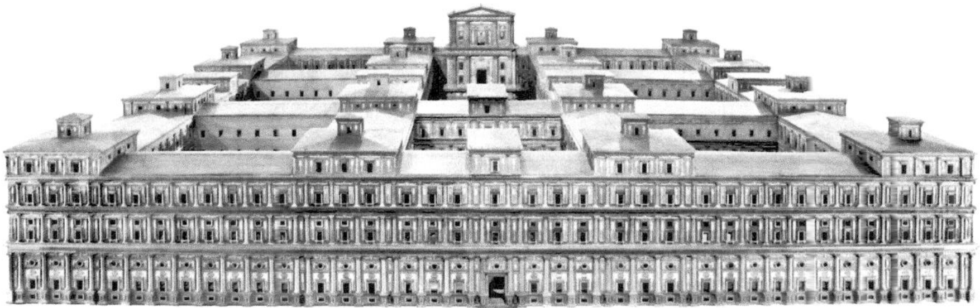

Figure 32. The Schott model (courtesy of Stiftung Historische Museen Hamburg).

In fact, King George I did not view the model until December 7, on his way to the opera at the Hay Market, but it was reported that he was very pleased with it.[3] However, the papers disagreed over whether the great model was twenty or thirty years in the making.[4]

The model was originally commissioned at the end of the 17th century by a Hamburg city councilor, Gerhard Schott (1641–1702). Schott was from a well-known Hamburg patrician family. He was one of the founders of the opera house on the Gänsemarkt in Hamburg and was a director of the opera house for over thirty years.[5] The guidebook that accompanied the model claimed that:

> The motive of forming this model of Solomon's Temple, which is now seen in London, was an opera representing the destruction of Jerusalem, acted at Hamburg; and as the Opera-house was built at the change of councillor Schott a man very learned and judicious, much renowned for the pains he took to represent his scenes in the most accurate manner, and altogether conform to antiquity. The decoration of the before-mentioned opera, where the city of Jerusalem, together with the Temple are represented, was brought by him the said councillor Schott to the highest degree of perfection. The same great man taking an extreme delight in the contemplation of this magnificent, and through the world renowned building, he at last resolved, not regarding the charges he would be at to form a proper model of so incomparable a piece of architecture.[6]

The model was over thirty years old by the time it reached London. It is known that the model was on display at the opera *The Destruction of Jerusalem*, which appeared in Hamburg in two parts in 1692. The first part deals, in three acts and a prologue, with the taking of the Temple and the second part, in three acts, deals with the conquest of Mount Zion. In the conclusion of the first part, the Temple was shown before and after its destruction by fire. The composer of the libretto was Christian Heinrich Postel, and the music was by the Kapellmeister, F. G. Conradi.[7]

Considering that it took twenty or thirty years to make and then another thirty years passed before it arrived in London, it is unlikely that the "ingenious mechanic a native of Hamburg" that built the model accompanied it to London, and by 1724, Schott himself had been dead for twenty-two years. It appears that after Schott's death, the model was stored and no longer used. Zacharias Conrad von Uffenbach, who visited Hamburg in 1710, claimed to have examined the model very carefully, but it then stood behind the theater.[8]

Schott's heirs appear to have sold the model to Mr. Combrecht Con,[9] who was reported to be an Englishman[10]; the year of this sale is not known. Combrecht Con brought the model to London, perhaps to find a buyer for it, and he also sent a model of the Tabernacle that had been built under Schott's direction. Although the English newspapers claimed that King George I was to be the buyer, nothing eventuated. Within a couple of weeks the model went on public display.

In the 18th century, private "collections" were opened to the public for a fee. The practice of displaying architectural models does not seem to have been unusual, and indeed appears to have been very lucrative. After Edmund Halley's death in 1742, his book collection was sold at auction and the catalogue featured:

> a very curious and complete Model, adorned with mosaic work, in mother of pearl etc. Whole Temple of Christ's Sepulchre at Jerusalem, as it was built by Helena, mother of the Emperor Constantine: with all the chapels, altars, and other observable buildings about it. From the showing whereof, the profits arising have been farmed at above 3000 Sterling per ann. This venerable curiosity is so artificially and commodiously contrived, that the inside and ground plan are rendered as visible as the elevation.[11]

The catalogue listed all forty-seven elements of the model, such as the belfry, the stairs, and the sepulchres, in detail. The model changed hands at auction in 1769[12] and 1774,[13] and by 1785, ended up in the museum of Margaret Cavendish Bentinck, the Duchess of Portland, as a part of a much larger collection.[14] After the Duchess's death, the collection was entirely dissolved at an auction in over 4,000 lots and the model's whereabouts is now unknown.

Advertisements for the exhibition of the Schott model were placed in many of the daily newspapers:

> The Temple of Solomon, lately brought over from Hamburg, which his majesty not long ago was pleased to see with great satisfaction, is every Day to be seen from eleven to Three-a-clock, in the Long Room of the Opera House in the Hay-Market. The complete masterpiece for its excellent architecture exact and perfect symmetry, and richness in gold, silver, jewels, carving and figures, has not its like in the universe; there being above 6700 pillars, 1500 chambers, and windows in proportion to be seen conforming to the original. The printed description of it, with several fine cuts, is to be had at the same place, at five shillings the book. The price for seeing the Temple is half a guinea. Every particular will be shown and explained by some persons attending there for that purpose. And whereas it is supposed that those who are curious in architecture and antiquity would be glad to see it more than once, the owner gives notice that those who pay a guinea shall see it as often as they please for the same.[15]

At half a guinea entrance fee, the exhibition was for a very elite audience. Later advertisements described the size of the model as being "13 foot high and 80 foot round."[16] The model was built to impress: a vast twenty by twenty by thirteen feet (6.096 × 6.096 × 3.963 meters).

Despite the mention of several fine cuts, presumably etchings, the book is not illustrated. Nevertheless, it was only a couple of months before two large prints, three feet three inches high and two feet wide (1 × 0.61 meters), of the Hamburg model were being advertised and sold by engravers in London.[17] It was also not long before the controversy of the debate over Villalpando's plan arose.

Within twenty months of the Schott model arriving in London, it was reported that "Mr. [William] Whiston has made a model of the Temple to show in opposition to that in the Haymarket."[18] How detailed, or how large, the model was is unknown, since neither the model nor any plans or drawings have survived. However, the reporter seems to have found the challenge to the Schott model exasperating, since he claimed that both models "pretended to be true models, yet are different. If our virtuosos can't agree upon corporeals, no wonder there is such a difference in speculative matters."[19]

Whiston had succeeded Newton as Lucasian Professor of Mathematics at the University of Cambridge but he lost his position because of his theological views. He was charged but not convicted of heresy in 1713 over these beliefs.[20] He had a keen interest in the Temple of Solomon, and in 1737, he published a translation of the complete works of Josephus into English. This translation achieved enormous popularity in the English-speaking world, and after nearly 300 years remains the most published translation of Josephus's works. This translation could have been stimulated by the arrival of the Schott model. The main source of Villalpando's reconstruction of the Temple of Solomon was Ezekiel. Whiston, however, stated that Ezekiel's vision was not of Solomon's Temple:

> As for Sir *I.N.*'s [Isaac Newton's] description of Solomon's Temple; (I think he should call it Ezekiel's Temple; for he takes it principally from Ezekiel, who describes neither Solomon's, nor Zorebabels, nor Herod's, but the Jews future Temple) I reserve its examination till I publish my own plan of all those Temples.[21]

Unfortunately, he did not publish his plan, but he continued to lecture on the Temples of Jerusalem in clear opposition to the Schott model. In his advertisement for his lecture, he distinguished between the Temples. Whiston lectured "upon sacred architecture past; of the models of the Tabernacle of Moses; of the Temples of Solomon, Zorobabel and Herod: And upon the sacred architecture future, of the model of Ezekiel's Temple."[22] For Whiston, Ezekiel's vision was a prophecy of the future and had not been built.

Whiston lectured at Grigsby's Coffee House, behind the Royal Exchange, on Wednesdays, and Button's Coffee House in Covent Garden on Friday. He lectured on both science and religion, and sometimes a mixture of both. In 1730, in a description of his lectures in a letter to a newspaper, he stated that his lectures would discuss

> the earliest date of the prediction of eclipses, and of other astronomical appearance; and show that Amos, Isaiah, and Jeremiah were the three first, who now appear to have foretold both eclipses and earthquakes; and Isaiah the first, who foretold the occultation of stars by the moon.... After all which I intend to produce my model[s] of Solomon's, Zeobabel's, Herod's, and Ezekiel's Temples and to compare that model with Sir Isaac Newton's description;...there and other the like curious and useful discoveries which I have made in astronomy and sacred architecture, may somewhat better deserve the attention of the inquisitive of this age.[23]

Unfortunately, this letter does not state whether he was establishing a connection between astronomy and sacred architecture, which many of his predecessors had done. However, the structure of the lecture does indicate this connection. Whiston's classified advertisement listed the eight lectures given, which began with "an examination of the pretences to astronomical characters before the Mosaic Creation"[24] and ended with three lectures on sacred architecture of the Temples of Jerusalem and his comparison of the Newton model.

Now Whiston had two models to refute—the Schott model and Newton's model in *The Chronology*, published posthumously in 1728—both of which were attracting public attention. Both models were based on Ezekiel's vision, but were extremely different. Whiston placed extra advertisements when the lectures were given that displayed the models,[25] and clearly, the public interest in the model remained active.

In June 1727, King George I died and the new reign of George II began. Perhaps the owners of the Schott model approached the new King to purchase the model, for in October of that year the newspapers reported, "We hear his majesty has purchased the famous model of the Temple of Solomon brought from Hamburg in the last Reign, and shown at the Hay Market, to make a present of it to one of the universities."[26] However, the advertisements resumed six months later, and within a few more months the usual advertisement had a note attached: "N.B. The Temple is to be seen till the 17th of the month and no longer, and then the Temple will be taken asunder, in order to be carried out of the Kingdom."[27] The Temple was put up for sale and was advertised in the newspapers for several months.[28] The advertisements claimed that in Hamburg

> it was seen by the late Czar, The King of Poland, and several Princes of Germany, by who large sums of money were offered but the original proprietor was then living and would not dispose of it on any account: since that time it was brought into England and allowed by his late Majesty, the Royal Family and most of the nobility and Gentry to be the exactest piece of architecture now examined.[29]

It is interesting that the original owner, Schott, was referred to as the "proprietor." These displays to the public were expected to be money-making enterprises, but were they seen as a religious education experience or as a novelty of miniature architecture? Whiston leaves no doubt that he did not perceive himself as proprietor but as educator, though his circumstances forced him to charge a fee.

However, the model did not sell. In early January 1729 the model went to auction,[30] but no buyer eventuated and it remained in the kingdom. It was moved to the Royal Exchange, where it continued to be on view every day, and to interest the public, the price was dropped to two shillings and the Sanctum Sanctorum, the holy vessels, and the windows of the court of the Gentiles had new gilt and all the floors of the Temple were painted so that "all appears finer and richer that before."[31] This brought a new audience to the exhibition and people continued to flock to it. The model remained on display until 1732 when it was purchased by Elector Friedrich August of Saxony, who was King of Poland and Grand Duke of Lithuania.

The model left London in August 1732, yet it took to until 10 January 1733 to reach Dresden. It was involved in a shipwreck, and progress was slowed down by the freezing over of the Elbe River near Hamburg and an accident in which the transport carriage overturned.[32] By 1734, the model was on display in the Wall Pavilion of the Zwinger Place in Dresden with a collection of other Jewish cultural pieces, including a model of the Tabernacle, a model of a full-sized rabbi, the Torah, a circumcision knife, and many other pieces. All of these pieces were displayed in a replica synagogue, which appears ironic given that the Jews of Dresden were forbidden to build their own synagogue.[33] In the nineteenth century the model changed hands several times. In 1836, with the breaking up of the collection, it was brought by a Jewish merchant, Samuel Elb, who sold it in 1846 to the Kreuzkirche (the Church of the True Cross). Thirty years later the model changed hands again; it was given to the Saxon Antiquarian Society, who sold it to the Hamburg Antiquarian Society in 1910. The model was put in storage in the Second World War and is now displayed in the Museum für Hamburgische Geschichte.[34] It has returned to its place of origin.

Jacob Judah Leon's (Templo) Model

While the Schott model was in London it was always on public display, and although an English buyer failed to eventuate, it did capture the public's attention, who continued to support its exhibition for close to eight years. However, there was a model of the Temple of Solomon that predated the Schott model, and may well have been the inspiration for it, that came to England twice (or possibly remained in England between exhibitions). This was the model by Jacob Judah Leon.

Few men have had as many aliases as the Rabbi Jacob Judah Leon: in Hebrew, Judah Arje, Aryeh, or Arye; in Europe, Leo, Leon Leonis, or Leonituis; and in England, Lion or Lyon. The surname Templo was given to him by contemporary scholars because of his life's work on the Temple of Solomon and the models that he exhibited.[35] However, Leon never used the surname Templo himself. He signed himself in Hebrew lettering as Yacob Yehuda Aryeh and is referred to in his literary works as Leon Hebreo.[36]

His birthplace is uncertain. Some claim that he was born into an old Portuguese-Jewish family in 1602, and although the family outwardly embraced Christianity to escape the attention of the Spanish Inquisition, they left Portugal and moved to Amsterdam, where they could live openly as Jews.[37] Others claimed that he was born in Hamburg and had a Spanish-Portuguese background.[38] Johannes Saubertus, a friend of Leon, claimed that he was Spanish,[39] there is no evidence to where he originated from. Throughout his life his work was translated into no fewer than eight languages—Dutch, Spanish, French, German, Hebrew Yiddish, Latin, and English. Leon settled in Middelburg, the Netherlands. However, although it is known that he lived in Middelburg, he claimed in a preface in 1646 that during his time in Middelburg he "taught in the holy Jewish community in the City of Hamburg."[40] It is also claimed that he succeeded the first rabbi of Hamburg, Isaac Athias, in 1628, returned to Amsterdam in the 1630s, and then moved to Middelburg.[41] Whatever the truth is, by 1643 he had moved to Amsterdam.

In the 17th century, the Dutch Republic, particularly the wealthy trading city of Amsterdam, was known for the acceptance of the settlement of Jews. It is recorded that a prominent member of the Amsterdam Sephardi community, David Curiel, was attacked by a German robber. Curiel was wounded but he managed to overcome his attacker with the help of his Christian neighbors. The robber was tried and executed. Later, the State of Holland expressed their regret at the incident in a letter to Curiel. Whether this is true or legend, it has been preserved in at least five different manuscripts in Jewish Libraries. This makes a striking contrast to the Inquisition of Portugal and Spain occurring at the same time.[42]

There were also intellectual collaborations between the Jewish and Christian communities. Dutch theologian and Hebrew scholar Adam Boreel and Leon published a vocalized Hebrew edition of the Mishnah together, with a Spanish translation in 1642 that was financed by Boreel. In this study the Temple plays an important role. Leon brought the study alive by constructing the model of the Temple, and building costs were also financed by Boreel.[43]

Leon became a rabbi and teacher for the Sephardi community, which yielded him little money. By 1642 he had completed a model of the Temple of Solomon, and published a book on the Temple in Spanish, *Retrato del Templo de Selomoh*,[44] and in Dutch, *Afbeeldinghe vanden Templel Salomonis*,[45] within the same year, and in French, *Portrait du Temple de Salomon*, the following year. The model was exhibited to the public and advertised by a leaflet, which briefly described the Temple and the surrounding buildings.

One of these leaflets from 1641 has been uncovered in Lincoln Cathedral Library. It is believed to have belonged to Dean Michael Honywood, who at the outbreak of the English Civil War in 1641 moved to Utrecht and devoted himself to the collection of books. He returned to England after the Restoration in 1660. Honywood commissioned Christopher Wren to erect a library to house his entire collection. In 1958, Wilfred S. Samuel uncovered one of Leon's leaflets, and it is thought to be the only one in existence.[46] At the top of the leaflet is an image of the Temple mount, revealing the Temple on the top. Underneath the Temple is a large image of Leon (see Figure 33), which is signed by Salom Italia, a Jewish engraver of Italian origin who was living in Amsterdam at the time. Leon briefly described the Temple in twenty-six numbered points, then the Palace of King Solomon in twenty points, followed by the Tower of Antonia in six points. At the end of the leaflet, the reader is encouraged to visit the model and buy the book between 9:00 and 11:00 a.m. or 2:00 and 5:00 p.m. Below this, a couple of lines are left blank to fill in the address for the exhibition.[47]

In the 1640s the model exhibition moved from place to place. On April 30, 1646, Leon received permission from the burgomasters of The Hague to show the model during a fair.[48] On June 6, 1646, the town government of Haarlem gave Leon permission to exhibit his model at the Fair of Saint Jan.[49] However, most of the exhibitions appear to have been held in houses, including his own. He established a museum at his house on Amsterdam's Korte Houtstraat and the model was admired by a large number of visitors: Jewish and Christian, locals, and many from all over Europe.

In a letter to Samuel Hartlib dated 1646, John Dury claimed to have seen

> the model of the temple with all the appurtenances thereunto, in a most exact way according to the description made thereof in the Scripture & after the sense of all the Rabbis that are of note & credit. This piece I have seen & amongst all the rarities & antiquities which are to be taken notice of, there is none to be compared

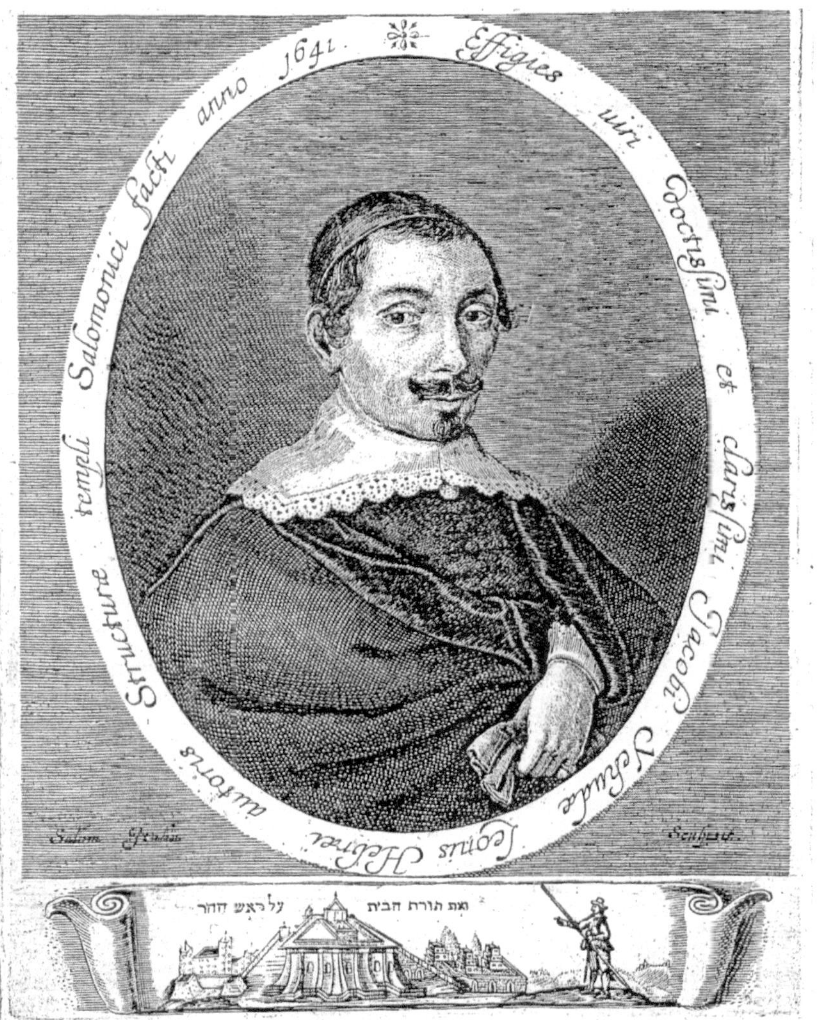

Figure 33. Portrait of Leon by Salom Italia (copyright © the Library and Museum of Freemasonry; used by permission).

thereupon, when once our antiquaries shall see the description thereof, they will find other objects of curiosities then hitherto have been minded.[50]

A German visitor described what the exhibition included:

Also, just in the same lane [i.e., Kurzholzgasse] as the Hebrew linguistic teacher Jakob Jehudah Leon, lived a Portuguese, who not only described but also formed very good in wood after their right and actual shape the Temple Solomon, the hut of the Stifi as well as the camp of the Levite and the whole Israel surrounds of these guardians, even the palace or the royal castle just of the same king after instructions of the old Hebrew history books. And these wooden illustrations will all age here in his house, who desires, granted to view, and may get explained the weirdest parts.[51]

Clearly, the exhibition of the model and the sale of his books supplemented Leon's meager income as a rabbi and teacher, and it would appear that this supplementation was significant. The model was exhibited for many years and brought Leon fame and fortune. It is known that one of his daughters, Abigail, and his son-in-law David Jesurun, who were living in the same house (which was the Temple museum) were asked to leave by Leon, but Jesurun refused. Jesurun took his complaint to a notary, and he claimed a share of the profits of the Temple model. The profits must have been significant and Leon eventually backed down.[52]

Leon's exhibition was very popular, not only with the public, but also with royalty and the scientific community. In 1642, Frederick Henry, Prince of Orange and Stadtholder of the Provinces of Holland, visited the new synagogue in Amsterdam. He was accompanied by Queen Henrietta Maria, wife of King Charles I. They also visited the Temple exhibition, which was on display at Leon's house. According to an heir of Leon's, Moses De Castro, who continued to be the proprietor of the model over one hundred years later, Frederick had honored Leon "by his particular approbation of the model, in a letter of recommendation addressed to the states of Holland"[53] De Castro claimed that he still retained the letter. Encouraged by this royal visit, Leon dedicated his *Description of the Tabernacle*, published in 1647, to Frederick; however, although some patronage had been promised by Frederick, it does not appear to have eventuated.[54]

In his second edition of the Dutch *Afbeeldinghe vanden Templel Salomonis*,[55] Leon included two dedicatory poems; one is signed I. D Brune, who is thought to be the Christian poet, and the other was by Hebraist Johan de Brunes the Elder.[56] Constantijn Huygen, secretary to two Princes of Orange, Frederick Henry and William, who was also the first secretary to the Dutch Royal Society, supported Leon's work by writing him letters of introduction. This would have been an important contact for Leon, and indicates the respect that the Dutch scientific community had for him.

His lucrative "hobby" was taking up a great deal of time because of the travel required and the writing of his continuous stream of books. In 1649, Leon had taken over the sixth form (*medras*) of the school Ets Haim, but many of the students chose to have private lessons, much to the disgust of the school governors. By 1661, the governors of the school prohibited Leon from showing the model on Saturdays and holidays under penalty of dismissal.[57]

Retrato del Templo de Selomoh was a guidebook to the Temple that explained the model. It is only seventy-six pages long, and in the preface Leon emphasized that he was reconstructing a real building made by men:

> Do not be astonished I have made references to all the things which could be found in the Temple, whatever they were and although they were to be seen at different times, but I shall distinguish between them and declare in what times and in which manner they were to be seen in the book which I am preparing.... I intend to describe expressly all these things and to prove from the authority of sacred Scripture and many other authorities of consequence, and by research and the employment of the utmost diligence and with sparing work I have studied all the authors that I have been able to discover who have written on this matter. God give me his grace to accomplish what I promise and you his protection.[58]

Here he is not proposing the ideal vision of Villalpando. He rejected Ezekiel as a source for the Temple of Solomon and used Josephus's *Antiquitates Judaicæ* and *Bellum Judaicum*, I Chronicles, I Kings, and the *Midot* as his main sources.

Leon disagreed with Villalpando, claiming that the Temple needed to be considered in the context of Jewish tradition. Although Villalpando's reconstruction had been built using the principles of architecture, Villalpando, according to Leon, was more concerned with theology than with a literal interpretation of the architecture. Leon's emphasis was the Temple made by man, for the worship of God, not the God-given plan that Villalpando had stressed. Yet Leon's Temple foundations look exactly the same as Villalpando's, and thus Villalpando did have some influence on Leon; although the plan is different in style, the architecture is very similar to Villalpando's (compare Figure 20 and Figure 34).

Unlike the Schott model, Leon's models no longer exist. Leon's books are now extremely rare; they were becoming rare even before the close of the 17th century. In the leaflet advertising Leon's exhibition of the model, he stated, after describing the Temple and surrounding buildings, "The other particulars of these magnificent buildings, are mentioned in the book named pictures of the Temple of Solomon described

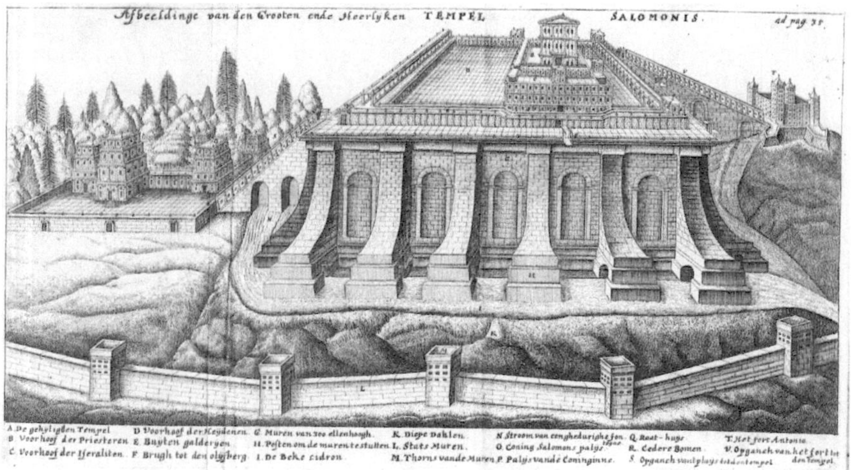

Figure 34. Jacob Judah Leon's Temple of Solomon (copyright © the Library and Museum of Freemasonry; used by permission).

by the author of this map."[59] A book entitled "Pictures of the Temple of Solomon" is not one of Leon's many publications,[60] and his earliest books had no illustrations and the latter ones had only a few. However, the illustrations were issued separately from the books and were inserted randomly by the owners.[61] Although there were a few images of the Temple in his text, Leon did not provide a floor plan of the Temple precinct to accompany the description in his books. If he did have a floor plan on a separate sheet, it has not survived.

The Schott model was of the whole Temple precinct and was built to the symmetrical plan of Villalpando. As stated previously, the foundations and the style of the architecture of Leon's Temple are very similar to that of Villalpando, but the plan of the precinct is very different. One noticeable element about Leon's plan of the precinct is that it is asymmetrical, whereas Villalpando's plan emphasized symmetry. Like Villalpando, Leon made his precinct square,[62] but the inner court and the Temple are placed to the northern side of the square precinct.

In Villalpando's reconstruction, the whole Temple precinct was built of stone, but in Leon's description it was built of marble. Leon claimed that

the form of the Temple was exactly square, built of very large and precious marble stones, the whiteness of which appeared afar off like a mountain covered with

98

snow, and the gold that was overlaid with stone with such a lustre when the sun was on it, that no person could look on it for its brightness.[63]

Leon emphasized the richness of the materials of the Temple throughout the book, often at the expense of the architectural description.

Leon claimed that the model dimensions were twenty by ten by seven feet (6.096 × 3.048 × 2.1336 meters) with a scale of 1:300. Jac Zwarts confirmed this measurement by claiming that the model was six by three by two meters,[64] but this size would have been far too large, since it would have been very difficult to travel with, and unlike Schott and his model, Leon traveled a great deal with it, and given that Leon appeared to have exhibited in private houses, there would have been few residences large enough to host such an exhibition. In a later English translation of Leon's original work of 1641, *Retrato del Templo de Selomoh*, published in 1778, the translator and proprietor of the model, Moses De Castro, claimed that it was seven by three and a half by one and a half feet[65] (2.1336 × 1.0668 × 0.4572 meters), which would be a more reasonable size for a model that was taken from fair to fair and exhibited in houses. However, all these measurements are rectangular, indicating that, unlike the Schott model, it was not a model of the whole Temple precinct but of the most sacred section of the precinct—either the inner courts and the Temple or the Temple alone.

Leon's fame spread, and he gained the support of Duke Augustus of Brunswick, who was an active intellectual and patron. Leon's book had been published in Dutch, Spanish, French, German, and Hebrew, but not in Latin, the language of scholarship. Duke Augustus commissioned Johanne Saubertus to prepare a Latin translation so that Leon's work would obtain a much wider audience. Leon's publications had been written as a guide to the Temple so that the viewer of the model could understand the architecture, the space, the vessels, and the rituals. Duke Augustus charged Saubertus with the production of a scholarly work based on Leon's original work. In a letter to Saubertus from Leon, he outlined the material that he was sending Saubertus to aid him in his translation. He sent a copy of *The Temple of Solomon* in a foreign language, but he does not say which one, with a Dutch translation in the margin. He also included an image of

the Great and Holy Temple which Solomon build on top of Mount Moriah; the Palace of the King on its right, and the Tower of Antonio on its left, both connected to the Sanctuary.... On the second leaf you will see the picture of the Holy

Tabernacle as it was shown to Moses the man of God on Mount Sinai and in addition the picture of all holy utensils which were needed in the services of the sanctuary, that is, the ark, table, the candle sticks, the two altars, the wooden structure and the carpets which covered it … the third leaf, you can see opposite facing you the layout of the camp of the children of Israel divided into twelve tribes surrounding the holy Tabernacle in the formation in which they journeyed on and stopped…. In addition to this I am sending you the book on the cherubim in a foreign language in which book is explained the true shape of the cherubim which are on the top of the Arc and the meaning of the name and the secret of their shape and why such a thing was made…. Also I am sending you a fourth leaf, a very large one, on which is drawn the resting place of all the standards of the twelve tribes when they were resting on the four sides of the compass (the world); also as they marched in the desert in a straight column; and everything which belonged to them; also the picture of the Tabernacle, of the Holy Temple and the garments of the priests; and the holy utensils set out round about. All this it does in detail and with care, with an explanation in Hebrew in the margin, also in a foreign language and in Dutch and in English.[66]

De Templo Hierosolymitano was published in 1665,[67] and although the book is attributed to Leon, it was greatly expanded by Saubertus. There are seven illustrations: (1) the title page (see Figure 35), with images of the Pope, Solomon, Dseru Babel, and Ezekiel in the corners, above the title plaque, a small image of the inside of the holy of holies that is badly executed but nevertheless with patterns and design that are reminiscent of Villalpando's illustration of the sacred sanctuary (see Figure 21), and below the title plaque, an image of the altar; (2) a portrait of the patron Duke Augustus of Brunswick; and (3) a portrait of Leon with the Tabernacles and Temple underneath, signed by Conr Buno, although it is clearly a copy of the image executed by Salom Italia in 1647 for the advertising leaflets. Illustration (4), the Temple on top of Mount Moriah, is the most interesting of the images, with the Palace of the King on its right and the Tower of Antonio on its left. This appears to be the image that was sent to Saubertus by Leon. It is very possible that this engraving was printed from the same copperplate as the earlier image; the inscriptions on the engraving are all in Dutch, which is out of context with the rest of the book, and the same spelling mistakes are repeated. Along with this engraving is an annotated floor plan and key to the annotations of the Temple by a prominent Dutch Hebraist, Constantijn L'Empereur. Of the final images, illustration (5) shows the robes of a rabbi, (6) some of the ornaments of the Temple, and (7) the Ark of the Covenant, which is completely different from the Ark in the title page.

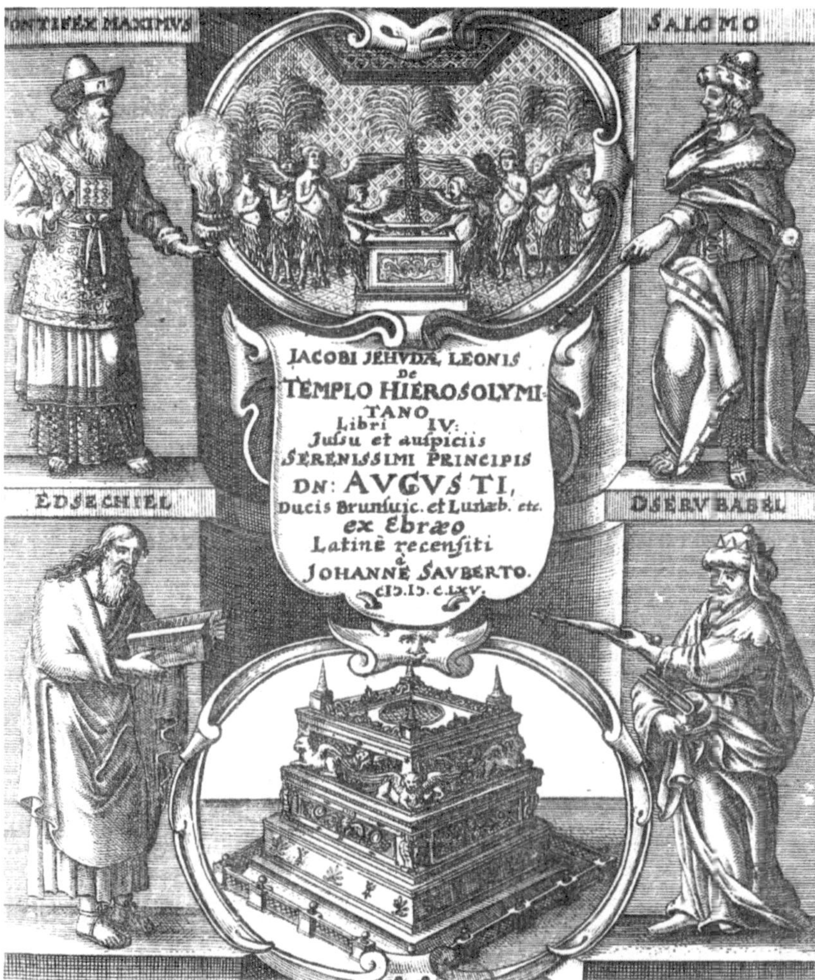

Figure 35. The title page of Saubertus' *De Templo Hierosolymitano* (author's collection).

The interesting thing about the illustrations in *De Templo Hierosolymitano*, in terms of style, consistency, and quality, is that they are executed by at least four different hands. Illustrations (5) and (6) are copied from the "fourth leaf, a very large one" sent by Leon. The original was printed as a separate leaf; it is a larger and more ornate image of the first Tabernacle image that he mentioned (see Figure 36).

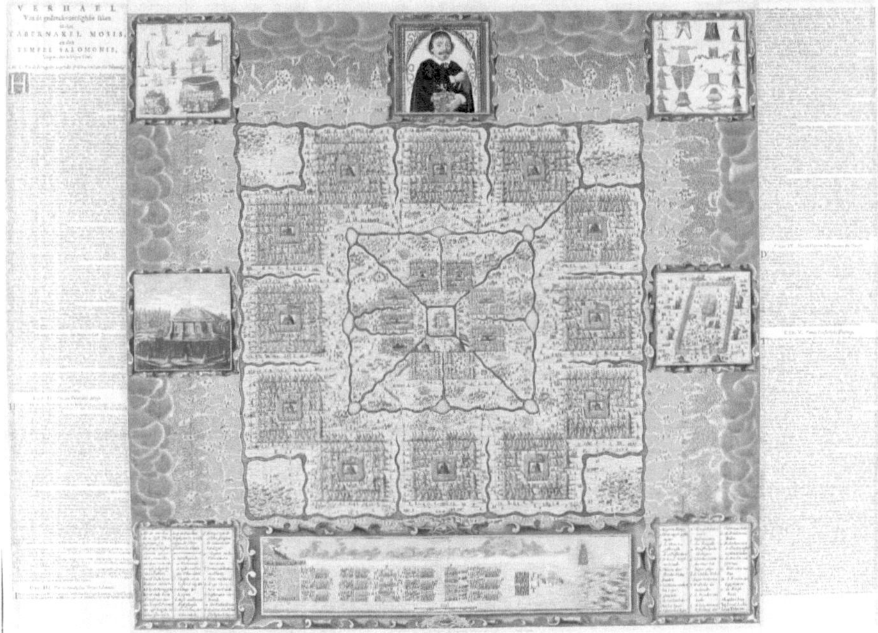

Figure 36. Leon's leaflet of the Tabernacle (courtesy of Bibliotheca Rosenthaliana, Special Collections of the University of Amsterdam).

Illustrations (5) and (6) are small boxed vignettes from the large image, but the copies are of a much poorer quality.

After Leon's death, his son donated over 200 illustrations belonging to Leon to the Hebrew School of the Portuguese Jews, where he was chief master.[68] They are not itemized but it has been assumed that these were images of his Temple design and that he executed most of them himself. However, none of the surviving illustrations, Temple or otherwise, are signed by him. Salom Italia executed the three engraved portraits of Leon, one of these with the images of the Temple and surrounding buildings, in 1641, 1647, and 1654. He also engraved the cover for Leon's book of the cherubim,[69] *Tratado de los Cherubim*,[70] in 1654, which was subsequently reissued in *An Accurate Description of the Grand and Glorious Temple* published in 1778 (see Figure 37). It is impossible to know whether Leon did any of the drawings himself. However, he does not claim to have done them, and given the different styles of the various unsigned etchings, they appear to have been done by several

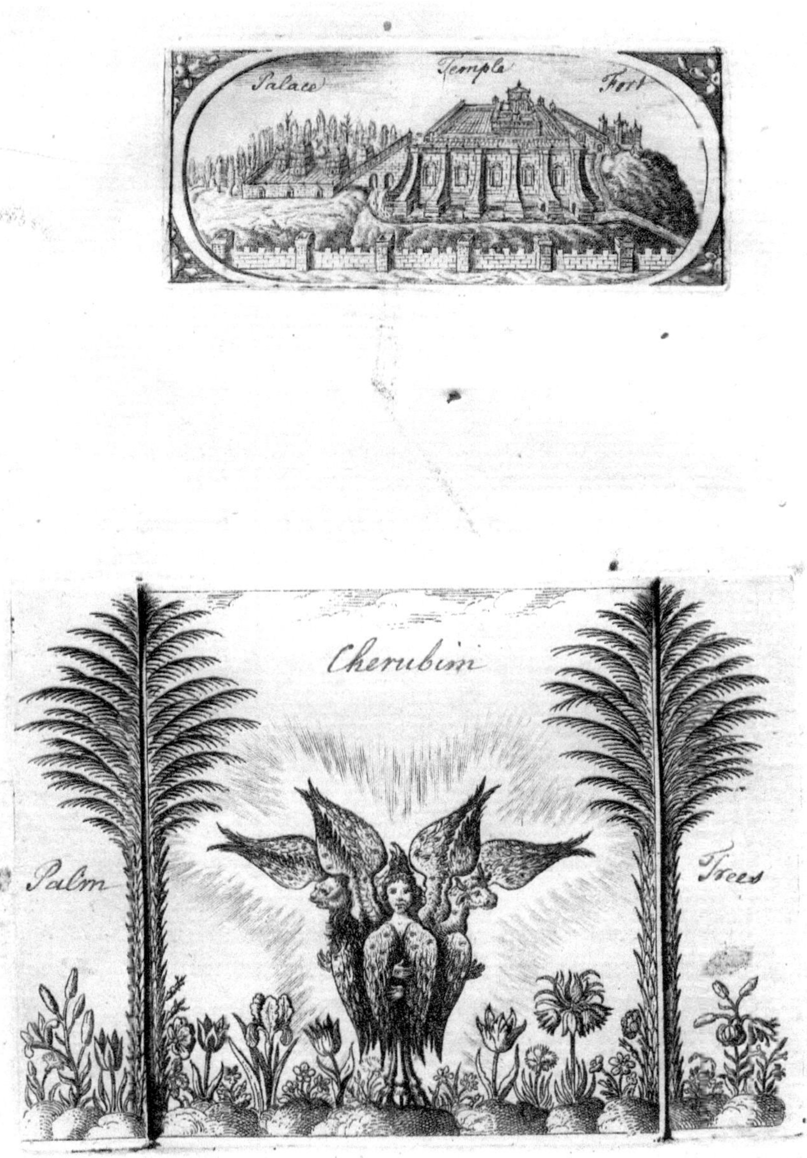

Figure 37. The cover page for Leon's book *An Accurate Description of the Grand and Glorious Temple* (copyright © the Library and Museum of Freemasonry; used by permission).

different hands, not only in Saubertus's Latin translation, but also in Leon's other books.

It was clear that Duke Augustus commissioned Saubertus to complete a scholarly work based on Leon's original work; however, the emphasis is different, and although the Temple's architecture is still significant, it is not as dominant as in Leon's 1640 work. In Leon's original work, there is a sense of rebuilding and "seeing" the Temple in all its richness, but Saubertus's version seeks to explain the Temple and its parts in a more academic sense.

Saubertus kept Leon's four sections; however, he expanded them, particularly the section on the description of the Temple, to up to five times their original length. In addition, Saubertus used some surprising references—Villalpando and Ezekiel—which explain Ezekiel's appearance on the title page. Saubertus added the plan and key to the Temple by Constantijn L'Empereur. L'Empereur died in 1648, almost twenty years before the publication of *De Templo Hierosolymitano* (see Figure 27). Perhaps Saubertus thought that the well-respected name of L'Empereur would give Leon's Temple more authority. In the wealth of paper reconstructions of the 17th century, which range from a simple floor plan to the elaborate plans, section and elevations of Villalpando, Leon differs in that he did not supply a floor plan. It seems unlikely that the plan would have been a separate sheet, but it does appear a strange oversight for Leon not to include one, or for Saubertus not to have asked him for one, particularly if he was keen to include one. From Leon's original description, it is impossible to draw an accurate floor plan because he did not provide measurements for many areas, particularly distances between features.

As with Leon's original work, it is difficult to construct a complete floor plan from Saubertus's extended version because of the absence of measurements between features. However, a couple of questions arise with the Latin translation. Since it is over five times the size of Leon's work and used sources that Leon did not use, how much of this work is Leon's? Leon does not use Ezekiel as a source, whereas Saubertus used Ezekiel's Temple and measurements throughout his "translation."[71] It is clear from the title page, with the image of Ezekiel that his prophecy was going to be given prominence. Although Saubertus did retain the Jewish sources, the addition of Ezekiel makes it a different reconstruction from Leon's.

Is Leon's reconstruction the same as L'Empereur's? L'Empereur derived his reconstruction from the same sources as Leon. Therefore, it is possible that there is a similarity with Leon's. The lack of a floor plan for Leon's reconstruction makes it impossible to decide. However, using the same sources does not necessarily guarantee a similarity, considering that Villalpando's and Newton's floor plans, despite both using Ezekiel as their main source, they have no similarities (see Figure 9 and Figure 20). Leon would not have been in a position to object if the reconstruction was dissimilar; it is very unlikely that he would have risked upsetting a powerful patron such as Duke Augustus. Such a patron would have been helpful to Leon, particularly when he planned to travel to England with the model.

Constantijn Huygen wrote letters of introduction for Leon for a trip to England to exhibit his models. A copy of the letter sent to Christopher Wren is preserved in Koninklijke Bibliotheek, The Hague, and is dated October 7, 1674:

> This bearer is a Jew by birth and profession, and I am bound to him for some instructions I had from him, long ago, in the Hebrew literature. This maketh me grant him the addresses he desireth of me, his intention being to show in England a curious model of the Temple of Solomon, he had been about to contrive these many years, where he doth presume to have demonstrated and corrected an infinite number of errors and parallelisms of our most learned scholars, who had meddled with the exposition of that holy fabric, and most specially of the Jesuit Villalpando, who, as you know, Sir, has handled the matter *ingenti cum fastu et apparatu, ut solent isti* [with enormous display and complexity]. I make no question but many of your divines and other *virtuois* will take some pleasure to hear the Israelite discourse upon his architecture and the conformity of it with the genuine truth of the holy text, but, Sir before all, I have thought I was to bring him acquainted with yourself, who are able to judge of the matter upon better and surer grounds than any living man. I give him also letters to the Portuguese ambassador, to my lord Arlington and M. Oldenburg that some notice be taken of him, both at court, and amongst those of the Royal Society. If you will be so good as to him unto my lord Archbishop of Canterbury his Grace, even in my name, I am sure the noble prelate will take it *pro more suo* [according to the custom of men] friendly and remember with me the Psalm, *Laetatus sum in his quae dicta sunt mihi, in domum domini ibimus* [I rejoiced when they said to me, let us go into the house of the Lord]. I pray, Sir, let his Grace find here my humble and most devoted respect, and for your part I believe I do still remember your excellent merits, and in consideration of them and will always show to be.[72]

Leon clearly intended an extensive visit, with introductions to the court, and the scientific and religious communities. Huygen must have regarded him highly to write such an introduction to such an eminent figure as Henry Bennet, 1st Earl of Arlington, Henry Oldenburg, the secretary of the Royal Society, and Christopher Wren. In the nineteenth century, Lucien Wolf suggested that Leon's visit in 1675 was not his first visit, and that he had previously made some good connections,[73] and presumably intended to build on them. Unfortunately, this is has proved impossible to verify.

The Restoration in Britain was a time of great religious friction, not only between Catholics and Protestants, but also between the factions of Protestants. In the England of the Restoration, it was perilous to worship as a Catholic publicly, particularly after the Great Fire in 1666. However, Jews could worship openly at a synagogue in London. Samuel Pepys visited a synagogue, perhaps out of curiosity to see the difference in worship, and London society seems to have shared his curiosity. The Jewish community of London prospered under Charles II. This could have been because the Jews of Amsterdam had advanced Charles 1,000 gulden to assist him in returning to England, and in return, he had granted them a charter that permitted them to settle in England.[74]

In 1675, Leon published *A relation of the most memorable thinges in the Tabernacle of Moses and the Temple of Solomon According to text of Scripture*, written in English, which is a summary of his works on the Temple and Tabernacle. It is little more than an extended leaflet and does appear to be more of a souvenir of the exhibition; it would not really stand as a work on its own. It begins with a prayer for the prosperity of His Royal Majesty and a dedication to Charles II.

In this dedication, Leon reminisced about the visit of Queen Henrietta Maria thirty years previously, and he stated, "the holy vessels, garments, and utensils thereof are delineated and set forth to the life, and which was graciously owned with devout affection thirty years ago and upward that serene Queen, your Majesty's mother; so be pleased, most noble prince, to imitate her pietie."[75] It has been suggested that "graciously owned" meant that Henrietta Maria had purchased these objects on her visit in 1643,[76] which is highly unlikely since she was in Amsterdam to raise money to support King Charles I's campaign in the Civil War. She attempted to sell the crown jewels in Amsterdam; however, Cromwell prevented that. Then she attempted to sell her own jewelry, and was equally unsuccessful. It would be very doubtful that she would have spent any of the money that she did eventually raise from the royalists in Amsterdam on a model or the ornaments of the Temple. It has also been suggested that Leon presented them to her as a gift,[77] which seems equally unlikely. It is more likely that by "owned" he meant that the Queen acknowledged the correctness of the model,[78] thereby giving his model royal approval.

There is little contemporary discussion on Leon, but he is credited with many things; it is often claimed that he was a teacher, writer, Freemason, architect, and draftsman. His models came to England twice, and on the first visit, Leon intended to come with the model. After visiting the models during their second visit to England in 1759, Masonic writer Lawrence Dermott claimed in the second edition of *Ahiman Rezon*

> the free masons arms in the upper part of the front piece of this book, was found in the collection of the famous and learned Hebraist, architect and brother, Rabi Jacob Jehudah Leon. This gentleman, at the request of the states of Holland, built a model of Solomon's Temple. The design of this undertaking was to build a temple in Holland, but upon surveying the model it was adjudged, that the united provinces were not rich enough to pay for it; whereupon the states generously bestowed the model upon the builder, notwithstanding they had already paid him his demand, which was very great. This model was exhibited to public view (by authority) at Paris and Vienna, and afterwards in London, by a patent under the great seal of England, and signed Killigrew in the reign of King Charles the second. At the same time, Jacob Judah Leon published a description of the tabernacle and the Temple, and dedicated it to his Majesty, and in the years 1759 and 1760 I had the pleasure of perusing and examining both these curiosities.[79]

Although not contemporary, this is the only description of Leon in England. Dermott mentioned that he was a "brother," indicating a Freemason. He studied the papers of Leon that were in the possession of Leon's grandson and claimed that they reiterated Charles II's Masonic role, and that Leon reportedly met and conversed with the king as a Masonic friend and fellow Mason.[80] This raises three questions: First, did the models come to England? Second, did Leon go to London with the models? Third, was he a Freemason and friend of King Charles?

There seems to be no doubt that Leon intended to go to London in 1675 and exhibit both the model of the Tabernacle and that of the Temple. This is backed up by the publication of an English booklet, *A Relation of the Most Memorable Things in the Tabernacle of Moses and the Temple of Solomon*, and the introduction letters. However, it appears that the book was not patented for the exhibition of the model in England. Whereas Leon had patented his other books for exhibition, for this book

> [the] patent was granted 21 June 1642, by *Les estats genevaux des Provinces Vnis*, for fifteen years, granting the right of publication of the book describing the models. This patent was confirmed by *Les Estates de Hollande et de West-Frise* on the 28 June 1642, and on February 17th of the same year *Les Estats de la comite de Zeland*, granted a similar patent for five years.[81]

The lack of a patent for the English translation indicates that the exhibition did not go ahead. However, the Temple model did reach England. A. Lewis Shane reported two contemporary accounts of the model being in England. Wilhelmus Goeree, a Dutch Biblical historian, wrote in 1683 that it had been some time since the Temple model had left Amsterdam,[82] and Peter Chyle referred to the Temple being displayed in London. In a manuscript on the history of Wells Cathedral written by Chyle in about 1680, he observed,

> That the model of Solomon's Temple composed by Rabbi Leon, a Jew of the Hebrew nation, which has been, and still is, common to be seen in London; and if we may believe their papers and report, was seven years in contriving, making, finishing, doubtless very exact, and worth any inquisitive person's view and contemplation.[83]

No contemporary newspaper accounts or English advertising leaflets have survived. Given the impact in the Netherlands of Leon's model and Schott's model in London fifty years later, the lack of accounts or reports of the exhibition in London does seem very strange.

Although it is clear that Wren, Lord Arlington, and Oldenburg received the introductory letter from Constantijn Huygen, there is no mention of their having received Leon. There is no surviving account of Leon's meeting with the king, nor mention of Leon or the Temple in the publication of the Royal Society's *Philosophical Transactions*. From the complete absence of any mention of Leon's visit, it would appear likely that he did not go. Leon died in July or August 1675, so if he did come to England, this must have taken place in the first half of the year. In September that year, Robert Hooke, scientist, architect, and later the president of the Royal Society, claimed in his diary, "With Chr. Wren. Long discourse with him about the module of the Temple."[84] This brief statement of Hooke's is tantalizing. If they were discussing the measurement of the Temple, perhaps they were discussing the model of Leon, but Hooke was very brief in all of his comments and did not give any details.

Dermott called Leon "brother" and it has been assumed that this means a Freemason.[85] In the 17th century, the Masons were stonemason guild members, and a precondition of being a member was that they were stonemasons. There were no Jewish stonemasons in Leon's time in England. The oath that candidates were obliged to take to become freemasons effectively limited the membership to Christians, and Leon's visit to England, if he came at all, was simply too short a period for him to have been made a Freemason. In addition, Freemasonry did not spread to the Continent until the 18th century, the first "Dutch lodge" being founded in The Hague in 1733. That Dermott's "brother" reference inferred Freemason membership was virtually impossible in Leon's time.

Dermott claimed that Leon designed the Masonic coat of arms, and this claim is repeated in early biographies. In 1893, the Hebrew scholar Lucien Wolf backed up Dermott's claim by stating that the story that the original design was found in Leon's paper was "in my opinion, very well grounded."[86] However, he does not say why, except to say that Leon had written a book on cherubim, the winged creatures that were placed by the Israelites in the holy of holies, in both the Temple and the Tabernacle, to protect the Ark of the Covenant. The Masonic coat of arms shows two cherubim flanking a shield that bears the symbols of a lion, an ox, an eagle, and a man. According to Wolf, Leon associated them with "the four traditional standards of the quadrilateral Hebrew encampment by which the 'tent of meeting' was surrounded in the wilderness—the lion of Judah, the man of Reuben, the eagle of Dan and the ox of Ephraim."[87] Dermott used the same description of the four standards.[88] These four symbols of lion, ox, man, and eagle are the symbols of the Christian Evangelists, and elements of the cherubim, who had four faces—of a man, a lion, an ox, and an eagle—the stature and hands of a man, the feet of a calf, and the wings of an eagle. The combination of these four symbols served both Christian and Jewish traditions. However, Wolf and Dermott clearly stated that the four symbols were the emblems of the four main tribes of Israel; but the symbol of Dan in Jewish tradition is of a scorpion, not an eagle, a tradition that Leon kept in his *Retrato del tabernaculo de Moseh*[89] In Villalpando's justification of the plan of the Temple, he also replaced the scorpion with the eagle, so that the four corners of his plan would represent the Evangelists. However, Villalpando went to great lengths to show that, although the emblem for Dan was a scorpion, it was eagle-like.[90] Wolf's article is often referred to as proof that Leon did design the Freemason's original coat of arms. Had Leon been the designer, the four traditional standards of the quadrilateral Hebrew encampment would have been the lion, man, scorpion, and ox, in keeping with Jewish tradition.

The claims that Leon went to London, met and conversed with King Charles II, was a Freemason, and designed the original Masonic coat of arms all seem to have originated with Dermott in 1764, and are repeated in many bibliographies and articles to this day.

On the title page of the 1788 English translation of Leon's 1642 work, *An Accurate Description of the Grand & Glorious Temple of Solomon*, De Castro stated, "First printed in Hebrew and Spanish at Middleburgh, by that celebrated architect Jacob Juda Lyon: In the year MDCXLII."[91] De Castro, a relative of Leon, who had inherited the models and continued to exhibit them, had translated the work from a Hebrew edition into English, and he seems to have assumed that Hebrew was the original language of the book. This is the first time that Leon was referred to as an architect. However, there is nothing to indicate that Leon had any training as an architect or that he was versed in architectural theory. In the reconstructions of Villalpando and Newton, they were interested to show that the Temple was a building constructed to architectural rules. Although Villalpando emphasized the divine origins of these rules, his reconstruction consisted of elevations, sections, and a floor plan with a great deal of architectural detail. Yet Leon was only interested in describing the building and its use. The building's proportions or harmonies held no interest for him. In addition, he supplied no floor plan or elevations, which would have been expected if Leon had been an architect, and he had only the one view of the Temple (see Figure 34).

There is no proof of many of the things that Leon is credited with; most appear to be untrue or at least unfounded, but they have been incorporated through time into his biographies, where the same claims are repeated. What is known about the model is that it came to England, perhaps in 1675, or maybe a little later, and it was exhibited again in the years 1759–1760 by a relative of Leon's, De Castro. There appears to be no mention of the model between these times, either in Holland or in

England. It may have remained in England in storage rather than being exhibited.

In 1771, in The Hague, an advertisement for the sale of the models was placed in the *'s Gravenhaegse Courant*. It stated,

> Here has arrived the very splendid and well-wrought Temple of Solomon, in three part, to wit, the Temple, the King's palace, and the citadel of Mark Antony [Antonia Tower], with its mountains and all its accessories, which has not been exhibited for eighty years, built over 130 years ago according to the architectural plan of the late gifted teacher Jacob Juda, a Hebrew, which will be shown with a complete explanation every day in the month of May (except for Saturday and Sunday), next to the house where hangs out the sign of the Paradise, opposite the Kalkstraetje near the Voorhout in the Hague; each visitor will be charged 11 stuivers, but in the case of a particular society each visitor will be charged one guilder.
>
> N.B. This Temple can be purchased by anybody interested.[92]

However, it did not sell. Seven years after this advertisement, De Castro published the English translation of Leon's original text. De Castro stated in the preface that the four chapters of the book "will give a distinct idea of whatever the curious may desire to know of this wonderful building; the model of which I have in my possession, made all of wood."[93] This is the last known mention of the model; all traces of Leon's model have disappeared, seemingly to Brazil.[94] In 1821, diamond merchants Samuel and Philips presented to the young regent and future emperor of Brazil D. Pedro I the famous model of Leon's Temple. However, whether it was the original or a copy is unknown.[95] The model was to be part of the regent's museum. However, there seems to be no trace of the model (if it was the model) after this; after 1821 it literally disappeared.

Conclusion

When the Schott model arrived in England in 1724, Newton was elderly but extremely active, and he was still the president of the Royal Society; despite his age, he walked long distances. Five months before Newton's death, Dr. Thomas Hunt, the Hebrew professor of Oxford, wrote to the Bishop of Rochester, Zachary Pearce, "I had the honor of a visit from him at my house in St. Martin's Church-yard, to which he walked, at his great age, from his house near Leicester Fields."[96] Hunt recorded that he and Newton spoke about Newton's work on chronology, which included a small chapter on the Temple of Solomon. Given the public fanfare in the newspapers and his interest in the Temple of Solomon, it would appear likely that the professor of Hebrew and Newton would have discussed the Schott Temple model.

Did Newton know of the model of Leon? It seems likely that he did, since Solomon's Temple was a topic of discussion by men of both religion and science in London. However, Newton does not refute it or even acknowledge its existence. Leon's model would not have appealed to Newton because Leon's floor plan could not be perceived as the "frame of the world." The lack of symmetry of the model makes that impossible. In addition, Newton strongly believed that the prophets held the ancient knowledge of the Temple, and Leon had not acknowledged Ezekiel's vision as the Temple of Solomon. Although Newton was interested in the prophecies early in his academic career, in the 1660s, he did not begin to work on the Temple until the late 1670s or early 1680s. He did go to London occasionally to attend Royal Society meetings, so it is possible that the Leon model stimulated his interest and a lifetime interest in the Temple. Models fascinated him when he was a child and may have done so as an adult. However, unfortunately, this will never be known and will remain speculation.

Villalpando's book was expensive and written in Latin, as were many of the commentaries. The Schott model book and Leon's books were inexpensive and were written in the vernacular. They had wide and common appeal. The reconstruction and the realization of Solomon's Temple in the 17th and early 18th centuries were important to both scholars and the public. The guidebooks that were sold at the exhibition reveal an interesting aspect of the exhibition. They were more than a catalogue or a souvenir of the exhibition; their purpose was to instruct the viewer in what they were seeing beyond the scale of the model.

5

The Model Guidebooks

The guidebooks were an important element of the exhibitions of the models of Solomon's Temple. Training tools that explained the details and the architecture of the Temple, they were ordered sequentially to guide the viewer through the Temple as though the viewer was physically located within the Temple. In their descriptions of the Temple, the guidebooks differ in their layout and in the sources they use. However, both Leon's guidebooks and the guidebook for the Schott model create a series of images for the viewer or reader's "mind's eye."

The purpose of seeing and moving through the Temple in this way could have been to create a form of religious meditation through the Biblical building. By visualizing and understanding the Temple by meditating on the building itself, and by verifying the building through the sacred texts, the guidebooks' writers approached the work in a similar fashion to that of Villalpando's "architecture of theology." However, unlike *Ezechielem Explanationes*, they were inexpensive and written in the vernacular, which made them more accessible to the public, and they were very popular.

The use of movement through a building as a tool for religious meditation and as a memory aid has ancient precedents. Cicero used a building as a memory background to plan his speeches; Thomas Aquinas used them as a tool for contemplation; and Francis Bacon and René Descartes explored these systems of mnemotechnics in search of the new scientific methodology. Newton had an interest in memory early in his studies. Although the work is incomplete, related works appear to have led to his interest in the reconstruction of the Temple. This chapter examines the guidebooks and their differences. It considers systems that used buildings and models as memory models. It then turns to Newton's work on memory and finally asks the question, did

Newton use his reconstruction of the Temple of Solomon as a memory model?

The Guidebook to Architecture

Leon's was the first of the guidebooks. *Retrato del Templo de Selomoh* is only seventy-six pages in length and is divided into four chapters. Chapter 1 is a general discussion of the Temple. This is followed by a chapter on the building itself and this chapter forms the bulk of the book. The third chapter considers the interior detail, including vessels and the altar, and the final chapter is on the buildings near the Temple, such as Solomon's palace and Antonia's Tower. Each chapter contains numbered paragraphs that explain all of the elements of the Temple's construction and its structure.

The 1675 book for the English exhibition of Leon's model is a summary of two of his books on the Tabernacle and the Temple; it was prepared and printed in Amsterdam and dedicated to Charles II. In a different format to his previous books, which had proved so successful, it is also very brief at only twenty-seven pages. Most of the booklet is about the material of the Tabernacle, the Temple, and the material of which the vessels were made. Leon listed the richness of the colored cloths of purple and scarlet, and the amount of gold, silver, and brass that was needed to make the vessels, but he said little about the structure of either the Tabernacle or the Temple. He was almost dismissive of the structure of the Tabernacle, and after describing the costly materials used, he stated,

> The manner how the Tabernacle was reared or raised, and again taken down is a most sweet and curious speculation but because that doeth require much writing we refer the reader to the treatise of the Tabernacle of Moses, which we have published where you shall find all the same at large.[1]

Again, he has a preoccupation with the materials used in the construction of the Temple. With respect to the construction itself, the entire description of the Temple is only three pages in length; even his advertising leaflet had more description of the Temple than this booklet. At the end of the three pages, he stated, "Concerning the other appendences of the building so wonderful, so precious, and so holy, I refer you to the treatise concerning the portraiture of the Temple, where I have laid forth everything most plain."[2] The 1675 volume is out of context with his other works, and it appears to have been prepared in haste because of his visit to London. Whatever the reason for its brevity and absence of detail, it does not act as a guidebook to the Temple model.

However, the portraiture of the Temple is more than a description of the Temple: his description "sees" the Temple and the ritual ornament are explained as though they were going to be used. It was an instruction book for the Temple and its use. For Leon, the model and the book create the reality of the Scriptures. The book begins thus:

> The architect of this edifice was the great and wise King Solomon, of whose great wisdom and riches the scripture gives an account: yet with all his wisdom and riches, he was not permitted to do it merely by his own skill and industry, but through the express order and model of God himself, who was the principal and essential architect of the great and wonderful building; having revealed to his servant Moses the model of the Tabernacle, and afterwards to the prophet King David, the plan and description of that grand fabric, with a command, that he should leave his son Solomon to build it without any alteration.[3]

Leon's motivation was to bring alive the plan that was built by man, and to celebrate the richness and color of the rituals and the ornaments of the rituals.

The book that was published for the Schott exhibition also has numbered paragraphs, but it emphasized the "movement" through the Temple and the Tabernacle. It is in fact two books bound together. The first, *The Temple of Solomon*, is dated 1725, and the second, *A Description of the Tabernacle*, is dated 1724. The anonymous writer or writers clearly stated their intention for writing the guide:

> Although the description and draughts of the Holy Land, the city of Jerusalem, and the Temple of Solomon, may in a great measure help to form a not on of the places; yet to see them represented in a material construction or model, as here is done of Solomon's Temple, must needs create a more distinct and lively idea there of: By which not only several dark words and passages concerning the said Temple are rendered clear and intelligible, but the circumstances of facts that happened there, will make a deeper impression in the mind, and the spectator be the more convinced *de material facti*.
>
> For there may be seen the very place where the sacrifices were killed and slaughtered; the place and altar upon which they consumed by fire; there we discover the steps in the Holy place next to the altar of incense, where Zacharia turned mute; where the Virgin Mary offered the infant Jesus to the Lord; thus we may follow Christ step by step, find him in the Synagogue fitting among the elders; disputing in the Hall of Solomon with the Jews; overthrowing the bankers tables; and driving out of the Temple the buyers and sellers.

> Hence all these that would dive into the knowledge of the scripture as to circumstances of places concerning the Holy Temple, which being here traced with the utmost care and labour, may by inspection of its model, get more knowledge in one hour's observation, than in reading the most authentic authors several years.[4]

The "dark words and passages concerning the said Temple" was a reference to Ezekiel. Both Newton and Villalpando noted the difficulty and the obscurity of Ezekiel's language. However, this did not stop either of them from going on to interpret him and using him as their main source for their reconstructions of the Temple.

Villalpando's massive, three-volume *Ezechielem Explanationes* was not only a lengthy scholarly work, it was extremely expensive. Perhaps because of this, the work was often known more through the commentators on the book, rather than by the original work. Especially quoted was the commentary of Louis Cappella in Brian Walton's *Biblia Sacra Polyglotta*. Newton owned *Biblia Sacra Polyglotta*[5] but did not own a copy of *Ezechielem Explanationes*. Unfortunately, Newton does not quote Villalpando directly; thus, it is difficult to clarify what his source was—whether the original text or a commentary on the text. In short, the expense and the scholarship would have made *Ezechielem Explanationes* inaccessible to the public and to many scholars, it is also clear that many writers believed that by spending an hour with the guidebook and the model, the viewer would be enlightened about the building, its architecture, and its religious significance. For both Newton and Villalpando, the measurements were important for understanding the Temple. The writer of the Schott model book acknowledged that the "Temple must be measured by calamus (rule, measure, reed) that contains six cubits, a cubit is six palmos, or hand-breath, the palm[os] of four inches."[6] Therefore, the sacred cubit was two feet and a calamus or reed was twelve feet. In contrast, for Leon the cubit of six palms was two feet and three inches, and a calamus thirteen feet and six inches.[7] This made a substantial difference to the size of the Temple precinct, and according to the writer of the Schott guidebook, it was 1,000 foot square, whereas Leon's was 1,125 foot square. Of course, this made no difference to the scale model, but it underlines the different interpretations of the dimensions of the Temple.

The Schott guidebook describes the foundations of the Temple, which reinforce and enlarge Mount Moriah. The foundations are built around the mount and then filled with earth

> so that by this means, an even space of 125 calamus was made, in the length and Breadth, whereupon the Temple and all its courts were built. The wall was 300 cubits high, 50 cubits thick for the better resisting the earth, and for preventing the giving way to its pressure, large buttresses were erected against it, which in the uppermost part were thick 50 cubits in the undermost 150 cubit[s], broad 50, and high 300 cubits. Such buttresses are on each side six, viz, two upon each corner, and two in the middle, expect the north side, where the two middle-most were left out, because the valley was not so deep there.[8]

This follows Villalpando's description. He regarded this massive structure as being unique, and it had no Biblical or secular precedent. Yet it was accepted and replicated by the writer of the Schott guidebook and by Leon in their reconstructions with no justification. Leon's description is very similar to that of Villalpando:

> The mountain was 300 cubits high, surround with deep valley, it had magnificent walls which reached to the top, the stones of which were white marble, ... there were pilasters, or supporters, 300 cubits high, 120 long and thick proportion, to support the walls on the outside, as from their great height they might have been in danger of falling.[9]

The writer of the Schott guidebook praised the great work of Villalpando, who demonstrated "to the world the truth of this building for it is without doubt 'the best pattern of architecture.'"[10] It was planned by the Divine Architect; therefore, it was the origin of all architecture, "as it is the basis of all that may be seen magnificent in architecture, now a-days, it may serve as a pattern throughout the whole, by which all the branches belong to architecture must be proved and ordered."[11]

After the introduction, which discusses the Biblical texts on how the Temple came about, the Temple precinct description is divided into two parts: first, a description of the courts, and second, a description of the Temple itself. Each of these sections has three chapters. The first section considers the three courts: the court of the Gentiles, the court of the Jews, and the court of the Priests. The second considers the three parts of the Temple: the porch, the holy place, and the most holy of holies.

The description is clearly walking the reader through the Temple from the outside of the Temple precinct into the heart of the holy of holies. The reader-viewer came "into the court of the Gentiles [that] was thro' a grate-work, which was surrounded by the whole Temple "[12] Continuing through the Temple precinct, the reader "entering thro' the

Balustrade" and then "entering through the opening," the description is at ground level. The reader-viewer comes

> out of the Court of the Priests, you come to the porch by a walk, which is twenty cubits broad, and surroundeth the Temple on all sides, where also the priests were used the pray. Therein are eight steps, whereby you come to the porch, and two steps more at the coming in, so that they are in all ten steps.[13]

The reader-viewer was taken on a mental journey into the Temple itself and into the holy of holies and out again. The measurements, the structure, the decoration, and its use are all described. The layout of the Temple from the description was clear and would have been assisted by knowing that the precinct was symmetrical. The book has no illustrations or plans. The writer was satisfied with the description alone, since he finished the book by stating, "And so much for the present about the construction of the Temple, where it is evident that this building was the greatest master-piece not only of architecture, but also of workmanship and magnificence."[14]

However, there are examples of copies that have been bound with illustrations from other sources. One example of this is a book that has ten illustrations and three maps bound at the end of the book.[15] The three plans are all of the Temple precinct and have slight variations, but are based on the Villalpando plan, and they appear to have been executed by three different artists. The first image looks like a broadsheet for the model, in a similar vein to Leon's but from another exhibition. It contains seven images: a section of the Temple that is executed according to Villalpando, a candlestick copied from the Triumphal Arch of Titus in Rome, the altar according to the learned Dean Prideaux, two images of the Brazen Molten Sea (one according to Villalpando and the other according to L'Amy), the Great Sanhedrin (the assembly of priests) in the Temple, the interior of the holy of holies according to Villalpando, and blocks of text in English to explain the illustrations. The other nine illustrations are all drawn by another artist. They depict the inside of the Temple, the outside of the Tabernacle, the Tabernacle with the court, the Ark of the Covenant, the golden altar of incense, the golden candlestick, the golden table, the brazen altar of burnt offering and the brazen laver in the court of the Tabernacle. All the titles are written in English and German. This collection of illustrations and plans demonstrates the level of interest in all things to do with the Temple and the diversity of the plans in which the readers were interested.

The Temple as a Memory Model

The guidebooks added an extra dimension to the models because they placed the reader-viewer's mental vision within the model and at the same scale as the model. Leon "sees" the Temple, and the writer of the Schott model book "moves through and sees" the Temple. Mentally moving through a building or complex of buildings was not a new idea; in fact, it is a very ancient one. Ancient orators used a system of mnemotechnics to aid in memorizing their speeches. This system deployed a specific place, usually a building, and images. The images would be the stimulus and the place was the background to the images. The mind's eye of the orator would travel through the building, a building that the orator had used many times as a background and with which he was very familiar. The images would be placed into the building to act as a mnemonic for the speech being given. They could be beautiful or grotesque images, whichever was needed to stimulate the mind, to guide the direction of the speech or to change the topic. The earliest work on this art of memory, *Ad Herennium*—originally attributed to Cicero, but now the author is considered to be anonymous—is dated ca. 86–82 BC. However, *Ad Herennium* contains references to earlier Greek mnemonic systems of place and image that have been lost, so this system could be very ancient.

In an intensive study entitled *The Art of Memory* published in 1966,[16] Frances Yates opened the field into the study of system of mnemotechnics. Yates followed the transformation of these systems and their use, from the writings of the ancient writers on place and images to the transformation into place, and corporeal similitudes of spiritual intentions, in the Middle Ages as a remembrance of the ways to heaven and to hell. "The *imagines agents* would have been moralized into beautiful or hideous human figures as 'corporeal similitudes' of spiritual intentions of gaining Heaven or avoiding Hell, and memorized as ranged in order in some 'solemn' building."[17]

While the traditional form of the art continued in the Middle Ages and beyond, an additional form of the art evolved. In around the year 1272, Ramond Lull claimed that if the attributes of God were infused with the whole of creation, an art could be constructed with these attributes that would be universally valid because it was based on reality.[18] In *Ars Magna* (The ultimate arts), published in 1305, Lull constructed a diagram of ten aspects of God. The diagram is in the shape of a geometric nonagon (nine-point star) indicating nine attributes of God—goodness, greatness, eternity, power, wisdom, will, virtue, truth, and glory—and the tenth is the diagram itself. Lull developed diagrammatic systems that used nine letters representing the nine attributes of God. This was one of the earliest attempts to develop a logical system to produce knowledge. Lull's work was further developed by Giordano Bruno in the 16th century and Lull also attracted works written in his name. One of these pseudo-Lull works, *Ars Magica,* which gained popularity in the 17th century, was written by an anonymous author and published in 1631 in Frankfurt; it devotes two chapters to memory and the use of astrological symbols to reinforce it.[19]

During the Renaissance, the culture of universal knowledge and encyclopedia making became entwined with the art of memory as part of that culture. Giulio Camillo's theater had become famous in Italy and France in the early 16th century. It was a wooden model of a theater that was crowded with images. It was reported to contain the world's knowledge and to act as a system of mnemotechnics to impart this knowledge. Eyewitnesses were amazed at its effectiveness.[20] Unfortunately, it is not known how it worked, and no plans of the theater have survived. What has survived is *L'idea del Theatro,* written by Camillo and posthumously published in 1550. However, it is a description of the images in the theater rather than of how the theater worked. It is enlightening insofar as it shows the Hermetic images, which are influenced by the work of Lull, and ideas that were the mnemonic triggers within the model, but it leads to no understanding of how they were used. What Camillo's theater does show is that memory backgrounds were not just virtual backgrounds but by the Renaissance they were physical models as well. The architectural model, whether physical or virtual, played a function in mnemonics in several ways: as a marker to remember speeches, for spiritual contemplation, and for the sorting of encyclopedic knowledge.

Much has been written in the past fifty years since Yates first opened this field to scholarship.[21] Most studies mention the decline in use of these systems in the 17th century; although they still survived, they were becoming redundant in the Age of Science. By the 17th century, the art of memory was less uniform than its ancient counterparts and many memory models that were less traditional have not been studied as memory models.

Villalpando's reconstruction of the Temple as an "architecture of theology," allowing his fellow theologians to visualize and meditate on the Temple and to discover divine truths, is similar to the place and corporeal similitudes of the Middle Ages. In addition, it represented the plan of the microcosm: it held the encyclopedic and universal knowledge of the cosmos. Despite this, in the past it has not been considered a part of the culture of the art of memory. Although not all of the reconstructions that were stimulated by Villalpando's work could be called memory models, the Leon and Schott models remained in the "architecture of theology" tradition through their guidebooks. Both Leon's and the Schott model's guidebooks were "architectures of theology" that were not designed for theologians, but for the public.

Villalpando, Leon, and the writer of the Schott handbook defined the vessels, the ritual objects, and the decorations of the Temple; place and image or corporeal similitudes come together in these works. Although Villalpando's *Ezechielem Explanationes* is a great deal larger and written for a different audience than the two small handbooks, they are written with the same feeling and intention.

There is no doubt that the Temple was significant to Newton. The importance of the central fire, the hearth of the Temple, in Newton's unpublished papers is demonstrated on several levels. First, he attached historical significance to it: it was the sacred space in the temples of the ancient and original religions.[22] Second, it demonstrated that the ancient religions had true knowledge of God since their temples were symbolic of the heliocentric system.[23] Third, in the ancient sacred architecture was encoded the celestial harmonies of the heliocentric planetary motions.[24] Finally, the sun—ancient emblem of divine power and the hearth in the center of the universe—was the "center of the penetrating gravitational attraction that held his heliocentric world together."[25] However, none of these points require a careful architectural reconstruction of the Temple.

One of Newton's earliest surviving manuscripts is "Of an Universall Language," dated ca. 1661.[26] In the 17th century, it was felt that Latin was no longer the language of scholarship, and that a new universal language—a more symbolic language, such as the one being developed for mathematics—was needed to fill the gap. This manuscript of Newton's was never finished, and he only developed 2,400 entries. However, it still constituted a significant amount of work. From Francis Bacon's *The*

Advancement of Learning (1605), where he outlined a system, to John Wilkins's *Essay towards a Real Character and a Philosophical Language* (1668), Newton's manuscript indicates that a substantial number of texts were published on the theme of a universal language. These universal languages have been strongly linked to the art of memory.[27]

Bacon closely connects a universal language with the art of memory. He claimed that there are two parts to the art of memory: "prenotation" and "emblems." Prenotation was needed first to set a limit to the research; otherwise, it would be boundless. This creates a framework in which the memory can work since memory requires boundaries, which are provided by ordering and arranging recollections in places of artificial memory. The places must be in an established order or placed in a sequence in which it is easy to evoke the emblems. The use of emblems "reduces intellectual conceptions to sensible images; for an object of sense always strikes the memory more forcibly and is more easily impressed upon it than an object of the intellect."[28] Bacon distinguished between hieroglyphs and real characters. Hieroglyphs "always have something in common with the thing signified" whereas real characters are "not at all emblematic." The Roman alphabet represented the conventional characters, but real characters would "represent not just letters or works, but things and notions,"[29] such as the ideogrammatic languages of China and the Far East.

Bacon claimed that memory was important for the new science of natural philosophy. He stated,

> This is particularly the case in inductive philosophy and the interpretation of nature; for a man might as well attempt to go through the calculations of an Ephemeris in his head without the aid of writing, as to master the interpretation of nature by the natural and naked force and memory, without the help of tables duly arranged. But not to speak of the interpretation of nature, which is a new doctrine, there can hardly be anything more useful even for the old and popular sciences, than a sound help for the memory.[30]

Bacon considered the use of the traditional art of memory—to enhance the memory to cite long verses or lists—as being nothing more than "tricks and antics of clowns and rope-dancers."[31] However, he turned the traditional form of the art of memory ordering into a tool for research into the new fields of natural philosophy and inductive thinking. The ordering and arranging of the emblems into classifications appears to be the basis of Bacon's method, although he does not explain the method very clearly.

Similarly, René Descartes considered the traditional art of memory "profitable trifles."[32] He believed that the art of memory was not based on order. In 1619, he proposed an alternative method:

> I have thought out another method: from interconnected images one can obtain new images which are common to each individual image, or at least from all of the connected images one could obtain a single image related to them all. And should not just consider the nearest image when composing a new image, but also the others in the series, so that the fifth is connected to the first by means of a stake driven into the ground, the image in the middle by means of the ladder by which they descend, the second by means of an arrow fired towards it, the third in the same analogous way, according to a true or fictitious means of signification.[33]

This is the work of the young Descartes, and although later his method changes in his seminal work, *Discourse on the Method of Rightly Conducting One's Reason and of Seeking Truth in the Sciences,* published in 1637, the method described above was the beginning of his search for a new art, for a new science, that had solid foundations. It also demonstrates his use of the corporeal and sensible images for the representation of abstract concepts that was developed in *Discourse on the Method.*

Both Bacon and Descartes searched for a new method for the new science of natural philosophy. The Royal Society was founded on Baconian principles. However, Newton does not allude to Bacon in his works, even though he did own many of Bacon's publications[34]; therefore, it is difficult to assess whether there was any direct influence. Descartes did have a strong influence on Newton, although he was critical of many aspects of Descartes's work.[35] Descartes's attention to detail in all things stimulated and left a lasting effect on Newton's later scientific sensibility.[36]

In the early 1660s, Newton wrote a manuscript that he entitled *Questiones Quaedam Philosophiae.* It contains thirty-seven topics of philosophical inquiry, and many of these he continued to study for the rest of his life. The topics included "Of the Sun, Stars, Planets, and Comets," "Of Light," "Of Minerals," "Of Meteors," "Of the Creation," "Of the Soul," "Of Memory," and many more. In this manuscript Newton posed problems, presented queries and considered responses. He claimed that memory is part of the soul:

> Memory is a faculty of the soul (in some measure) for else how can divers[e] sounds, or words excite her to divers[e] thoughts or 3. 4. 5 or more words beget the same thought in her. Perhaps she remembers by the help of characters in the brain, but then how doth she remember the signification of those characters[?][37]

It is clear that he is considering characters and the signification of the characters two different types of "images" in the brain, in a similar way to Bacon's real characters and hieroglyphs. Unfortunately, he does not consider a response about the characters and the signification of the characters. However, these characters and signification are not disconnected from experiences of the external world. Like Descartes, he distinguished between the corporeal and sensible (memory) images.

In his work on memory, he emphasized the relationship of the external world and the internal world of the memory. He claimed that, although memory can be affected by illness or physical trauma, other factors can affect the memory. Dreams can remember other dreams or events of the external world. Newton lists groups of things that are interconnected that can be recalled by association:

> Things seen & words heard at the same distance are distinctly remembered. So are distance & wideness or extension & bigness. So are things which enter not the senses as meditations, thoughts, dreams, & that a man hath remembered. Meditations remind a man of actions, & actions of meditation. Colours, actions, sounds loud softly, high & low, Time as that 2 things were done together or so long after one another reckoning how long since such a thing done by counting the time from one action to another until the present time.[38]

However, objects, events, or situations are soon forgotten if they are not thought about. Recollection is stimulated by thinking about it: "A man cannot remember what he never thought upon as a blow or prick or noise in his sleep the things & sounds which he hears & sees but minds not."[39] Although characters in the brain stimulate the memory, the repeated thinking upon the object also retained that recollection. It was not the characters in the mind that existed to stimulate memory, but "the soul remembers too, for she must remember those characters,"[40] because memory was the function of the soul and not a mere sense.

In 1666, Gottfried Leibniz, Newton's great rival, published *Dissertatio de arte Combinatoria* (Dissertation on the combinatorial art). Influenced by Lullism and building on the work of Descartes, he cited works on the art of memory in the prefatory pages. Leibniz suggested that all concepts are a combination of a small number of concepts, just as a word is constructed by a combination of letters. It follows that all truths or characters can be expressed by a combination of concepts. These characters are directly related to the art of memory insofar as the characters are derived from the search for the "image" for things and a universal language. It is possibly through his invention of new "characters" that he was able to operate the infinitesimal calculus, which was a fragment, of the never-completed "universal characteristic."[41] The search for the universal language that was derived from the ancient art of memory was seen as a basis for the new science that was emerging in both Europe and England. In the twenty-one years since the publication of Leibniz's *Dissertatio de arte Combinatoria*, Newton had established the mathematics of infinitesimal calculus. However, it is Leibniz's "characters" or notation that expresses modern calculus, not Newton's.

In the early 1660s, Newton showed interest in a universal language and the art of memory. Newton owned eight works of the (pseudo) Lull. Seven of these are texts on alchemy. The other one is *Ars Magna*, which used the attributes of God to construct a logical system to produce knowledge. Newton also referred to *Ars Magica* in the margins of another Lull book[42]; thus, he was aware of Lull's work on memory and the use of astrological symbols. In the 1670s and early 1680s, he interpreted the symbols of the Bible, particularly the Apocalypse in Revelation. By the mid–1680s he was writing on the language of the prophets:

> He that would understand a book written in a strange language must first learn the language & if he would understand it well he must learn the language perfectly. Such a language was that wherein the Prophets wrote, & the want of sufficient skill in that language is the main reason why they are so little understood. John did not write in one language, Daniel in another, Isaiah in third, & the rest in others peculiar to themselves; but they all wrote in one & the same mystical language as well known without doubt to the sons of the Prophets as the Hieroglyphic language of the Egyptians to their Priests. And this language so far as I can find, was as certain & definite in its signification as is the vulgar language of any nation whatsoever: so that it is only for want of skill therein that interpreters so frequently turn the prophetic types & phrases to signify whatever their fancies & hypotheses lead them to. He therefore that would understand the old Prophets (as all Divines ought to do) must fix the significations of their types & phrases in the beginning of his studies. Something in this kind has been done by former writers, & as I have endeavoured in the following discourse to carry on the design further so I hope others will bring it to more perfection. The rule I have followed has been to compare the several mystical places of scripture where the same prophetic phrase or type is used & to fix such a signification to that phrase as agrees best with all the places, & if more significations than one be necessary to note the circumstances by which it may be known in what signification the phrase is taken in any place & when I had found the necessary significations to reject all others as the offspring of luxuriant fancy for no more significations are to be admitted for true ones then can be proved.[43]

He continued on to significations or analogies from the whole of nature, the earth, and the world politique, the heavens. The earth was analogous to the heavens. Here he developed prophetic types and phrases that signify whatever researchers' "fancies & hypotheses lead them to." In this manuscript, Newton saw the Temple as being analogous to the universe,[44] and he described the language of the prophets as another universal language, if not the most important one, which is ordered and far more vivid than in his original work on universal language.

Conclusion

For Newton, the Temple was the plan of the universe: he clearly stated in his manuscript that all the parts of the Temple were analogous to the parts of the universe. He believed that within the plan of Temple were the secrets of the universe, nature, and God.[45] Newton's writings on the Temple clearly describe the Temple as a hieroglyph or symbol of the universe. In Newton's prophetic writings, the Temple is the background to the apocalyptic prophecy—it is a real building. In his manuscripts the Temple is both hieroglyph and building. Most of his manuscripts are working documents, and the occasional title throws some enlightenment on the direction of the study, but not all are enlightening. For instance, the title of Babson MS 434 is "A Treatise or Remarks on Solomon's Temple, Introduction to the Lexicon of the Prophets, Part Two: About The Appearance of the Jewish Temple," which would indicate that he was going to describe the architecture in more symbolic terms rather than carry out a careful reconstruction.

The title and content of this manuscript in the context of his work on prophetic and universal languages and memory does imply that Newton intended the Temple model as a memory model. Newton had agreed with the theological underpinning of Villalpando's model of the Temple, the architecture of theology, although he disagreed with his plan.[46] It is understandable that Newton would want to replace Villalpando's geocentric plan with a heliocentric plan of his own. Bacon began his inquiry into inductive reasoning and Descartes began his into deductive reasoning to assist in the art of memory. The differences between their ideas are great. Nevertheless, there is common ground, and they were the founders of the new science. Newton developed rules of reasoning in philosophy—inductive reasoning—in Book Three of the *Principia*, which was written at the same time as *Two Incomplete Treatises on Prophecy* and at the same time or within a couple of years of Babson MS 434. This leaves the question, did he also use the Temple model as a memory model to order his scientific hypotheses as well as his religious ideals?

6

The Architectural Model of Newton's Temple of Solomon

Newton did not build his reconstruction from his early work in Babson MS 434, nor did he publish it, and so it remained an unpublished manuscript. The description in Babson MS 434 follows the text of Ezekiel, who was guided through the Temple precinct. He moved through the Temple in the same way indicated in Schott's book. Although Babson MS 434 is a scriptural exegesis, it is also an architectural text. Newton's main purpose with this manuscript was to reconstruct the architecture. However, in other manuscripts he studied the vessels, objects, decoration, rituals, and meaning. The following text, "Newton's Unwritten Guidebook," is written from Newton's reconstruction, which he constructed from his manuscripts on the Temple and prophecy. In the guidebook, Newton's manuscripts have been related to images of the model built by the author from the text of his reconstruction.

Newton's Unwritten Guidebook

The Temple was the scene of the vision of the prophets[1] Daniel, Ezekiel, and John. It was in the Temple that Daniel was so deeply affected by his prophetic vision that the angel Gabriel said to Daniel, "But thou, O Daniel, shut up the words (of the prophecy), and seal the book, even to the time of the end: many shall run to and fro, and knowledge shall be increased."[2] Daniel's prophecy was shut away—only to be opened at the end of time. The seven seals that closed the book were later opened in the Temple. Before the seals were opened, John the Divine, in Revelation, lifted his head, "and the Temple of God was opened in heaven, and there was seen in his Temple the Ark of his Testament."[3] The Temple of God contained the Ark of his Testament or Covenant; thus, this Temple was the same plan as the Temple of Solomon that was a divine plan and was the only Temple to house the Ark of the Covenant.[4] John the Divine, in Revelation, prophesied the opening of the book, and as each seal was opened, he described its opening in symbolic language, with the Temple as the background to the Apocalypse.[5]

It was in the language of the prophets that lay the understanding of these prophecies. Newton believed that this prophetic language was an analogy between the "world natural," and a kingdom considered a "world politic."

> The whole world natural consisting of heaven and earth, signifies the whole world politic, consisting of thrones and people, or so much of it as is considered in the Prophecy: and the things in that world signify the analogous things in this. For the heavens, and the things therein, signify thrones and dignities and those who enjoy them; and the earth, with the things thereon, the inferior people; and the lowest parts of the earth, called Hades or Hell, the lowest or most miserable part of them. Whence ascending towards heaven, and descending to the earth, are put for rising and falling in power and honour: rising out of the earth, or waters, and falling into them, for the rising up to any dignity or dominion, out of the inferior state of the people, or falling down from the same into that inferior state; descending into the lower parts of the earth, for descending to a very low and unhappy estate; speaking with a faint voice out of the dust, for being in a weak and low condition; moving from one place to another, for translation from one office, dignity, or dominion, to another; great earthquakes, and the shaking of heaven and earth, for the shaking of kingdoms, so as to distract or overthrow them; the creating a new heaven and earth, and the passing away of an old one, or the beginning and end of the world, for the rise and ruin of the body politic signified thereby.[6]

The world politic that was considered in prophecy consisted of many kingdoms, but the most noble of all was the celestial frame—the universe.

At the center of the celestial frame was the sun, the continuous hearth of the universe, perpetually burning. The ancients planned their temple around a central hearth that kept a perpetual sacred fire in a consecrated place for sacrifices.[7] God ordered Moses to build him a sanctuary "according to all that I show thee, after the pattern of the tabernacle, and the pattern of all the instruments thereof, even so shall ye make it."[8] God described the plan of the Tabernacle and the vessels and instruments to Moses. Moses built it in the style of his ancestors. By placing the outward atrium and the inner atrium of the Tabernacle and the Temple of Solomon, the plan framed "the Tabernacle & Temple so as to make it a symbol of the world."[9] The Tabernacle and the Temple represented the true and real temple of God, and they were built "as in the fittest manner to represent the whole system of the heavens."[10] The Temple of Solomon was built to the same divine plan as the Tabernacle, only the measurements were doubled.[11]

Figure 38, Figure 39, and Figure 40—The Temple was not only the scene of the prophecies; it was also the frame or hieroglyph of the universe. The Temple precinct was built on Mount Moria, where God had told David the Temple should be built to the divine plan given to Moses. However, it was not to be built by David, since he was a man

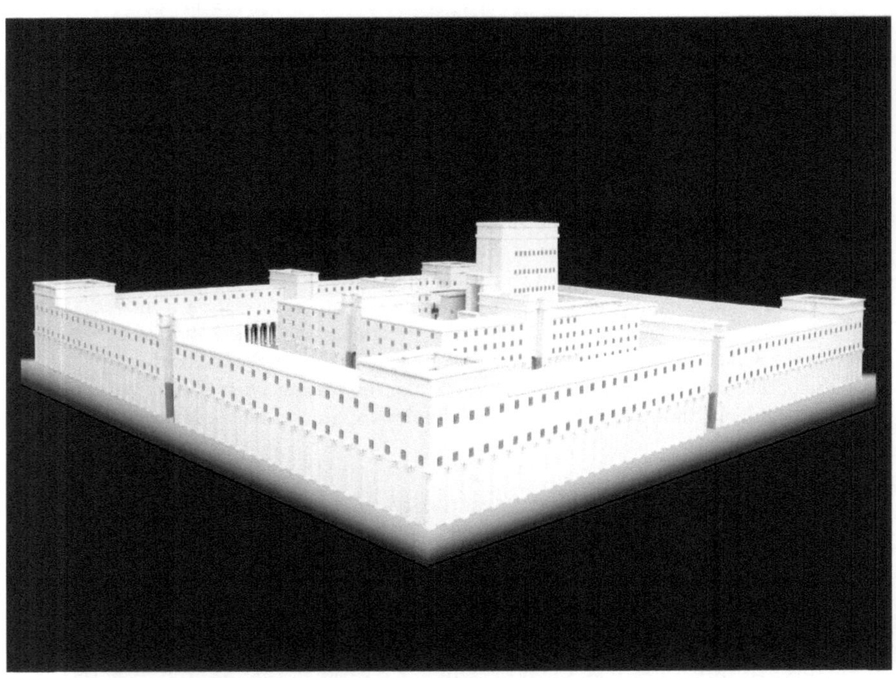

Figures 38, 39 and 40. Bird's-eye views of the Temple of Solomon.

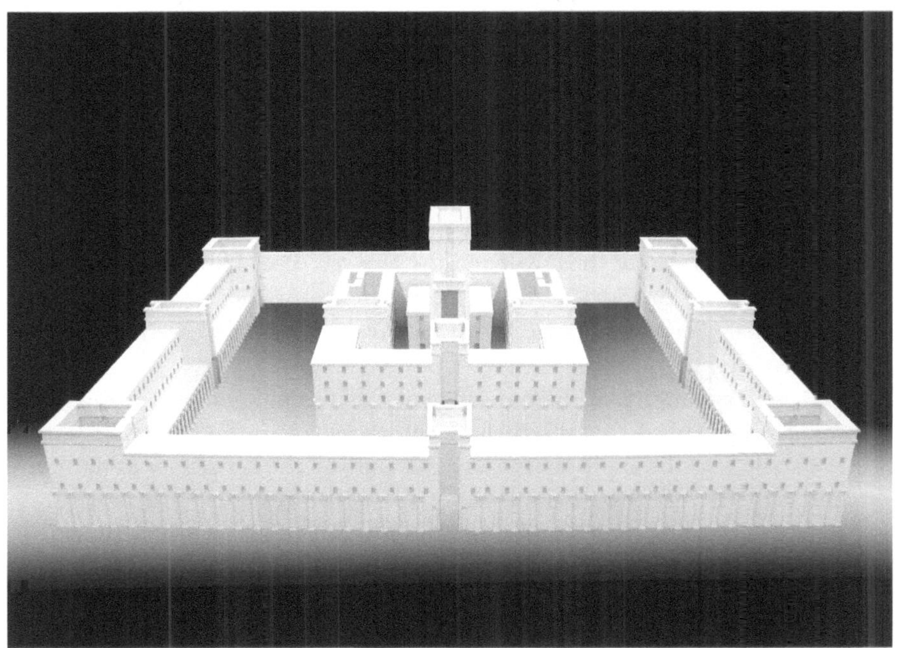

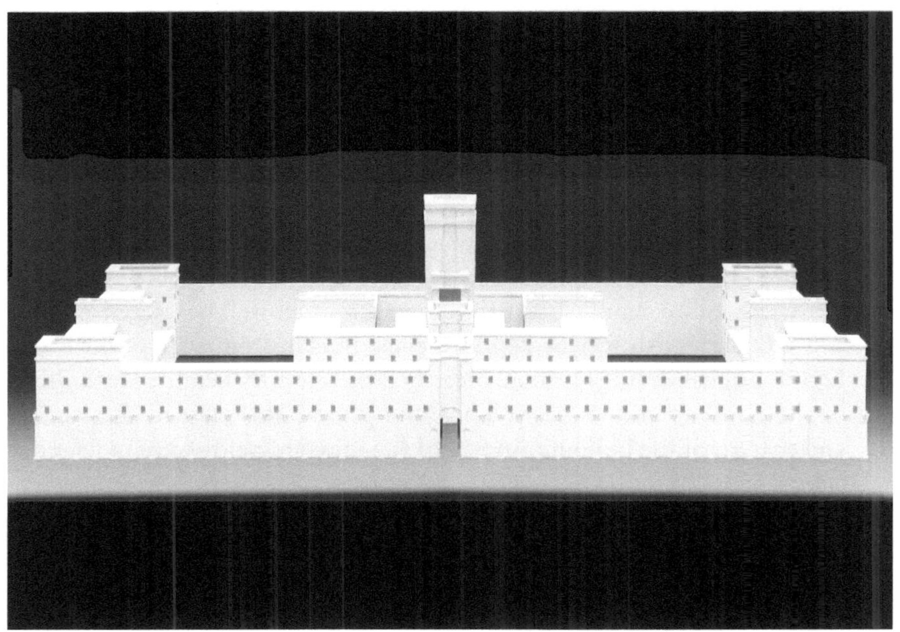

of war. Thus, David handed the task to his son Solomon. The top of the mount was of barely sufficient size to build the Temple; for this reason, an immense wall was built surrounding the hill to the south, the east, and the west. The hollow was filled between the wall and the hill to form the area required for the Temple precinct. Its size was 500 cubits square and it was built of stone. It had three main divisions: the great atrium or the people's court, and the inner atria that consisted of two sections: the court of the priest and the Temple. The altar was the central feature of the precinct and was in the center of the inner atria. The inner atria were surrounded by the great atrium, and these atria were concentric.

The symmetry of the buildings of the Temple precinct mimicked the divine plan of the universe. Harmony between the Scriptures and the analogies of the prophets was equivalent to the simplicity of nature, and this was reflected in the architecture of the Temple: "The structure is valued by such great simplicity and harmony of all its proportions."[12] The height of the buildings of the great atrium was almost sixty cubits, that is to say, half of the height of the Temple and equal to the height of the outer wall of the inner atrium. The exterior and interior gates were mutually corresponding so much in height as in length and in an equal width, and the heights of the adjacent chambers were maintained in this way to the double-sided gates and will also be equal. This perfect architectural harmony of the Temple represented in microcosm the perfect harmony of the macrocosm.[13]

Figure 41 and Figure 42—In Ezekiel's prophecy, he was taken to a high mountain by a man whose appearance was like that of brass. To the south of the mountain was the frame of a city—the Temple precinct. In the man's hand was a measuring reed of six cubits long by the cubit and a hand's breadth—the sacred cubit. The sacred cubit was 2.068 English feet or 24.816 inches; thus, his measuring rod was 12.408 English feet.[14] The man measured the breadth, height, and width of the building and its parts. Thus, the prophecies retained the truth and pattern of the building, and all of the measurements were in sacred cubits.

The precinct was laid out in a square and faced the east. Approaching the east gate of the great atrium, the symmetry of the building was highlighted. The eastern gate was in the center of the eastern side of the great atrium. On the outer wall were three times seven half columns

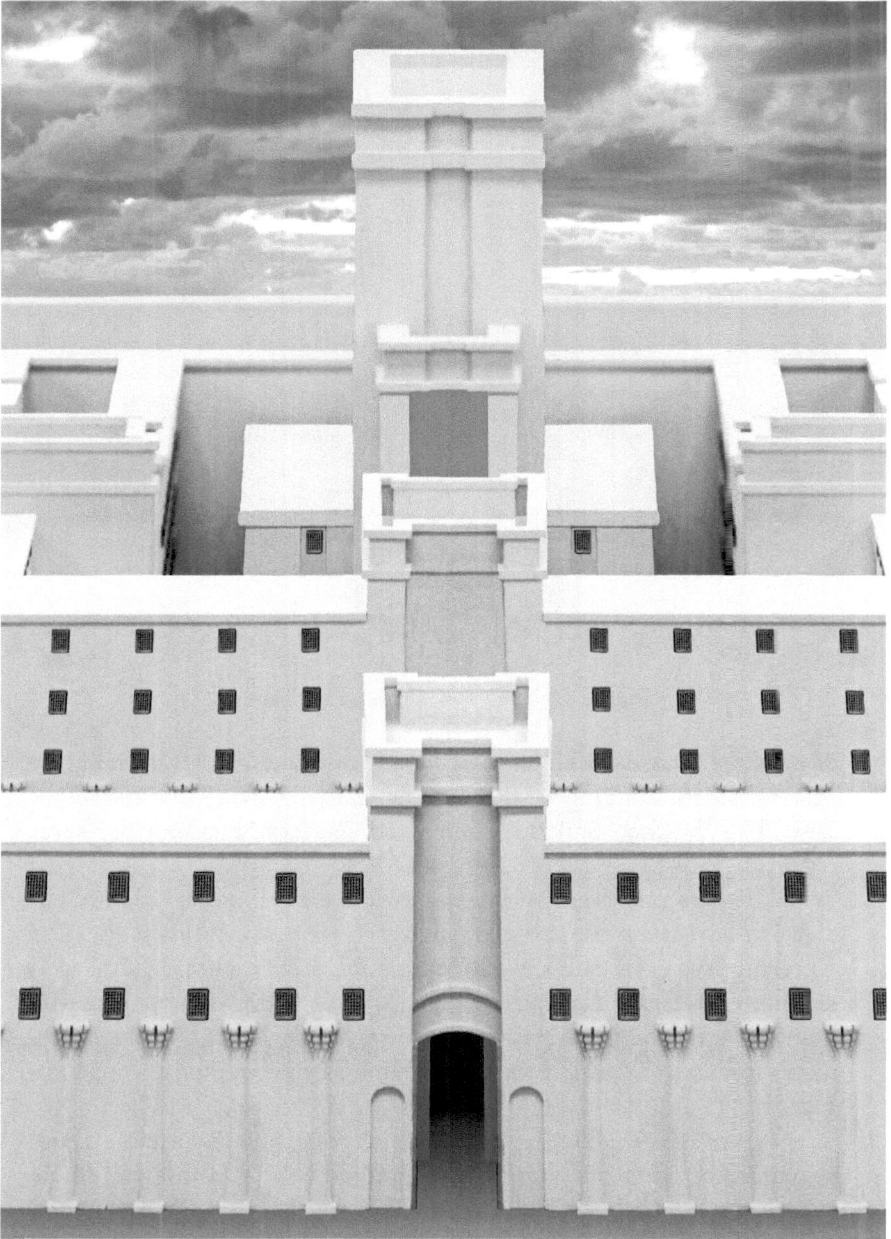

Figure 41. Looking over the Temple from the east.

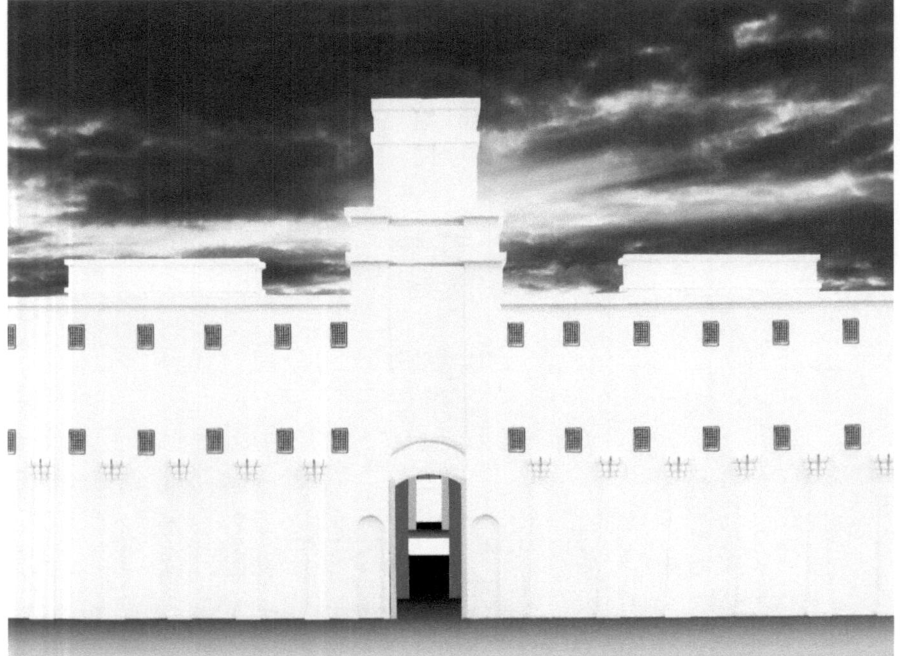

Figure 42. The eastern gate of the Temple.

or pilasters against a wall on each side of the gate. "And it is from here that Solomon, alluding to the Temple that was evidently marvelous, said, 'The Wisdom built her house and she had hewn out her seven columns (Proverbs 9:1).'"[15]

The gate was twenty-five cubits wide, fifty cubits in breadth, and close to seventy-five cubits in height, so its proportions were 1:2:3. Entering the gate, one saw three chambers on each side that were six cubits square, and in each of the chambers there was a narrow window. Between the chambers were archways that led out to the colonnades under the rooms that were visible as one walked through the gate.

Figure 43—Walking out of the gate, one saw the great atrium's pavement opening out. It was one hundred cubits to the wall of the inner court in the north, the east, and the south. From the east gate, it was possible to see towers on the northeast and southeast corners of the great atrium; two other towers were out of sight in the southwest and

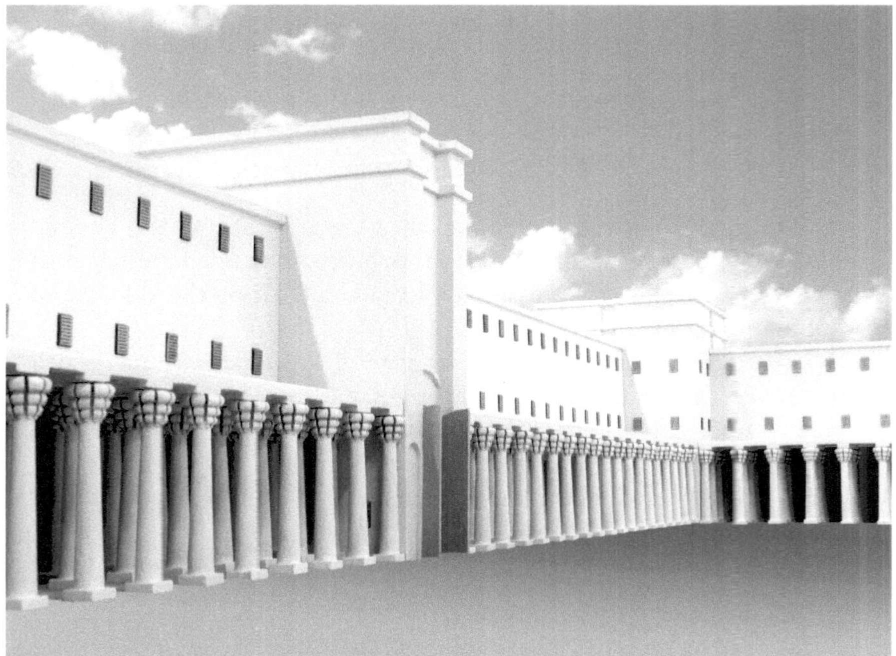

Figure 43. Inside the eastern gate in the great atrium of the Temple of Solomon.

northwest corners. These housed the kitchens of the people. In the towers were the stairs to the upper chambers. There were thirty large chambers in the great atrium, ten each on the north, east, and south sides, but none on the west side, which could not be seen from this point. These chambers, supported by a colonnade, were the chambers for the people. The colonnade next to the kitchen was dedicated to the banquet of the people. The atrium was kept for all of the people, and it was here that they consumed the sacrifices. The stairs were next to the kitchen, so that the people did not remove the food out into the courtyard. As one looked around the great atrium, the colonnade became one of the dominating features of the great atrium perimeter of the Temple precinct. Ezra 6:4 stated that the Temple was built "with three rows of great stones, and a row of new timber":

> Those three rows were of cylindrical stones of form, that is to say, columns. There were two rows of columns in the colonnade under the rooms; the third was in the external facade of the exterior wall of the rooms[;] these corresponded with the

columns of the colonnade of the Great Atrium. The series of beams of wood was found in the panelled ceiling of the colonnade, each one of them carried upon two columns and each one of these were skilfully cut so that together with the remaining one revetment of wood of the panelled ceiling presented a pleasant aspect to the ones that they looked at. Of that there was only one row of these assembled; there was only a colonnade in this outer wall.[16]

Moving toward the north corner of the great atrium and looking back at the exterior of the inner atriums, one saw seven pilasters against a wall on each side of the east gate, again emphasizing the Wisdom of Solomon (see Figure 44).

Turning back to enter the east gate of the inner atriums, which was raised five cubits higher than the great atrium, one saw eight steps leading up to the eastern gate of the inner atrium. This gate, as with all six gates of the Temple precinct, was identical to the eastern gate of the great atrium, emphasizing the elegant proportion and harmony with

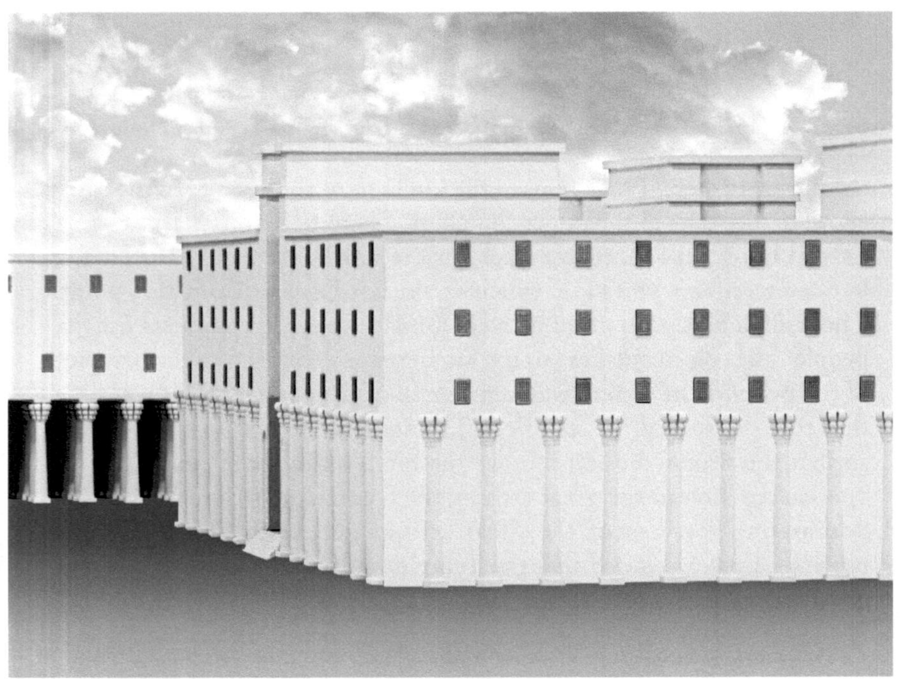

Figure 44. Looking at the wall of the inner sanctum from the great atrium.

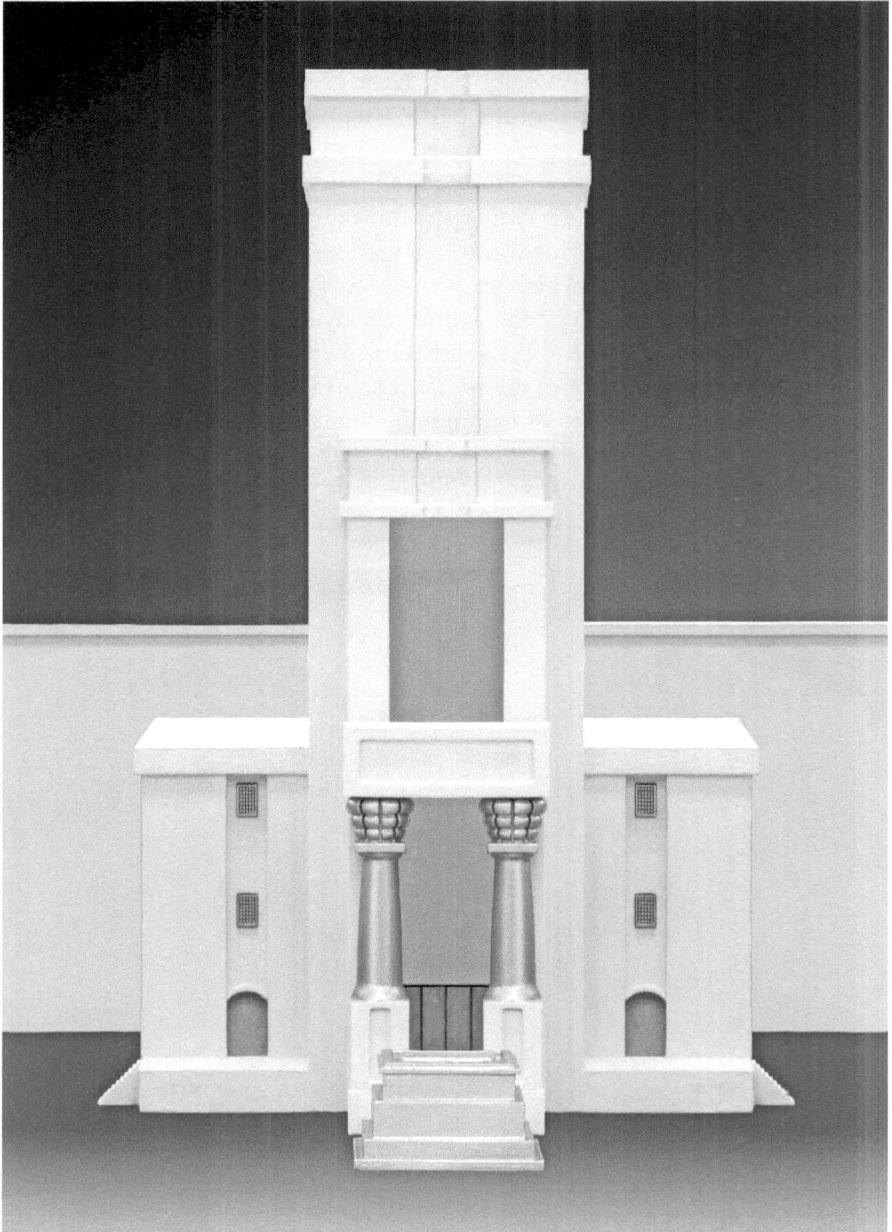

Figure 45. The altar of the burnt offering in front of the Temple.

the rest of the precinct. Only the priests could enter the inner atrium court; it was the place of the sacrifices and the burnt offerings.

Figure 45—After passing through the gate directly ahead, one saw the Temple with the altar of the burnt offerings. The altar was made of bronze and was twenty cubits in length and width, and ten cubits in height—twice the measurements of the altar in the Tabernacle of Moses.[17]

Figure 46—The entire inner atrium was two hundred by one hundred cubits and was divided into two sections: the court of the priests and the separate place, which were both one hundred cubits square. The court of the priests consisted of three identical gates, one to the north, one to the east, and one to the south; chambers for the priests; the altar of the burnt offerings; and the porch of the Temple. In the court of the priests were three floors of communal chambers above the colonnade for the lower priests, and this was where they ate the sacrifices and dressed in the sacred vestments. There were thirty chambers on each floor—ninety communal chambers altogether.

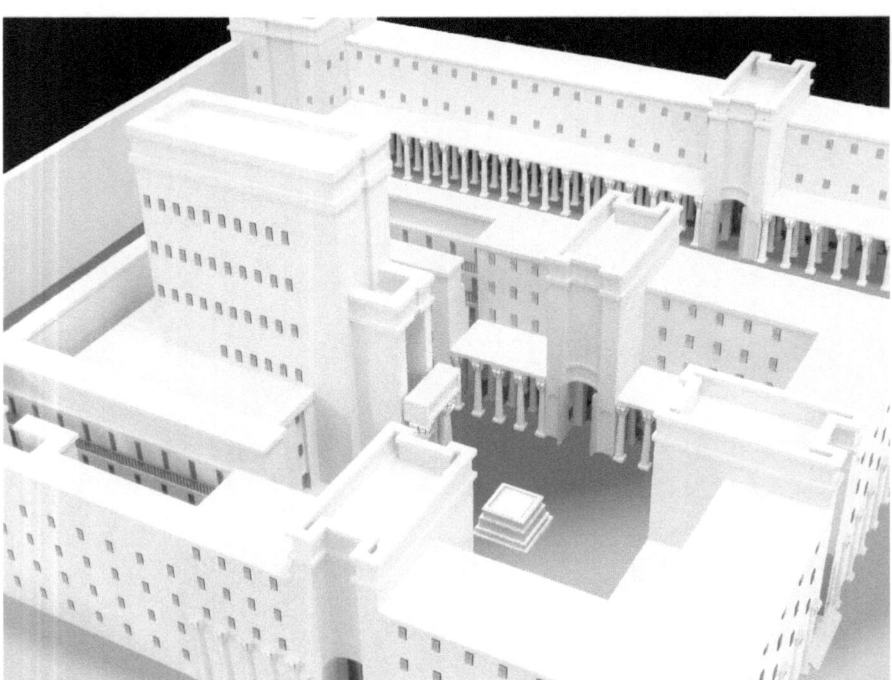

Figure 46. Bird's-eye view of the inner sanctum.

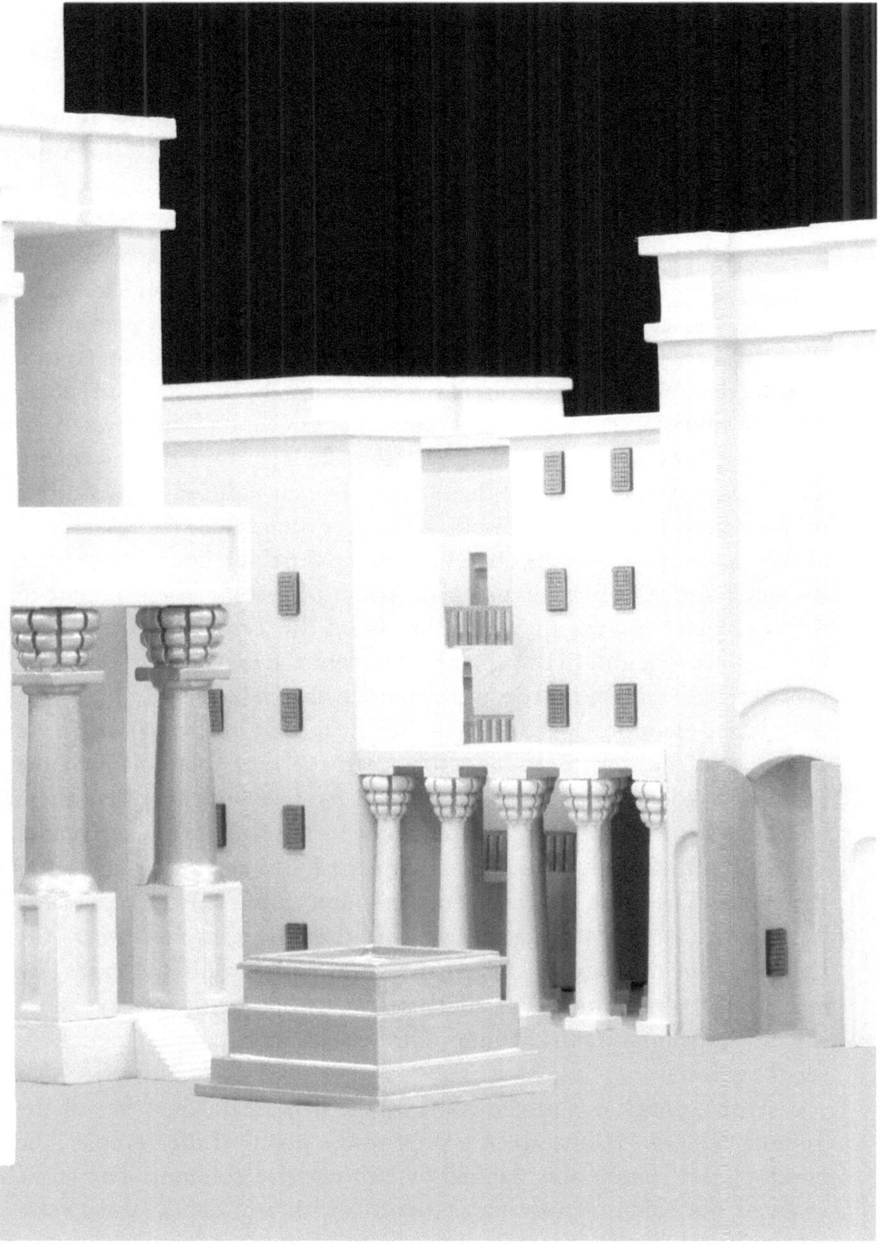

Figures 47. View of the inner sanctum.

Figure 47 and Figure 48—The separate place was divided into three sections. In the center was the Temple itself with fifteen cubits[18] of pavement to the right and the left of it. The Temple and the pavement occupied an area of fifty by one hundred cubits. On one side of the Temple were the chambers for the higher-ranking priests, who were the overseers responsible for the services of the Temple and of the altar of the burnt offerings. On the other side, the twenty-four principals of the priests had individual chambers in the sides of the separate place. The south and the north sides were architecturally identical. On each floor there were fifteen higher-priest chambers.[19] These chambers were accessible through a small colonnade beside the south and north inner gates. This section of the separate place was twenty-five by one hundred cubits. The chambers were divided by a walkway of ten cubits. There were four floors but no colonnade, and the bottom floor was on the pavement. The thickness of the walls of these chambers was reduced by two cubits for each floor and the three floors above the ground floor had a walkway of two cubits, to access the chambers. Since the three floors above were the same size, this formed a stepped structure letting in more light to the chambers whereas the walls that faced the Temple and the great atrium were straight. In the chambers toward the east, which were supported by a small colonnade, were stairs to the walkways.[20]

These chambers were of equal height to that of the atrium of the priests, and the four floors, together with the roof that occupied the space of a floor, arose to the height of fifty-five cubits, so that these buildings as much by their total height as by the heights of each one of the floors, would correspond exactly to the buildings of the atrium of the priests. However, the length of a hundred cubits on the side of the Temple had exactly ten chambers,[21] and there were five chambers the same size on the side of the great atrium and toward the east. The remaining fifty cubits in the southwest and the northwest corners of the inner atrium were the atriums of the cooks, which were the kitchens for the priests.

Moving back out to the court of the priests and in front of the Temple (Figure 45), one saw ten steps to the porch of the Temple. The porch of the Temple was flanked by two massive columns. The stone bases of the columns were six cubits in width and depth, and twelve cubits in height. The height of the body of the bronze columns was eighteen cubits and the capitals were five cubits, so that the total height

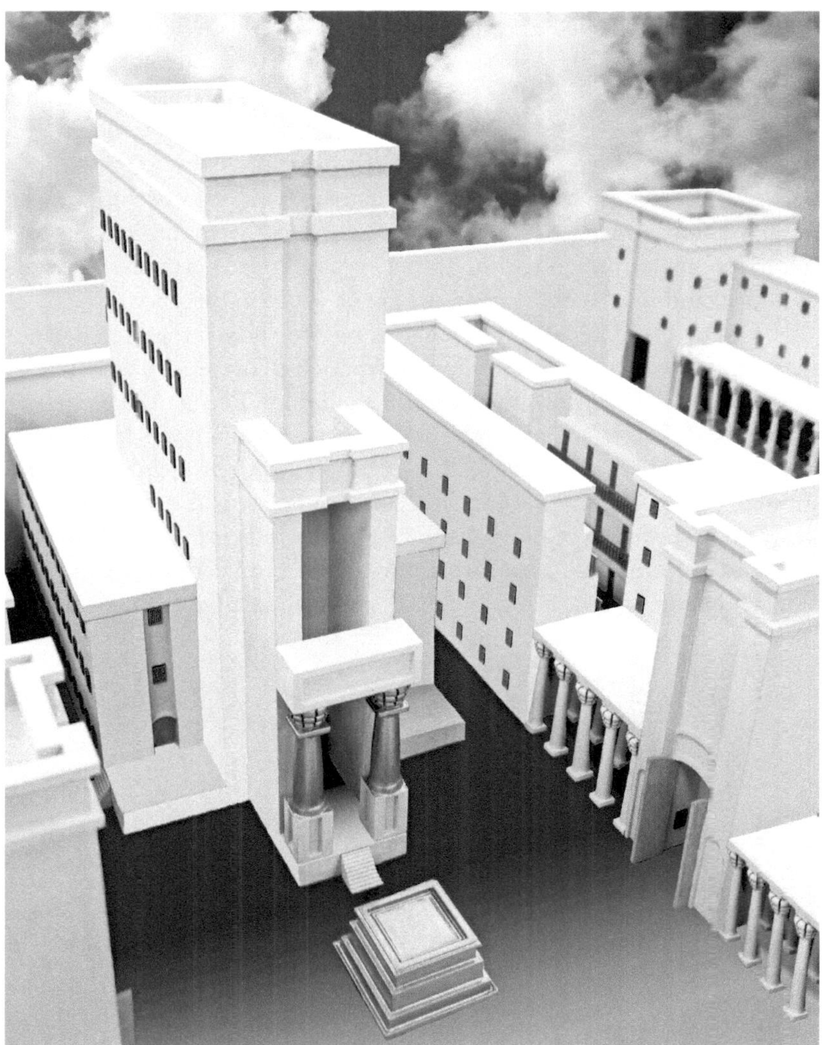

Figures 48. View of the inner sanctum.

of the base, columns, and capitals was thirty-five cubits. This supported an architrave that added another ten or twelve cubits. The bronze column and architrave were freestanding and the height of the porch was close to seventy-five cubits.[22] The height of the full Temple behind the porch was one hundred and twenty cubits.

On the north, west and south sides of the Temple were three floors of chambers. The main doors to these chambers were facing toward the east, but the priests could not access these chambers via the Temple steps, as there were separate sets of stairs on the side to the north and the south. There were thirty chambers, each with a storeroom across a passage. Thus, there were ninety chambers and ninety storerooms. The outer walls were thicker on the lower floor, so the rooms on the first floor were five cubits in width, on the second floor they were six cubits in width, and on the third floor they were seven cubits in width.[23]

Figure 49—The Temple consisted of two rooms: the sacred sanctuary and the holy of holies. Double wooden doors to the entrance of the Temple had two turning leaves in each door, one on the right and one on the left. Moving into the sacred sanctuary, which was forty cubits in length, twenty cubits in width, and thirty cubits in height, one was immediately struck by the interior. Near the door was a wooden altar of wood three cubits in height, and two cubits in length and width that had some protrusions. There were ten golden candelabras, five on each side of the sacred sanctuary, and each candelabrum held seven candles.

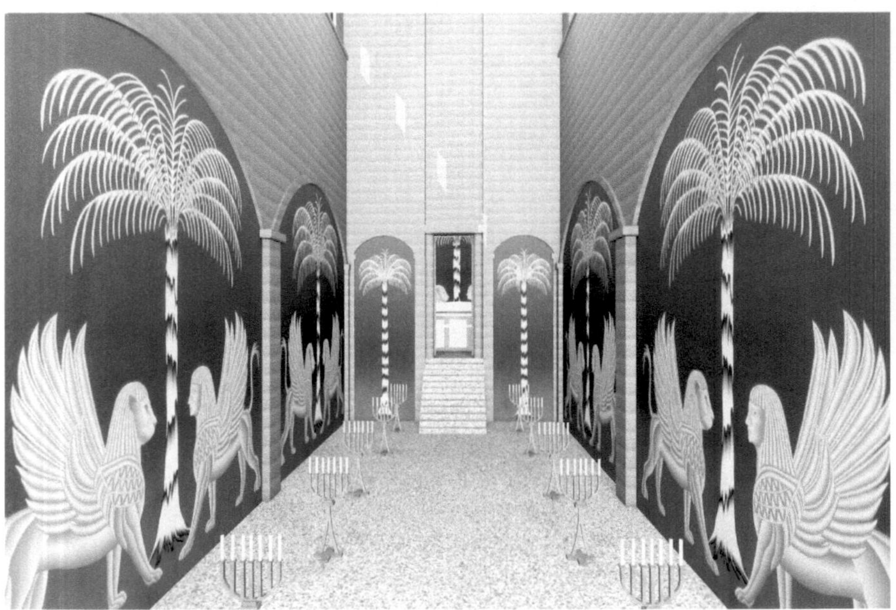

Figure 49. The sacred sanctuary of the Temple.

The walls were lined with timber and there were revetments in the walls, also made of wood. In the revetments were decorations of cherubim and palm trees. The palm trees were between the cherubim. Each of the cherubim had the body of a lion, the wings of an eagle, and two faces: one of a lion and the other of a man. Thus, the palm trees were looked upon by the face of a man on one side and the face of a lion on the other, throughout the house on every side.[24] The rooms were lit, not only by the candelabra, but also from a gallery of slanted windows that illuminated the sanctuary from above:

> In the Apocalypse the world natural is represented by the Temple of Jerusalem & the parts of this world by the analogous parts of the Temple: as heaven by the house of the Temple; the highest heaven by the most holy; the Throne of God in heaven by the Ark; the Sun by the bright flame of the fire of the Altar, or by the face of the Son of Man shining through this flame like the Sun in his strength; the Moon by the burning coals upon the Altar convex above & flat below like an half Moon; the stars by the Lamps; thunder by the song of the Temple & lightning by the flashing of the fire of the Altar; the earth by the Area of the courts & the sea by the great brazen Laver. And hence the parts of the Temple have the same signification with the analogous parts of the world.[25]

A priest took some fire from the great altar in the court of the priest and placed it in a silver censer or incense burner. Then he took the censer to the high priest, who brought it into the Temple to the small altar.[25] The sacred rituals were performed in the Temple away from the people, who could not come into the inner court.

Figure 50 and Figure 51—Directly ahead in the Temple were twelve steps that led to a door. This door was normally closed. Only the high priest could enter this domain and only once a year.[27] This was the holy of holies that contained the Ark of the Covenant. The room was a cube, the same shape as the divine city in Revelation, of twenty cubits. There are no windows and it is in total darkness.[28] Cherubim and palm trees decorated the walls. This was the sacred heart of the Temple. The Ark that contained the broken remains of the stone tables on which the Ten Commandments were written had been originally kept in the Tabernacle of Moses. However, the Temple of Solomon was the only temple to contain the sacred Ark. In 586 BC, the Babylonian king Nebuchadnezzar destroyed Jerusalem and the Temple of Solomon—the Ark of the Covenant was also destroyed.

With the porch, "the length of the entire Temple was a hundred cubits of the following form: the bases were six cubits; the front wall

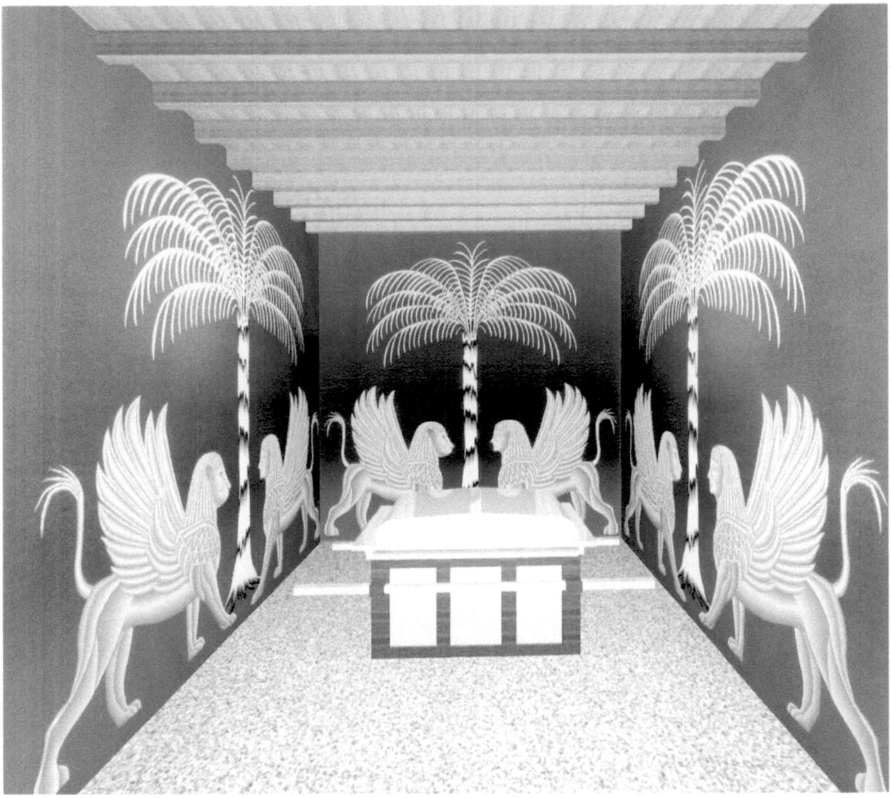

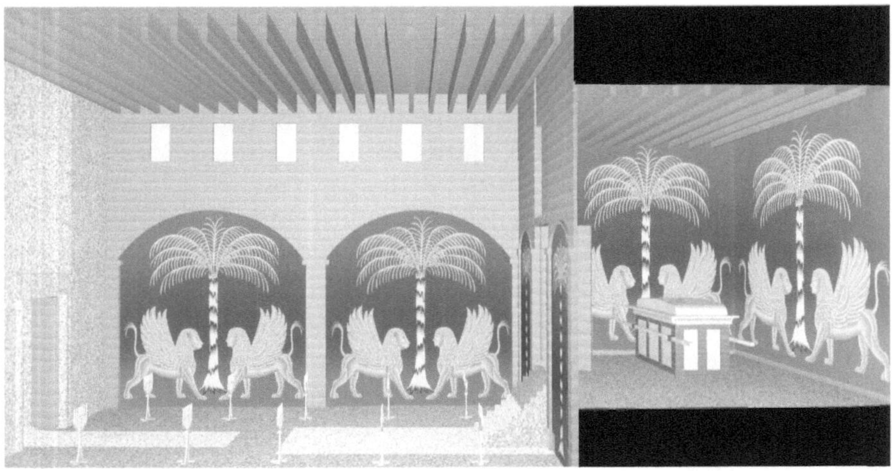

Top: Figure 50. Inside the holy of holies. *Bottom:* Figure 51. Cross-section of the Temple.

144

of the vestibule was five cubits; the remaining length of the vestibule was fifteen cubits; the front wall of the Temple was six cubits; the holy place was forty cubits; the most interior part was twenty cubits, and the western wall of the most interior part was six cubits. The total length was one hundred cubits."[29]

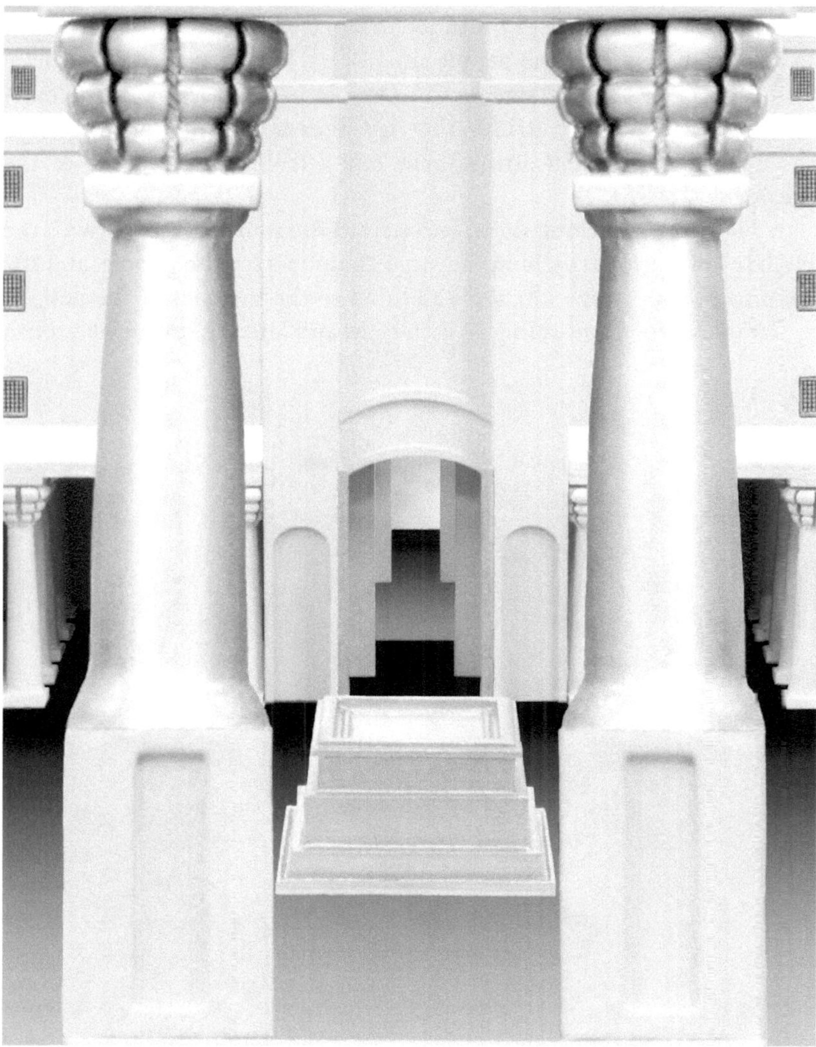

Figure 52. View from the porch of the Temple.

Figure 52—Leaving the Temple, from the porch one looked directly east toward the gates. From a bird's-eye view of the back of the Temple facing east, it was possible to see the chambers of the principals of the priests and the arrangement of the gates (see Figures 53 and 54). Moving down the steps of the Temple brought one down into the court of the priests again. Passing back by the altar of the burnt offerings and through the eastern gate of the inner atrium (see Figure 55), one returned to the great atrium of the people.

Figure 56—Before leaving the Temple precinct through the eastern gate of the great atrium that lay ahead, turning right to walk the circuit of the great atrium gave one a feel of the expanse of the precinct.

Figure 57—Turning right, one viewed the southeast tower with the kitchens of the great atrium, the large chambers for the people, and the colonnade next to the kitchen dedicated to the banquet of the people.

Figure 58—Continuing to turn right and looking toward the south

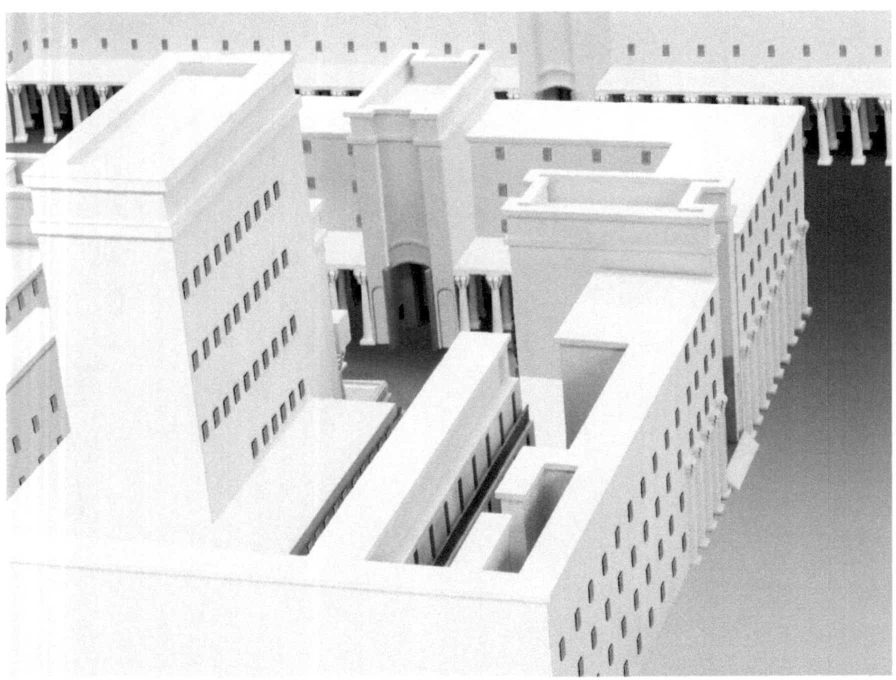

Figure 53. Bird's-eye view from the back of the Temple.

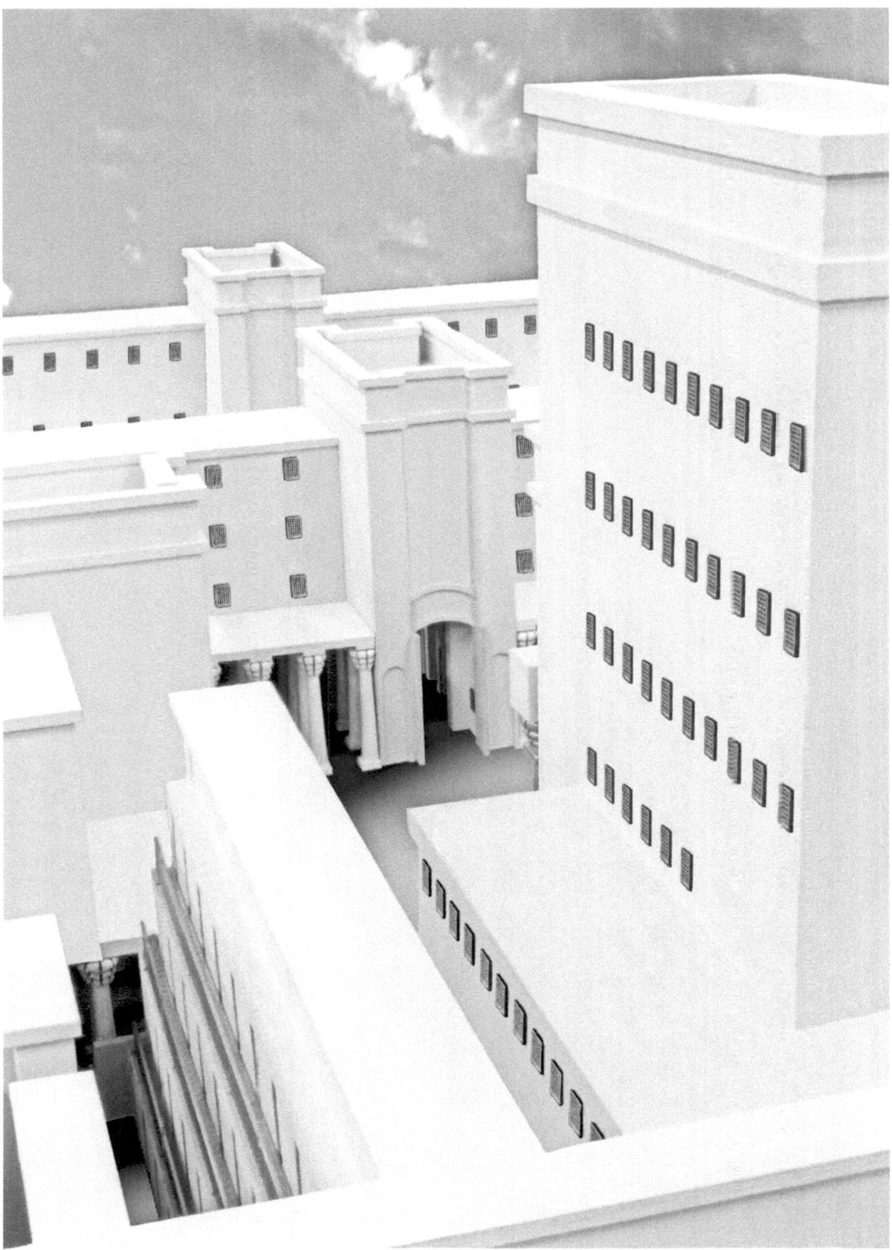

Figure 54. Bird's-eye view from the back of the Temple.

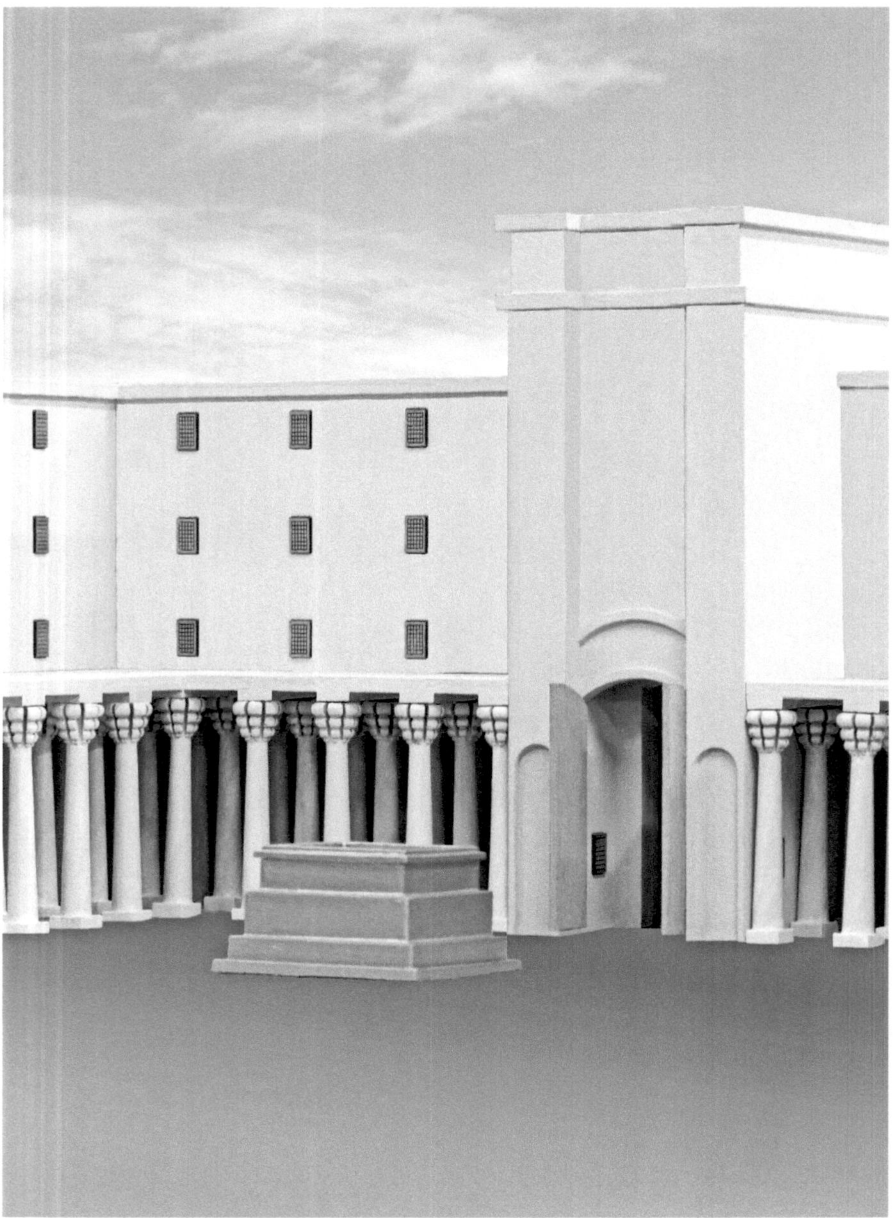

Figure 55. Passing the altar of the burnt offering through to the eastern gate of the inner atrium.

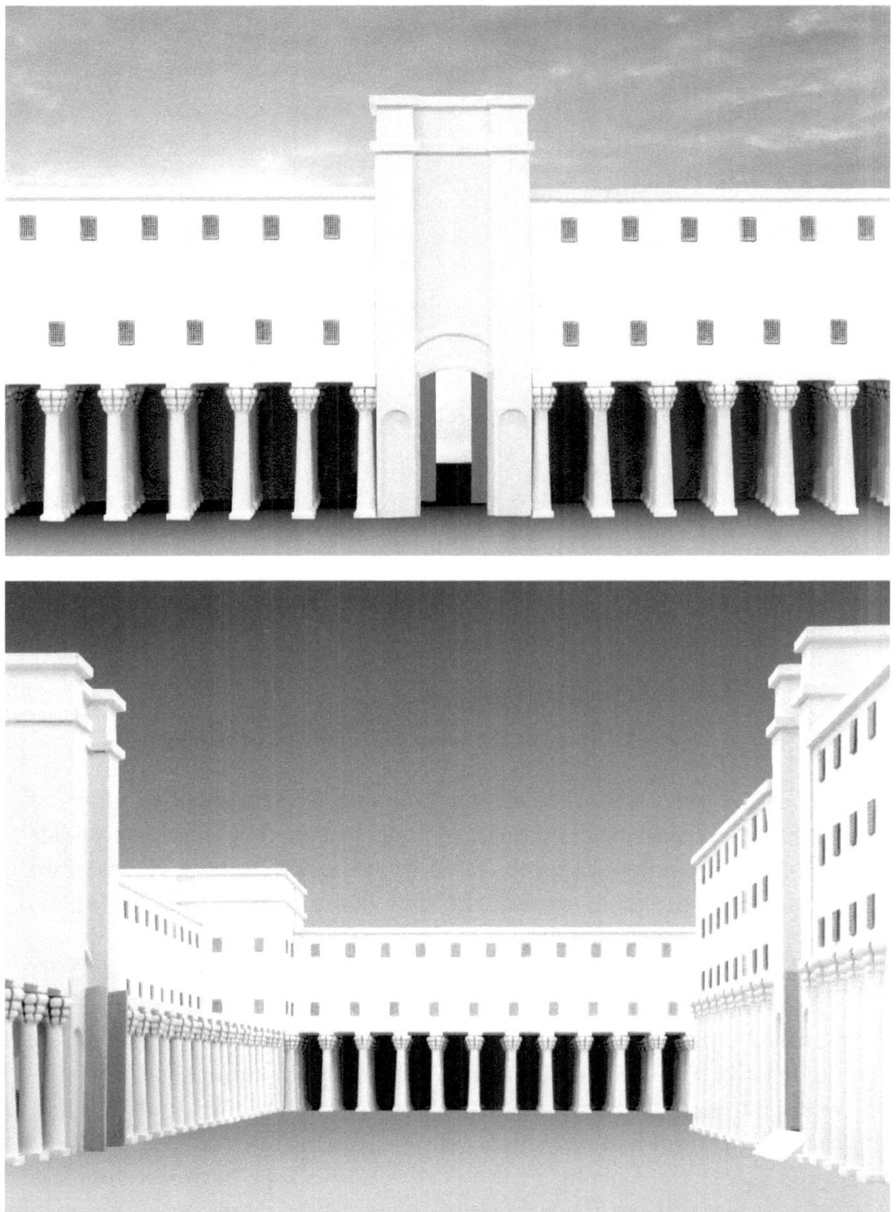

Top: Figure 56. The eastern gate from inside the inner atrium. *Bottom:* Figure 57. Inside the great atrium.

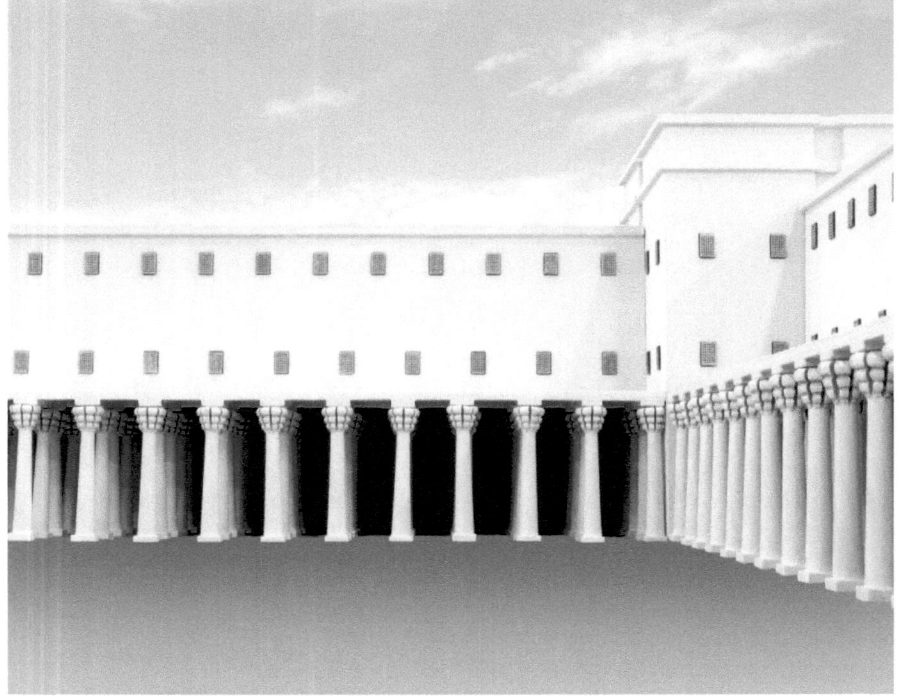

Figure 58. Towards the south side of the great atrium.

side of the inner atrium, it was possible to see the gridded windows of the priest's chambers: first, the three floors occupied by the minor priests on top of the colonnade, replicated by the pilasters against a wall on each side of the gate; second, the four floors of the chambers of the high priests and the principals of the priests.

Figure 59—Looking back toward the east at the tower, one saw the columns of the colonnade, which were twenty-one cubits in height. Remembering that a man's average height was two and a half cubits, the massive scale became apparent. Apart from the towers on the south-west and northwest corners of the western wall, the great atrium and the inner atrium had only high plain walls with no features.

Figure 60—Turning to the north and walking between the plain walls, one could see the northwest tower. Light from above the open tower lit the stairs to the upper floors that wound around the walls, with the kitchen around the walls under the stairs.

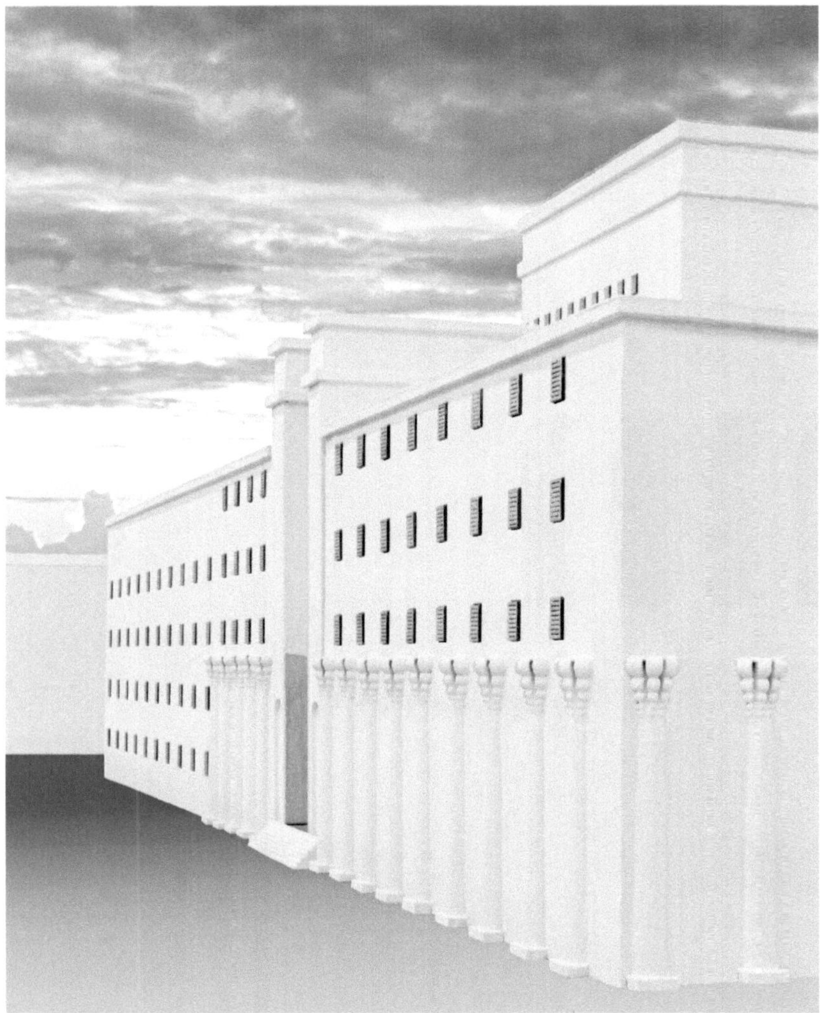

Figure 59. Looking towards the east.

Figure 61—Turning back toward the east, one viewed the eastern gate of the great atrium.

Figure 62 and Figure 63—When one stood at the northeast corner, the circuit of the great atrium was complete. Looking back, one saw the northwest tower in the distance and the inner atrium showing the seven pilasters, highlighting that this was the house of Wisdom.

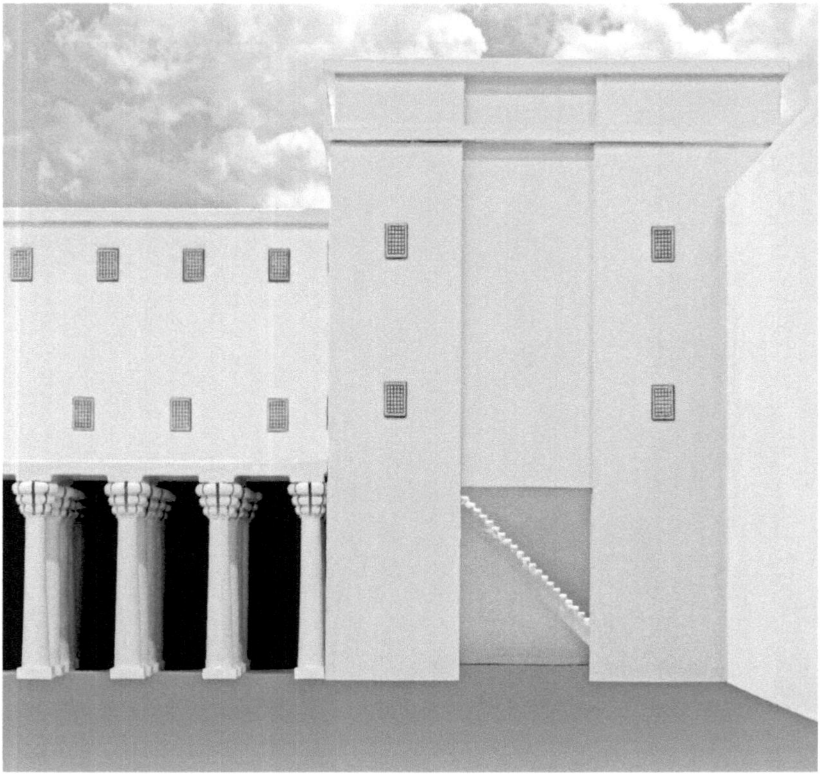

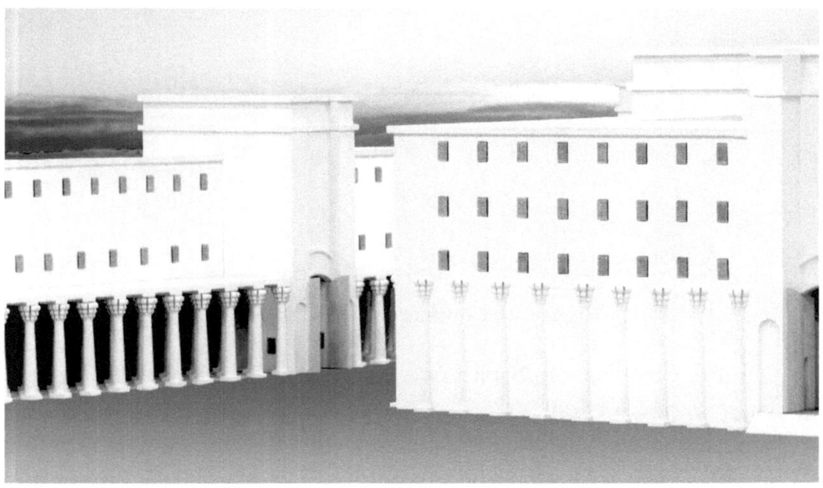

Top: Figure 60. The northern cornered tower with the staircase to the upper floors. *Bottom:* Figure 61. Towards the eastern gate of the great atrium.

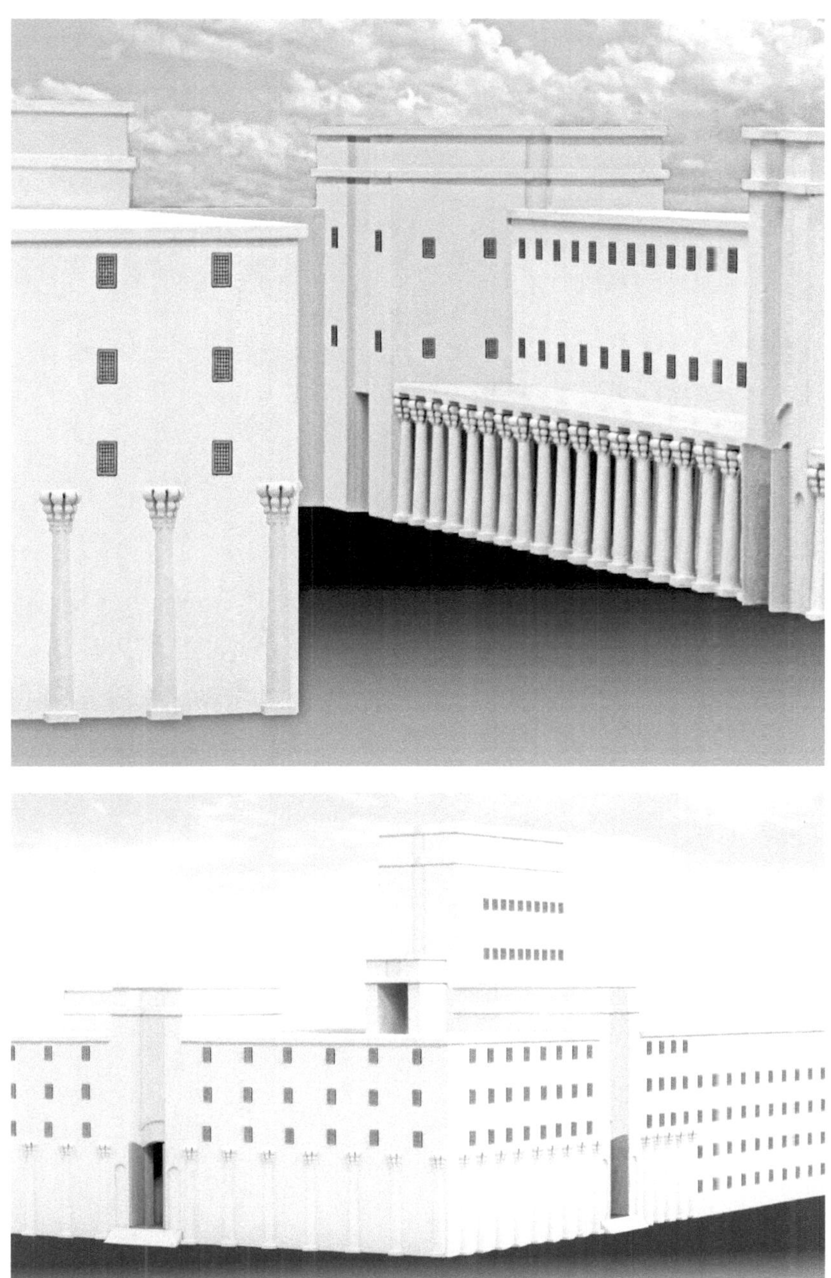

Figures 62 and 63. Views of the north-east corner looking towards the inner atrium.

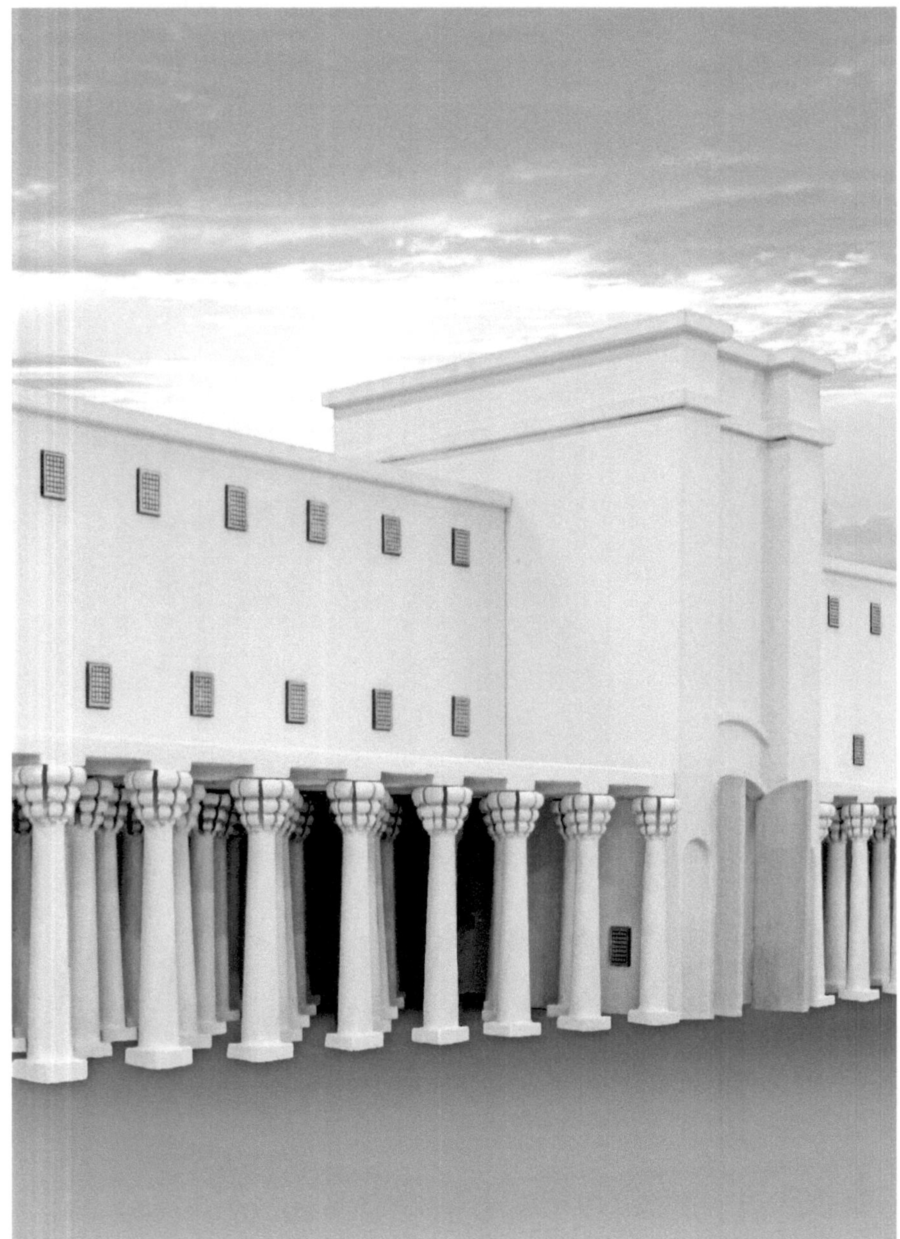

Figure 64. Returning to the outer eastern gate.

Figure 64—Turning to leave through the eastern gate of the great atrium for the last time, one leaves the Temple precinct.

Figure 65—Moving back to the high mountain to the north of the city and looking from the northeastern corner, one could appreciate the harmonious heights of the buildings, the towers, the temple, and the porch of the Temple.

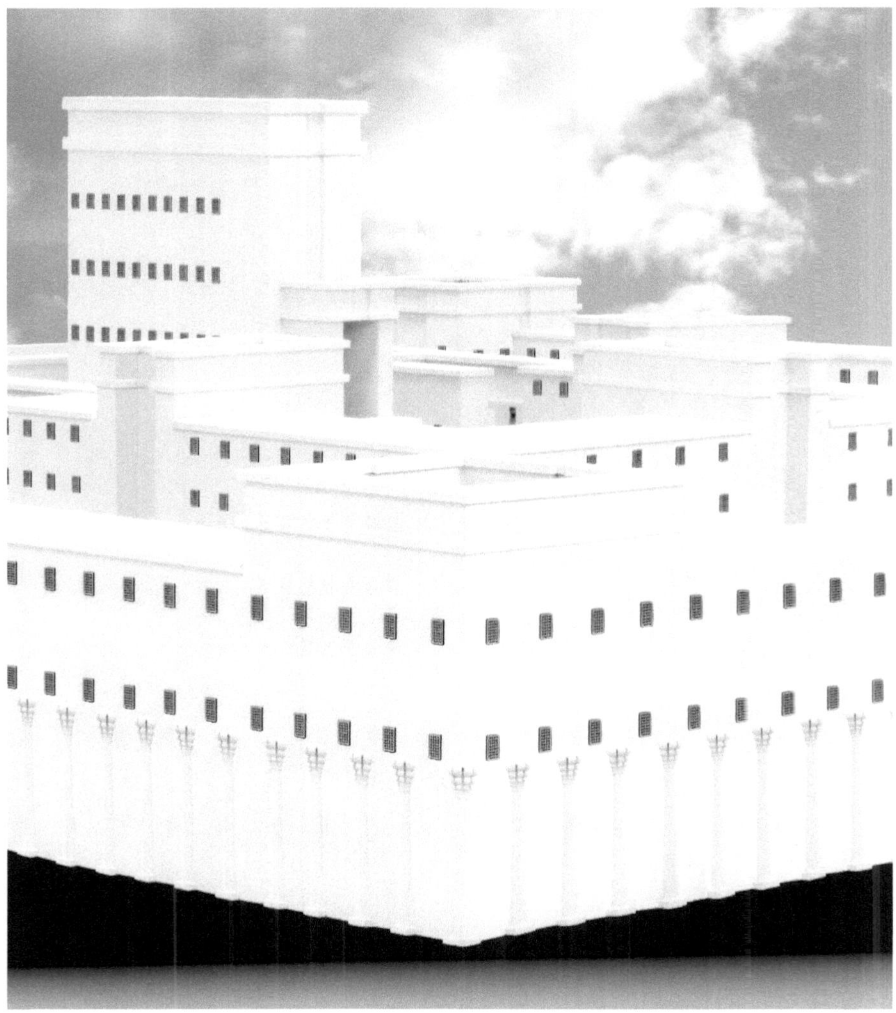

Figure 65. View from the north-east across the Temple precinct.

Figure 66 and Figure 67—The final glimpse of the Temple precinct from the north side revealed the four gates from the north to the south side of the precinct and the Temple. The architecture of the Temple as a whole and of its parts was the microcosm that had the same signification as the analogous parts of the universe—the macrocosm. To look upon the magnificent architecture of the Temple was to see the frame of the universe and the plan of God.

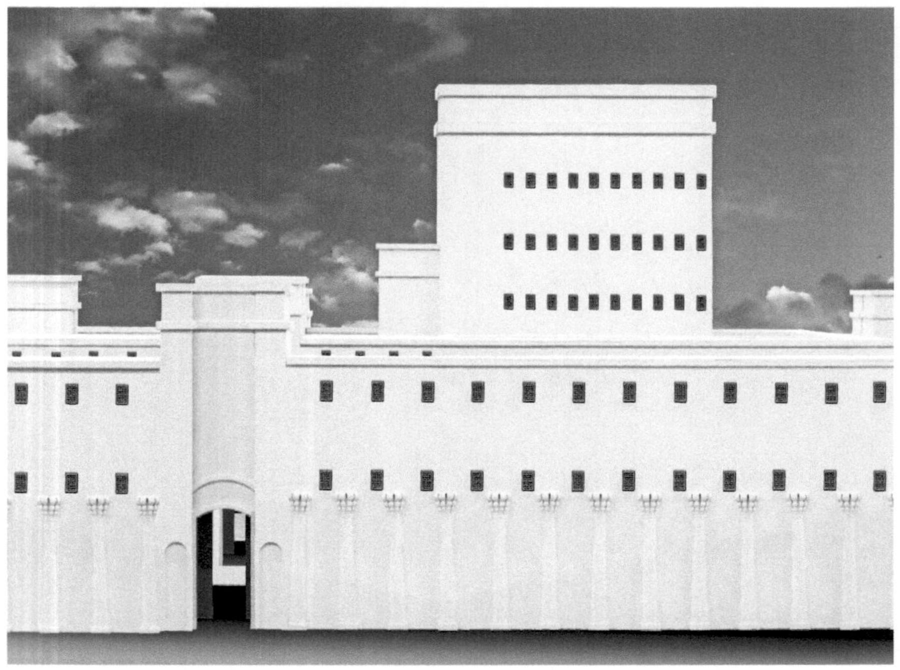

Figures 66 (*above*) and 67 (*opposite*). Looking north towards the Temple precinct.

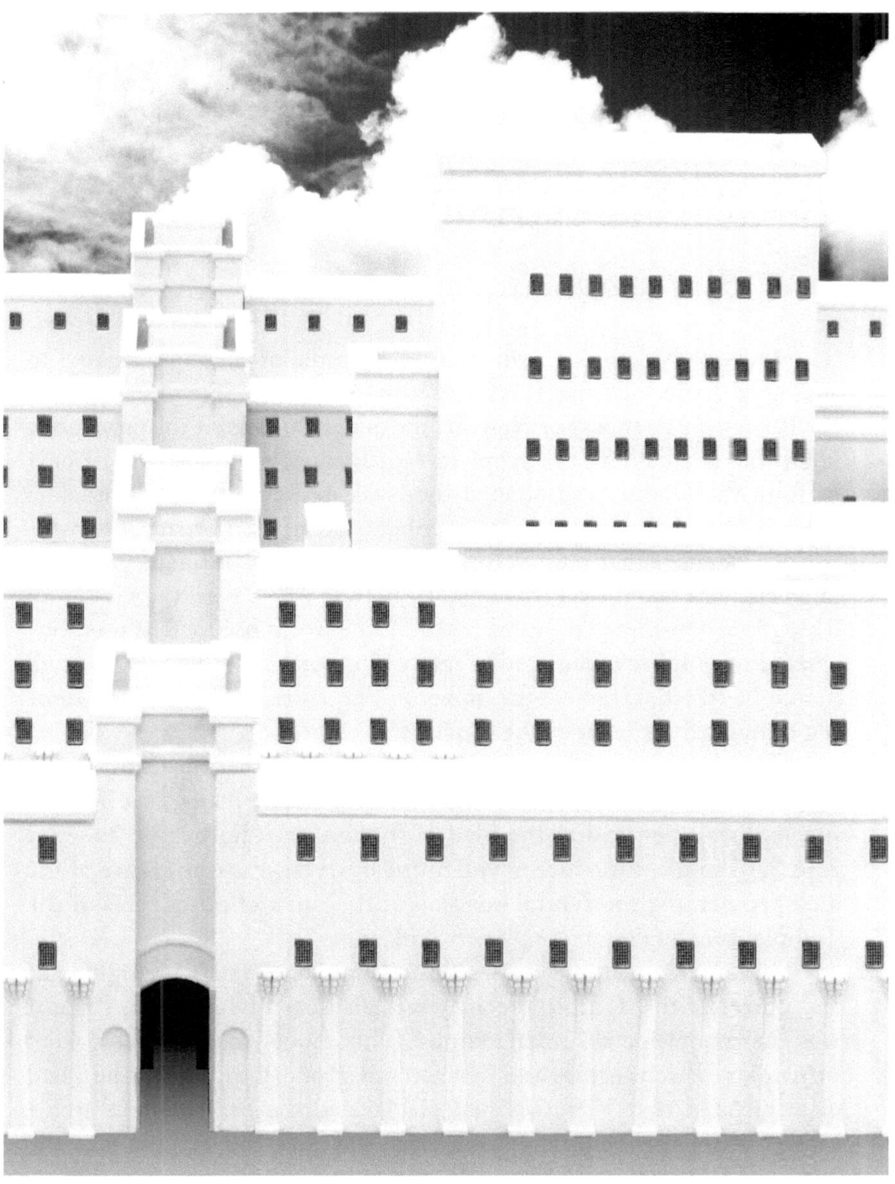

Conclusion

Most of Newton's writings on the Temple of Solomon related to the Apocalypse. The angels "moved" through the Temple as the seals of the Book were opened. For Newton, the understanding of the prophecies lay in the language of the prophets—of Daniel, who closed the Book, of John the Divine who opened the book in Revelation, and Ezekiel who described the Temple. The prophets had written of ancient truths but in a language that was not for everyone to understand. This prophetic language was taken from the analogy between the "world natural" and a kingdom considered a "world politic." The world politic that was considered in prophecy consisted of many kingdoms, the most noble of all being the celestial frame—the universe. Therefore, the plan of the Temple mimicked the plan of the universe.

Clearly, Newton, the man who demonstrated that the orbits of the planets were elliptical, did not mean that the square plan of the Temple precinct was identical to the plan of the universe. Rather, he believed that the Temple was a hieroglyph of the universe: the central fire of the altar represented the central position of the sun and other parts of the Temple were analogous to planets and stars.

Although Newton considered the Temple precinct a hieroglyph of the universe, the Temple precinct was also earthly and real, since it was the model for all other temples. This model was built using the principles of architecture and harmonious proportion. Villalpando had clearly stated that Vitruvius had plagiarized the principles of architecture from the Temple of Solomon and that the Temple was the origin of architecture. Newton does not state this as clearly as Villalpando does. However, it is implied throughout his work that the tenth century BC Temple was built to the principles that were codified by the first century BC architectural theorist Vitruvius. In *The Chronology*, he stated that he had not heard any mention of fine temples before the Temple of Solomon. In this text he also made the Kingdom of the Israelites the first "civilized" kingdom—for its technology—even though he does not dedicate a chapter to the Kingdom of the Israelites.

Newton studied no topic that would require knowledge of Vitruvius except for the study of the Temple and the cubit that was the measurement used for the Temple. This reinforces the view that his study of the Temple was not just as a hieroglyph or religious symbol. He clearly desired a realistic reconstruction of the Temple. In the *Principia*, Newton wrote that nothing would please him more than if the principles laid out in the *Principia* confirmed people's belief in God.[1] By making the Temple real, perhaps to Newton, this would confirm his and others' belief in the Wisdom of Solomon that was derived from the ancient knowledge of Moses and the original religion. Yet his study of Vitruvius and the architecture of the Temple does not appear to have continued beyond the early 1690s. Although he continued his study on the Temple and the prophecy concerning the Temple, he integrated this work with his later apocalyptic writings. The small chapter in *The Chronology* shows no interest in architecture. The plan of the Temple cannot be reconstructed from the text of *The Chronology*. The plans that illustrate the chapter are not the work of Newton and they were produced after Newton's death by an unknown artist. The only known full reconstruction of Isaac Newton's Temple of Solomon is from Babson MS 434.

Although Newton was interested in chronology as early as the 1660s, he showed no interest in the Temple until the late 1670s or early 1680s, when Leon's model was in London. This raises the question, "did Newton see or know of Leon's Temple exhibition?" It is known that Newton attended some meetings of the Royal Society in London within the appropriate time frame. Given his emerging interest in the Temple, it would seem likely that he did see it. It is even possible that the Leon model stimulated his interest in the Temple. However, it is impossible to establish whether he did or did not see it.

Certainly, Newton would not have agreed with Leon's design of the Temple. Although there is no plan of Leon's Temple, it is clear from the images that it was asymmetrical. Newton strived to demonstrate that the plan of the Temple was symmetrical and that the altar was centrally placed to mimic the plan of the universe.

Conclusion

When the Schott model arrived in London in 1724, Newton was living in central London. The model was a media sensation. It is very probable that he did see it, particularly since he was still interested in the Temple and at the time was revising his *The Chronology*. He had also been interested in Villalpando's design. Both the Leon and the Schott models would have interested Newton, but he would not have agreed with either one. The Schott model was built to the plan of Villalpando—a plan that Newton strongly disagreed with. He pointed out that, although Villalpando's main source was the Book of Ezekiel, his gridded plan contradicted some of the main features that Ezekiel described. At the same time, Newton strongly agreed with Villalpando's rational and theological underpinnings that saw the Temple as the microcosm of the macrocosm.[2] At Christmas time 1725, Stukeley and Newton discussed their respective plans of the Temple of Solomon,[3] and it does seem inconceivable that they did not discuss the Schott model, given the fanfare that it had received in the previous year when it had arrived in London, and its ongoing exhibition.

The Leon and the Schott exhibitions were not the only exhibitions on the Temple of Solomon. A model was built by Lutheran preacher Christoph Semler in 1718, and he also wrote a very comprehensive guidebook that allowed the reader to "travel" through the Temple. This model never left Halle, Germany, as it was housed in a school and was used as a teaching aid.[4] Although it was viewed by the community and was a significant part of that community, it did not have any impact outside of Halle. However, the Leon and Schott models traveled and were on exhibition for a relatively long time, and both were housed in public exhibition spaces for maximum exposure. These exhibitions were unique and were viewed by royalty, the gentry, the scientific community, and the public. They were early examples of public museums that at the time were beginning to take their place in English culture.

Cabinets of curiosities—encyclopedic collections of an array of objects whose categories, such as natural history, archaeology, ethnography, and many other areas, had not yet been defined—were a fad of the time. They were also a forerunner of museums and were generally an eclectic collection of natural and manufactured objects. Thomas Howard, Earl of Arundel, was an ardent collector during the reigns of James I and Charles I, as well as a patron of Inigo Jones. He amassed a huge collection of artworks. However, although Howard made his treasures accessible to scholars,[5] it could not be said that they were open to the public.

In an introduction to the catalogue of a private collection published in 1656, the collector John Tradescant described his collection of nature as consisting of "birds, four-footed beasts, fish, Shell-creatures, insects, minerals and outlandish-fruits" and his manufactured collection consisting of "utensils, household stuff, habits, instruments of war used by several nations, rare curiosities of art."[6] These collections were perceived as the proof of a harmonious universe and they acted as the microcosm of universal nature.

In a letter at the end of the 16th century from Francis Bacon, the counselor of Britain, to the second counselor, on the study of philosophy, Bacon expressed what such a collection should consist of. He stated that, first,

> the collecting of a most perfect and general library, wherein whosoever the wit of man hath heretofore committed to books of worth, be they ancient or modern, printed or manuscript, European or of the other parts, of one or other language, may be made contributory to your wisdom. Next, a spacious, wonderful garden, wherein whatsoever plant the sun of divers climates, out of the earth of divers moulds, either wild or by the culture of man brought forth, may be with that care that appertaineth to the good prospering thereof set and cherished: This garden to be built about with rooms to stable in all rare beasts and to cage in all rare birds; with two lakes adjoining, the one of fresh water the other of salt, for like variety of fishes. And so you may have in small compass a model of universal nature made private. The third, a goodly huge cabinet, wherein whatsoever the hand of man by exquisite art or engine hath made rare in stuff, form, or motion; whatsoever singularity chance and the shuffle of things hath produced; whatsoever Nature hath wrought in things that want life and may be kept; shall be sorted and included. The fourth such a still-house, so furnished with mills, instruments, furnaces, and vessels as may be a palace fit for a philosopher's stone.[7]

This collection, "in small compass a model of universal nature made private," Bacon perceived as essential to the study of philosophy.

Elias Ashmole was a man of considerable standing in both the scientific community and at court. He was comptroller of the excise, Windsor herald, an astrologer whom King Charles II consulted, a founder member of the Royal Society, and an author of several historic and alchemical books. Ashmole had a large collection that mainly consisted of books, manuscripts, coins, medals, and some rarities, including some prehistoric flint implements. Ashmole had inherited the Tradescant collection, which significantly increased the size and the breadth of his collection.[8]

By the second half of the 17th century, these "cabinets of curiosities" had become widespread. They came in all sizes, from small cabinets to the more extensive collections of Tradescant, Bacon, Ashmole, and the Earl of Arundel. The curiosity of the collectors showed no bounds. After Ashmole presented his sizable collection to the University of Oxford, it became the Ashmolean Museum. Opened in 1683, it was the first public museum in Britain.

Although the opening of the Ashmolean Museum postdates the Leon exhibition, the elements of a museum culture were already present in Britain, and instead of an eclectic collection that represented the macrocosm, the model of the Temple took that role in these exhibitions. After 1732, the Schott model became part of a private museum in Germany, but while in England, it was of sufficient interest to the public to be viewed as a complete exhibition.

The initial entrance fee of half a guinea for the Schott model exhibition restricted the number of visitors to the exhibition, but the later price of two shillings, although still expensive, opened up the exhibition to the general public. The guidebooks clearly walked the reader or viewer through the Temple. The books went beyond being a souvenir of the exhibition; they offered the viewer an experience of the architecture, the vessels, and the ritual objects. Leon's model was exhibited in his house, and he also traveled with the model to other houses to exhibit it, and to local fairs. The price he charged is not recorded; however, its appearance at local fairs indicates that the price was set at a reasonable level and thus more accessible to the public.

These models with their guidebooks created a collective memory landscape. Like Villalpando's "architecture of theology," the models of the Temple arranged the architecture and the vessels before the eyes of the viewer, and the guidebook not only walked the viewer through the Temple, but allowed the viewer as reader of the guidebook to reconstruct the Temple at will, at a later time, in the mind's eye. According to Leon, the architecture of the Temple did "express [the] order and model of God himself."[9] The writer of the Schott guidebook stated,

> It is the basis of all that may be seen magnificent in architecture, now a-days, it may serve as a pattern throughout the whole, by which all the branches belonging to architecture must be proved and ordered: and can there be a more convincing

> proof, since God himself, who is the Creator of the great building of the world, has been the immediate projector and architect thereof.[10]

He believed the Divine Architect built all things to a pattern, proved and ordered as He did in the great building of the world. The Temple was built according to the pattern of the universe. The celestial pattern and the order and model of God were encoded in the architecture of the Temple.

Newton's early work on the architecture of the Temple reveals that he was also working on a memory landscape, which he drew upon in his apocalyptic works, even late in his life. Although his work on *The Chronology* does not reveal a continuation of his memory landscape, it is known that as he was preparing *The Chronology* for publication, he sanitized it and burned some of his manuscripts to hide his heretical religious beliefs. Given the importance that Newton gave the reign of Solomon throughout *The Chronology*, and his disinterest in the description of the Temple, it would appear that concealing his beliefs is a possible reason for the change. In short, he was looking toward preserving his scientific legacy and not being remembered for his heretical beliefs.

Newton agreed with the concept of Villalpando's "architecture of theology," and Newton's work on the Temple clearly shows that his model was for his own religious contemplation. However, the careful reconstruction of it according to the architectural principles of Vitruvius, which would have been particularly studied for the reconstruction, implies that it was much more than a religious hieroglyph to Newton. His early questions and thoughts on memory in the 1660s were only searching for ideas—he had not formulated any theory—but they do demonstrate that he distinguished between characters and the signification of characters. Memory was not just a mere sense, such as sight; he located memory in the soul that had to remember the characters. He distinguished between external and internal images and listed groups of things that were interconnected and could be recalled by association. These ideas could have been copied out of an art of memory book. Newton's work of the mid–1660s on universal language is another questioning and incomplete work, but it is in the process of formulating ideas about an abstract and universal language. Twenty years later this had become an analogous prophetic language of signification that related to the world natural and the world politic—the Temple's plan reflected the plan of the universe and therefore the mind of God.

This prophetic language was created in the mid–1680s, and the Temple landscape around the mid–1680s to the early 1690s—at the same time as, or in the case of the latter, within a few years of the publication of the *Principia*. This timing is hard to ignore. The *Principia* revealed the laws and the form of the universe; the Temple landscape revealed the plan of the microcosm–Temple based on the macrocosm-universe. Both the real and the memory landscapes were important to Newton, and his writing on the prophets, the Apocalypse, and the Temple greatly outweighs his scientific writing, even in the most productive scientific periods of his life.[11]

Newton continued to refine his work on the prophetic language, but all of these manuscripts remain incomplete.[12] Some of the manuscripts reveal tables of contents, implying that Newton intended them to be more than private studies, perhaps a publication, of which the Temple was intended to be a chapter. Babson MS 434, or "A Treatise or Remarks on Solomon's Temple, Introduction to the Lexicon of the Prophets, Part Two: About the Appearance of the Jewish Temple," was part of that study, and an intended chapter. It is a significant document of over eighty pages of small and tight handwriting, and the second, more refined, reconstruction comprises seventy percent of the manuscript. This would have made a substantial chapter, quite unlike the mean, unintelligible 3,000-word chapter it became in *The Chronology*.

The mirroring of the Temple and the universe is a strong theme in Newton's prophetic manuscripts. This was not an unusual topic at the time. There is no doubting the religious importance of the Temple to Newton, but to Newton, as with many other scholars of the time, there was no line between religion and science. Science proved the existence of God and religion revealed the mind of God—the pattern of the universe. It was an indivisible circle. Whether Newton intended his reconstruction of the Temple to be more than a memory landscape or model, defined in the mid–1680s in his work on the prophetic language, is impossible to say. However, in the 17th century, the art of memory was a practice that was evolving with the new science of natural philosophy. It was the basis of Bacon's and Descartes's inductive and deductive reasoning, respectively, that was later continued by Leibniz. Bacon, Descartes, and Leibniz published prolifically in their lifetimes and they articulated their theories to the scientific community. Newton did not. He published the *Principia* after considerable encouragement from

Edmund Halley—even then, he took a few years to complete it—and *Optics* was not published until 1703, twenty-five years after he had written it. He had waited to publish it until after the death of his nemesis, Robert Hooke, who had criticized the work when it had been originally written and presented to the Royal Society. As a consequence of his lack of desire to publish, many of Newton's manuscripts remained incomplete. Therefore, if Newton did use the Temple as a tool to order his scientific concepts, to facilitate a new philosophical ideal, he did not articulate his theory in written form. However, his manuscripts on the language of the prophets, in which he defined place and signification, do leave the possibility open.

John Maynard Keynes's comments on Newton are generally paraphrased as "Newton was the first scientist and the last magician." However, this implies two eras and two different personas and Newton's studies in alchemy, prophecy, and theology were not of the past era; they were very much embedded on his own era. His studies were based on reason and logic as he attempted to reconcile Biblical texts and natural philosophy. Although his scientific achievements were beyond the era in which he lived, he was a man of that era and continued to study and probe into the topics that were important at the time. Through his studies of alchemy, prophecy, theology, and particularly the Temple, it is possible to see the Newton of the late 17th and early 18th centuries by keeping him in context with his era.

Chapter Notes

Introduction

1. William Stukeley, "The Creation, Music of the Spheres K[ing] S[olomon's] Temple Microco[sm] and Macrocosm Compared &C," 1721–1724, FM MS 1130 Stu (1), London: Freemasons Library, London, 44, 127.

2. "Advertisement," *Daily Journal* London, December 8, 1724, Issue 1212: 2.

3. James Thomson, *The Works of Mr James Thomson* (London, 1802), 243.

4. *Ibid.*, 248.

5. "Advertisement," *Daily Courant*, Issue 7238, December 28, 1724: 3; *The Temple of Solomon with All Its Porches, Walls, Gates, Halls, Chambers, Holy Vessels, the Altar of Burnt-Offering, the Molten-Sea, Golden-Candlesticks, Shew-Bread Tables, Altar of Incense, the Ark of the Covenant, with the Mercy-Seat, the Cherubims Etc* (London, 1725), 3; "Advertisement," *Mist's Weekly Journal* London, Issue 67, August 6, 1726: 2; "Advertisement" *Daily Post* London, Issue 2359, April 15, 1727: 1

6. Patricia Fara, *Newton: The Making of Genius* (London: Picador, 2002), 161.

7. John Gage, "Blake's Newton," *Journal of the Warburg and Courtauld Institutes* 34 (1971): 373.

8. Harold Bloom, *William Blake* (London: Chelsea House, 2006), 22.

9. Tessa Morrison, *Isaac Newton's Temple of Solomon and His Reconstruction of Sacred Architecture* (Basel: Springer, 2011). See Figure 8.1 bar chart, which demonstrates the amount of literature written on natural philosophy, theology, and alchemy.

10. Lawrence M. Principle, *The Aspiring Adept: Robert Boyle and His Alchemical Quest* (Princeton, New Jersey: Princeton University Press, 1998).

11. Jose Faur, "Newton, Maimonidean," *Review of Rabbinic Judaism* 6, no. 2/3 (2003): 229.

12. John Maymard Keynes, "Newton the Man," in *Essays in Biography*, ed John Maymard Keynes (Cambridge: Cambridge University Press, 1972), 363–64.

13. William Wotton, quoted in Palmira Fontes da Costa, *Singular and the Making of Knowledge at the Royal Society of London in the Eighteenth Century* (Newcastle upon Tyne: Cambridge Scholars, 2013), 7.

14. Margery Purver, *The Royal Society: Concept and Creation* (London: Routledge, 2013), xvi.

15. Neil Kenny, *The Uses of Curiosity in Early Modern France and Germany* (Oxford: Oxford University Press, 2004), 111.

16. Barbara M. Benedict, *Curiosity: A Cultural History of Early Modern Inquiry* (Chicago: University of Chicago Press, 2001), 27.

17. Morrison, *Newton's Temple of Solomon*. See Figure 8.1 bar chart that demonstrates the amount of literature written on natural philosophy, theology, and alchemy.

18. Quoted in Chloë Houston, *The Renaissance Utopia: Dialogue, Travel and the Ideal Society* (Farnham: Ashgate, 2014), 121.

19. Joseph Mede, *Clavis Apocalyptica or a Prophetical Key* (London, 1651), 6.

20. Philip C. Almond, "Henry More and the Apocalypse," *Journal of the History of Ideas* 54, no. 2 (1993).

21. Isaac Newton, "Yahuda," n.d., MS 1.1, Jewish National and University Library, Jerusalem, p. 15r.

22. Almond, "Henry More"; Jeffrey K Jue, *Heaven Upon Earth: Joseph Mede (1586–1638) and the Legacy of Millenarianism* (Dordrecht: Springer, 2006).

23. Roy Porter, *Enlightenment Britain and the Creation of the Modern World* (London: Penguin, 2000), 99.

24. Jeremy Black, *Eighteenth Century British 1688–1783* (London: Palgrave, 2001), 150.

25. Derek Gjertsen, *The Newton Handbook* (New York: Kegan Paul, 1986), 88–90; Frank E. Manuel, *A Portrait of Isaac Newton* (Cambridge, MA: Belknap Press of Harvard University Press, 1968), 213–25; and Michael White, *Isaac Newton: The Last Sorcerer* (London: Fourth Estate, 1998), 222–53.

26. White, *Isaac Newton: The Last Sorcerer*, 262.

27. Isaac Newton, "Prolegomena Ad Lexici Propretici Partem Secundam: De Forma Sanctuary Judaici," n.d., mid-1680s–early 1690s, Babson MS 434, Babson College, Wellesley, MA.

28. "Drafts Concerning Solomon's Temple and the Sacred Cubit," n.d., ca. 1680, National Library of Israel, Jerusalem; "Untitled Treatise on Revelation," n.d., ca. 1670s–1680s, Yahuda MS 3, National library of Israel, Jerusalem; "Fragments on the Kingdoms of the European Tribes, the Temple and the History of Jewish and Christian Churches," n.d., ca. 1675–1685, Yahuda MS 28, National library of Israel, Jerusalem.

29. Isaac Newton, *The Chronology of Ancient Kingdoms Amended* (London: Histories & Mysteries of Man, 1988).

Chapter 1

1. http://www.newtonproject.sussex.ac.uk/prism.php?id=1.

2. Tessa Morrison, "The Paradox of the Divine Architecture in Dante's *La Divina Commedia*," *International Journal of Humanities* 8, no. 2 (2010); Tessa Morrison, "Planning to Welcome the Pilgrims of the Middle Ages," *The Journal of the Australian Early Medieval Association* 5 (2009).

3. Frank E. Manuel, *Isaac Newton: Historian* (Cambridge: Cambridge University Press, 1963), 48–49.

4. Isaac Newton, "Translation and Transcription of the 'Tabula Smaragdina' of Hermes Trismegistus," n.d., ca. 1680–1690, King's College, Cambridge.

5. Isaac Newton, "The Seven Chapters," n.d., ca. late 1680s, King's College, Cambridge.

6. Frances A. Yates, *Giordano Bruno and the Hermetic Tradition* (London: Routledge, 2002), 8.

7. Betty Jo Teeter Dobbs, "Newton's Commentary on the Emerald Tablet of Hermes Trismegistus," in *Its Scientific and Theological Significance, in Hermeticism and Renaissance: Intellectual History and the Occult in Early Modern Europe*, eds. Ingrid Merkel and Allen G. Debus (London: Associated University Presses, 1988).

8. Isaac Newton, "Appendix A 'Of natures obvious laws & processes in vegetation,'" in *The Janus Faces of Genius*, ed. B.J.T. Dobbs (Cambridge: Cambridge University Press, 2002), 276–277.

9. *Ibid.*, 269.

10. Isaac Newton, "Two Incomplete Treatises on the Vegetative Growth of Metals and Minerals," 1670–1675, NMAHRB MS 1007 B, Dibner Library, Smithsonian Institute, Washington, 1r.

11. Hermes Trismegist, "Tabula Smaragdina," in Dobbs, *Janus Faces of Genius*, 274.

12. Isaac Newton, "Commentarium," in Dobbs, *Janus Faces of Genius*, 275–277.

13. *Ibid.*, 277.

14. Bishop of Rochester, "An Account of Want Related to the Publishing of Sir Isaac Newton's Chronology of Ancient Kingdoms Amended (London, 1770)," in Newton, *Ancient Kingdoms Amended* (London, 1770), 7–8.

15. William Whiston, *Memoirs of the Life and Writings of Mr William Whiston* (London, 1749), 39.

16. For example, Newton, "Fragments on the Kingdoms" (see chap. 1, n. 28); Isaac Newton, "Notes from Buxtorf," n.d., National Library of Israel, Jerusalem; Isaac Newton, "Notes on Villalpando," n.d., National Library of Israel, Jerusalem.

17. Newton, *Ancient Kingdoms Amended* (1988), 1.

18. *Ibid.*, 8.

19. Vaughan Hart, *Art and Magic in the Court of the Stuarts* (London: Routledge, 1994), 32.

20. Newton, *Chronology of Ancient Kingdoms Amended* (1988), 15, 19.

21. *Ibid.*, 43.

22. *Ibid.*, 191.

23. *Ibid.*, 202.

24. *Ibid.*, 14.

25. *Ibid.*, 16.

26. *Ibid.*, 11.

27. *Ibid.*, 16.

28. *Ibid.*, 56.

29. *Ibid.*, 62.

30. *Ibid.*, 147.

31. *Ibid.*, 68.

32. *Ibid.*, 213.

33. Exodus: 25.

34. Newton, *Chronology of Ancient Kingdoms Amended*, 220.

35. *Ibid.*, 332.

36. *Ibid.*, 332.

37. *Ibid.*, 342.

38. In the floor plan of the Temple precinct in *The Chronology*, an external wall encloses the entire precinct wall. This external wall has four gates on the Western side, which were the Gate of Shallecheth, the Gate of Parbar, and the two Gates of Assupim. This wall and the gates belong to the Second Temple (1 Chronicles 26:16–18).

39. Isaac Newton, "Fair Copies of the 'Short Chronicle' and 'Chronology of Ancient Kingdoms Amended,'" n.d., Additional MS 3988, Cambridge University Library, Cambridge.

40. Maurizio Mamiani, "Newton on Prophecy and the Apocalypse," in *The Cambridge Companion to Newton*, ed. I. Bernard Cohen and George E. Smith (Cambridge: Cambridge University Press, 2002), 387; A. Rupert Hall, *Isaac Newton: Adventurer in Thought* (Cambridge: Cambridge University Press, 1992), 372–373; Michael Murrin, "Newton's Apocalypse," in *Newton and Religion: Context, Nature, and Influence*, ed. James E. Force and Richard H. Popkin (Dordrecht: Kluwer Academic, 1999), 209n32.

41. Gjertsen, *Newton Handbook*, 88–90 (see chap. 1, n. 25); Manuel, *Portrait of Isaac Newton*, 213–22 (see chap. 1, n. 25); White, *Isaac Newton: The Last Sorcerer*, 222–53 (see chap. 1, n. 25). At conferences, this is a commonly expressed sentiment at papers given by the author on this topic.

42. Almond, "Henry More," 189 (see chap. 1, n. 20); Jue, *Heaven Upon Earth*, 4–6 (see chap. 1, n. 22).

43. Florian Cajori, "Sir Isaac Newton's Early Study of the Apocalypse," *Popular Astronomy* XXXIV, no. 2 (1926).

44. Isaac Newton, *Observations on the Prophecies of Daniel and the Apocalypse of St. John* (Lewiston: Edwin Mellen Press, 1999), 259; Isaac Newton, "Irenicum," n.d., Keynes MS 3, King's College, Cambridge, fol. 48.

45. Isaac Newton, "Treatise on Revelation (Section 2)," n.d., Yahuda MS 9.2, National Library of Israel, Jerusalem, 2r.

46. *Ibid.*

47. *Ibid.*, 2r–3r.

48. Isaac Newton, "Two Incomplete Treatises on Prophecy," n.d., Keynes MS 5, King's College Library, Cambridge, v.

49. *Ibid.*, 6v.

50. Isaac Newton, "Extract from 'the Original of Religions,'" n.d., Yahuda MS 41, National Library of Israel, Jerusalem, 6v.

51. Exodus 25.

52. Tessa Morrison, "Bede and the Temple of Solomon," *The Journal of the Australian Early Medieval Association* 3 (2007): 243.

53. Bede, *On the Temple*, trans. Sean Connolly (Liverpool: Liverpool University Press, 1995).

54. See Tessa Morrison, "Villalpando's Sacred Architecture in the Light of Isaac Newton's Commentary" in ed. Kim Williams, *Nexus VII: Architecture and Mathematics* (Turin: Kim Williams, 2008), 79–91.

55. Isaac Newton, "A Treatise or Remarks on Solomon's Temple," n.d., ca. mid-1680s, Babson College, Wellesley, MA, 53r. All quotations from Babson MS 434 are translated from Latin by the author.

56. *Ibid.*, 29r (*Intervalla harum basium ex rationibus architectonicis non debent esse minora basibus*).

57. *Ibid.*, 36r (*quam posuerim sextuplam crassitudinis more Dorico*).

58. *Ibid.*, 45r (*Erat autem latitudo decem cubitorum et altitudo justa regulas architectarum debet esse dupla latitudinis.*); Vitruvius, *The Ten Books on Architecture*, trans. Morris Hicky Morgan (New York: Dover, 1960), IV, vi, 6.

59. Newton, "Remarks on Solomon's Temple," 10r (*Architecturae ratio postulat*).

60. For full translation of Babson MS 434 see Morrison, *Newton's Temple of Solomon* (see chap. 1, n. 9).

61. Newton, "Remarks on Solomon's Temple," 31rff.

62. Newton, "Treatise on Revelation (Section 2)"; Newton, "Incomplete Treatises on Prophecy," 28v.

63. Ezekiel 40:5.

64. Newton, "Drafts Concerning Solomon's Temple" (see chap. 1, n. 28).

65. Newton, "A Dissertation Upon the Sacred Cubit of the Jews" in *Miscellaneous Works of John Greaves Professor of Geometry at Oxford* (Londres, 1737).

66. See chap. 5 in Morrison, *Newton's Temple of Solomon* (see chap. 1, n. 9).

67. Newton, "Remarks on Solomons Temple," 27.

68. *Ibid.*, 43.

69. Newton, "Sacred Cubit of the Jews," 422.

70. Vitruvius, *Ten Books on Architecture*, 3.1.3.

71. Tessa Morrison, "The Body, the Temple and the Newtonian Conundrum," *Nexus: Architecture and Mathematics* 12, no. 2 (2010).

72. Richard Westfall, *Never at Rest: A Biography of Isaac Newton* Cambridge: Cambridge University Press, 1980), 346; Dobbs, *Janus Faces of Genius*, 153.

73. Newton, "Solomon's Temple and the Sacred Cubit" (see chap. 1, n. 28).

74. John Harrison, *The Library of Isaac Newton* (Cambridge: Cambridge University Press, 1978).

Chapter 2

1. Martin S. Briggs, "Architectural Models I," *The Burlington Magazine for Connoisseurs* 54, no. 313 (1929): 175.

2. Tessa Morrison and Michael Ostwald, "Shifting Dimensions: The Architectural Model in History," in *Homo Faber: Modelling Architecture*, ed. Mark Bury et al. (Melbourne: SIAL, Melbourne Museum and Archadia Press, 2007), 143.

3. J.A. Sakellarakis, *Herakleion Museum* (Athens: Ekdotike Athenon, 2001), 54.

4. Vitruvius, *Ten Books on Architecture*, I, I, 14 (see chap. 2, n. 58).

5. *Ibid.*, X. xvi, 3.

6. *Ibid.*, X, xvi, 6.

7. *Ibid.*, X, xvi, 12.

8. Plato, *Plato's Republic*, trans. G.M.A. Grube (Indianapolis: Hackett, 1974), 65.

9. Giorgio Vasari, *Lives of the Most Eminent Painters, Sculptors and Architects*, trans. Gaston du C. de Vere (New York: Harry N. Abrams, 1979), 114.

10. Cesare Guasti, ed. *Santa Maria del Fiore: La costruzione* (Firenze: M. Ricci,1887). See documents 150, 169, 170, 176, and 341.

11. Vasari, *Lives*, 354.

12. Henry A. Millon and Vittorio Magnago Lampugnani, *The Renaissance from Brunelleschi to Michelangelo: The Representation of Architecture* (London: Thames and Hudson, 1994), 19.

13. Vasari, *Lives*, 398.

14. *Ibid.*, 400.

15. *Ibid.*, 402.

16. *Ibid.*, 403.

17. Millon and Lampugnani, *Brunelleschi to Michelangelo*, 21.

18. *Ibid.*, 408–409.

19. Leon Battista Alberti, *On the Art of Building in Ten Books* (Cambridge Massachusetts: MIT Press, 1988), 33–34.

20. Vasari, *Lives*, 1398.

21. *Ibid.*, 1279.

22. *Ibid.*, 1280.

23. Millon and Lampugnani, *Brunelleschi to Michelangelo*, 35.

24. Vasari, *Lives*, 1889.

25. *Ibid.*, 1889, 1891, 1896, 1899, 1908, 1910–1912 and 1916.

26. James A. Ackerman, *The Architecture of Michelangelo* (London: A. Zwemmer Ltd., 1966), 7–8.

27. Vasari, *Lives*, 1909.

28. *Ibid.*, 1908.

29. Ackerman, *Architecture of Michelangelo*, 9.

30. John Wilton-Ely, "The Architectural Model," *Architectural Review* 104 (1967): 27.

31. Briggs, "Architectural Models II," 246.

32. *Ibid.*

33. Henry Wotton, *The Elements of Architecture* (Amsterdam: Da Capo Press, 1979).

34. Hooke was later a professor of geometry at Gresham College and after the Great Fire of London in 1666 became an architect and clerk of work with Christopher Wren.

35. Stephen Inwood, *The Man Who Knew Too Much* (London: Pan Books, 2002).

36. *Ibid.*; Robert Lomas, *The Invisible College: The Royal Society, Freemasonry and the Birth of Modern Science* (London: Headline, 2002).

37. Kerry Downes, *The Architecture of Wren* (Over Wallop: Granada, 1988), 31.

38. Pratt, quoted in John Wilton-Ely, "The Architectural Model: English Baroque," *Apollo* 88 (1968): 252.

39. Inwood, *Knew Too Much*, 96.

40. Robert E. Stillman, *The New Philosophy and Universal Languages in Seventeenth Century England* (London: Associated University Presses, 1995), 24.

41. Briggs, "Architectural Models II," 246.

42. Downes, *Architecture of Wren*, 45.

43. Briggs, "Architectural Models II," 247.

44. John Summerson, quoted in Lomas, *Invisible College*, 44.

45. Lomas, *Invisible College*, 43; Wilton-Ely, "Architectural Model: English Baroque," 28.

46. Christopher Wren, quoted in Wilton-Ely, "Architectural Model: English Baroque," 253.

47. Christopher Wren, *Parentalia: Memoirs of the Family of the Wrens* (Londres,1750), 280.

48. *Ibid.*

49. *Ibid.*, 282.

50. *Ibid.*

51. Downes, *Architecture of Wren*, 48.

52. Wren, *Parentalia*, 283.

53. Wilton-Ely, "Architectural Model: English Baroque," 254.

54. *Ibid.*

55. William Stukeley, *The Family Memoirs of the Rev William Stukeley MD and the Antiquarians and Other Correspondence of William*

Stukeley, Roger and Samuel Gales Etc (Edinburgh: William Blackwood, 1883), 320, 470.

56. Tessa Morrison, *The Origins of Architecture: An English Sixteenth to Eighteenth Century Perspective* (Champaign, IL: Common Ground, 2014).

Chapter 3

1. Bede, *On the Temple*, 4.3, 13.1, 18.5 (see chap. 2, n. 53).

2. Mary Carruthers, *The Craft of Thought: Mediation, Rhetoric, and the Imaging of Images, 400–1200* (Cambridge: Cambridge University Press, 2000), 184.

3. Bede, *On the Temple*, 1.1.

4. Bede, *On the Tabernacle*, trans. Arthur G. Holder (Liverpool: Liverpool University Press, 1994), 2.1.42–43.

5. *Ibid.*, 2.1.43.

6. Exodus 25.8–9.

7. Bede, *On the Temple*, 3.5.

8. Bede, *The Ecclesiastical History of the English People*, trans. Judith McClure and Roger Collins (Oxford: Oxford University Press, 1994), 1.7.

9. *Ibid.*, 1.33.

10. *Ibid.*, 2.14.

11. *Ibid.*, 3.23.

12. *Ibid.*, 3.25.

13. *Ibid.*, 5.16.

14. *Ibid.*, 5.20.

15. Otto von Simson, *The Gothic Cathedral: Origins of Gothic Architecture and the Medieval Concept of Order* (Princeton: Princeton University Press, 1984), 37–38.

16. M.T. Clanchy, *Abelard: A Medieval Life* (Oxford: Blackwell Publisher, 1999), 30; von Simson, *Gothic Cathedral*, 37.

17. Philo, "On the Life of Moses," in *The Works of Philo*, ed. C.D. Yonge (Peabody,: Hendrickson, 2004), II, 115.

18. von Simson, *Gothic Cathedral*, 38.

19. Plato, *Plato's Republic* (see chap 3, n. 8).

20. Carruthers, *Craft of Thought*, 258.

21. von Simson, *Gothic Cathedral*, 134.

22. Erwin Panofsky, *Abbot Suger* (Princeton: Princeton University Press, 1948), 61.

23. Sumner McKnight Crosby, *The Royal Abbey of Saint-Denis: From Its Beginnings to the Death of Suger, 475–1151* (New Haven: Yale University Press, 1987), 222.

24. Harold W. Turner, *From Temple to Meeting House: The Phenomenology and Theology of Places of Worship* (New York: Mouton, 1979), 191.

25. Helen Rosenau, *Vision of the Temple: The Image of the Temple of Jerusalem in Judaism and Christianity* (London: Oresko, 1979), 37.

26. Reproductions can be seen in Walter Cahn, "Architecture and Exegesis: Richard of St.-Victor's Ezekiel Commentary and Its Illustrations," *The Art Bulletin* 76, no. 1 (1994), fig. 6 and 7; Rosenau, *Vision of the Temple*, plate 25.

27. See the Trinity Apocalypse in J. Williams, *The Illustrated Beatus: A Corpus of the Illustrations of the Commentary on the Apocalypse* (London: Harvey, 1998).

28. Rosenau, *Vision of the Temple*, plates 41, 43, 45.

29. *Ibid.*, plate 38.

30. Cahn, "Architecture and Exegesis."

31. Joseph Rykwert, "Theory as Rhetoric: Leon Battista Alberti in Theory and in Practice," in *Paper Palaces: The Rise of the Renaissance*, ed. Vaughan Hart and Peter Hicks (New Haven: Yale University Press, 1998), 45.

32. Francis Wromald, "The Throne of Solomon and St. Edward's Chair," in *De Artibus Opuscula XI: Essays in Honor of Erwin Panofsky*, ed. Millard Meiss (New York: New York University Press, 1961), 539.

33. F. Donald Logan, *A History of the Church in the Middle Ages* (London: Routledge, 2002), 337.

34. George Anthony Bull and George Bull, *Michelangelo: A Biography* (London: St Martin's Press, 1998), 12.

35. L.D. Ettlinger, *The Sistine Chapel before Michelangelo: Religious Imagery and Papal Primacy* (Oxford: Clarendon Press, 1965), 93.

36. Ian Campbell, "The New St Peter's: Basilica or Temple?," *Oxford Art Journal* 4, no. 1 (1981): 3–4.

37. Turner, *Temple to Meeting House*, 195.

38. Rudolf Wittkower, *Architectural Principles in the Age of Humanism* (London Academy Editions, 1988), 2.

39. Turner, *Temple to Meeting House*, 206.

40. John Calvin, *Institutes of the Christian Religion*, trans. Henry Beveridge (Grand Rapids: W.M.B. Eerdman, 1957), iv, I. 5.

41. Calvin, *Institutes of the Christian Religion*.

42. *Ibid.*, iv, ii, 3.

43. *Ibid.*, III, xx, 30.

44. Calvin, quoted in Ronald S. Wallace, *Calvin, Geneva and the Reformation* (Edinburgh: Scottish Academic Press, 1988), 134.

45. Calvin, quoted in Turner, *Temple to Meeting House*, 207.

46. Hubert Jedin, *Crisis and Closure of the Council of Trent* (London: Sheed and Ward, 1967), 6.

47. Robert E. McNally, *The Council of Trent, the "Spiritual Exercises," and the Catholic Reform* (Philadelphia: Fortress Press, 1970), vi.

48. Mendell Lewittes, ed., *The Code of Maimonides (Mishneh Torah): Book Eight, the Book of Temple Service* (New Haven: Yale University Press, 1957).

49. Ptolemy, *The Almagest*, trans. R. Catesby Taliaferro (Chicago: Encyclopaedia Britannica, 1955).

50. Juan Bautista Villalpando and Hieronymus Prado, *Ezechielem Explanationes Et Apparatus Urbis Hierosolymitani Commentariis Et Imaginibus Illustratus* (Romae, 1604), 417.

51. R. Wishnitzer, "Maimonides' Drawing of the Temple," *Journal of Jewish Art* 1 (1974).

52. Rosenau, *Vision of the Temple*, 92.

53. Claude Perrault, *Ordonnance Des Cinq Especes De Colonne* (Paris, 1683), xviii.

54. Wolfgang Herrmann, "Unknown Designs for the Temple of Jerusalem," in *Essays in the History of Architecture*, ed. Douglas Fraser, Howard Hibbard, and Milton J. Lewine (Bath: Pitman Press, 1969).

55. Herrmann, "Unknown Designs," 146; Morrison, *Origins of Architecture* (see chap. 3, n. 56).

56. Hanno-Walter Kruft, *A History of Architectural Theory: From Vitruvius to the Present* (New York: Princeton Architectural Press, 1994), 177.

57. Kruft, *History of Architectural Theory*; Herrmann, "Unknown Designs," 146.

58. Peter van Rooden, "The Jews and Religious Toleration in the Dutch Republic," in *Calvinism and Religious Toleration in the Dutch Golden Age*, ed. Ronnie Po-chia Hsia and Henk van Nierop (Cambridge: Cambridge University Press, 2001), 135.

59. Peter T. van Rooden, *Theology, Biblical Scholarship and Rabbinical Studies in the Seventeenth Century* (Leiden: Brill, 1989), 166.

60. Villalpando and Prado, *Ezechielem Explanationes*.

61. These examples are only a few of the most influential and significant reconstructions from the seventeenth century to highlight the differences in the reconstructions. For a wide view of the reconstructions of the Temple see Rosenau, *Vision of the Temple*.

62. Samuel Lee, *Orbis Miraculum, or, the Temple of Solomon, Pourtrayed by Scripture-Light Wherein All Its Famous Buildings, the Pompous Worship of the Jewes, with Its Attending Rites and Ceremonies, the Several Officers Employed in That Work, with Their Ample Revenues, and the Spiritual Mysteries of the Gospel Railed under All, Are Treated of at Large* (London: Printed by John Streater for Abell Roper, 1659), Preface.

63. Lee, *Orbis Miraculum*, Preface.

64. Christopher Wren, *Life and Works of Sir Christopher Wren. From the Parentalia or Memoirs by His Son Christopher* (London, 1750), 250.

65. *Ibid.*, 242.

66. Stukeley, "Music of the Spheres," 74.

67. Drawn by author from *ibid.*., 91.

68. William Stukeley, *Memoirs of Sir Isaac Newton's Life.*

69. Stukeley, "Music of the Spheres," 44.

70. Stukeley, *Family Memoirs*, 262 (see chap. 3, n. 55).

71. Isaac Newton, *Miscellaneous Notes and Extracts on the Temple, the Fathers, Prophecy, Church History, Doctrinal Issues, Etc.*, n.d., National Library of Israel, Jerusalem, 32r.

72. *Ibid.*

73. *Ibid.*, 12.

74. *Ibid.*, 46.

75. *Ibid.*, 46.

76. *Ibid.*, 56.

77. Marsha Keith Schuchard, *Restoring the Temple of Vision* (Leiden: Brill, 2002), 186.

78. Roy Strong, *Britannia Triumphans: Inigo Jones, Rubens and Whitehall Palace* (Hampshire: Thames and Hudson, 1980), 61.

79. Ignatius of Loyola, *Personal Writings: Reminiscences, Spiritual Diary, Selected Letters Including the Text of "the Spiritual Exercises,"* trans. Joseph A. Munitiz and Philip Endean (London: Penguin, 1996).

80. *Ibid.*, 294.

Chapter 4

1. Helen Rosenau, "Jacob Judah Leon Templo's Contribution to Architectural Imagery," *Journal of Jewish Studies* XXIII, no. 1 (1972): 73; John Wilton-Ely, "The Architectural Models of Sir John Soane: A Catalogue," *Architectural History* 12 (1969): 6.

2. "Advertisement," *London Journal* London, Issue CCLXVI, August 29, 1724: 2.

3. "Advertisement," *Daily Courant* London, Issue 7222, December 8, 1724: 2.

4. "Advertisment," *London Journal*, 2; "Advertisement," *Daily Courant*, 2.

5. George J. Buelow, "Opera in Hamburg 300 Years Ago," *The Musical Times* 119, no. 1619 (1978): 26.

6. *All Its Porches* (see chap. 1, n. 5).

7. Harry Ryland, "Schott's Model of Solomon's Temple," *Ars Quatuor Coronatorum* 13 (1900): 24.

8. *Ibid.*

9. Harry Ryland, "Rabbi Jacab Jehudan Leon," *Freemason* 22, July (1882): 414.

10. Ryland, "Schott's Model," 25.

11. Thomas Osborne (Bookseller), *A Catalogue of a Choice and Valuable Collection of Books: Being the Libraries of a Late Eminent Serjeant at Law, and of Dr Edmund Halley, Late Astronomer Royal ... Which Will Begin to Be Sold, the Price Marked in Each Book, at T. Osborne's Shop ... On Thursday the Twentieth of May ... Where Is Also to Be Sold as It Was Sent from the Holy Land, as a Present to the Said Late Doctor, a Most Curious and Compleat Model of the Whole Temple of Christ's Sepulchre at Jerusalem* (London, 1742), n.p.

12. "To Be Sold by Auction," *Gazetteer and New Daily Advertiser* London, April 27, 1769: 3.

13. "To Be Sold at Auction," *Public Advertiser* London, Issue 14063, October 26, 1774: 3.

14. "For the Public Advertiser," *Public Advertiser* London, Issue 16196, April 19, 1786: 3.

15. "Advertisement," *Daily Courant*, Issue 7238, December 28, 1724: 2.

16. "Classified Advertisement," *Daily Courant* London, Issue 9088, November 12, 1730: 2.

17. "Advertisement," *Daily Post* London, Issue 1690, February 24, 1725: 2.

18. "Advertisement," *Mist's Weekly Journal* London, Issue 67, August 6, 1726: 2.

19. "Advertisement," *Mist's Weekly Journal*, August 6, 1726: 2.

20. *The Tryal of William Whiston, Clerk for Defaming and Denying the Holy Trinity before the Lord Chief Justice Reason* (London, 1740).

21. William Whiston, "A Collection of Authentick Records Belonging to the Old and New Testament," (London: The British Library, 1727), 1070.

22. "Advertisment," *Daily Courant* Tuesday, December 8, 1724: 2.

23. William Whiston, "To Caleb Dánvers," *Country Journal or the Craftsman* London, Issue 185, January 17, 1930: 2.

24. "Classified Ads," *Daily Courant* London, Issue 9149, February 2, 1731: 2.

25. "Classified Advertisements," *Daily Post* London, Issue 3608, April 12, 1731: 2.

26. "Advertisment," *Daily Courant*, December 8, 1724: 2.

27. "Classified Advertisement," *Daily Post* London, Issue 2772, August 9, 1728: 2.

28. "Classified Advertisement," *Daily Post* London, Issue 2887, December 24, 1728: 2;

"Classified Advertisement," *Daily Journal* London, Issue 2517, January 31, 1729: 2.

29. "Advertisement," *Daily Journal* London, Issue 2115, October 24, 1727,).

30. "Classified Advertisements" *Daily Journal*, January 31, 1729: 2.

31. "Classified Advertisement," *Daily Courant* London, Issue 9080, November 12, 1730: 2.

32. Michael Korey, "The Temple of Solomon and the Jewish Cabinet in the Dresden Zwinger: A Search for Their Historical Traces," in *Fragments of Memory*, ed. Michael Korey and Thomas Ketelsen (Dresden: Deutscher Kunstverlag, 2010), 15.

33. *Ibid.*, 21.

34. *Ibid.*, 35.

35. W.J. Chetwode Crawley, "Rabbi Jacob Jehudah Leon," *Ars Quatuor Coronatorum* 12 (1899): 153.

36. Al L. Shane, "Jacob Judah Leon of Amsterdam (1602–1675) and His Models of the Temple of Solomon and the Tabernacle," *Ars Quatuor Coronatorum* 96 (1983): 149.

37. *Ibid.*, 148.

38. A.K. Offenberg, "Jacob Jehuda Leon (1602–1675) and His Model of the Temple," in *Jewish-Christian Relations in the Seventeenth Century*, ed. J. van den Berg and Ernestine G.E. van der Wall (Dordrecht: Kluwer Academic Publishers, 1988), 95.

39. *Ibid.*, 98.

40. Richard H. Popkin and David S Katz, "The Prefaces by Menasseh Ben Israel and Jacob Judah Leon Templo to the Vocalised Mishnah (1646)," in van den Berg and van der Wall, *Jewish-Christian Relations*, 152–53.

41. Offenberg, "Jacob Jehuda Leon," 32.

42. van Rooden, "Jews and Religious Toleration," 133 (see chap. 4, n. 58).

43. Offenberg, "Jacob Jehuda Leon," 32.

44. Jacob Jehudah Leon, *Retrato Del Templo De Selomoh* (Amsterdam, 1642).

45. Jacob Jehudah Leon, *Afbeeldinghe Vanden Templel Salomonis* (Amsterdam, 1642).

46. Lewis Edwards, "Notes," *Ars Quatuor Coronatorum* 73, no. 1961 (1996): 52.

47. *Ibid.*, 54.

48. Offenberg, "Jacob Jehuda Leon," 105.

49. Gary Schwartz, "The Temple Mount in the Lowlands," in *The Dutch Intersection: The Jews and the Netherlands in Modern History*, ed. Yosef Kaplan (Leiden: Brill, 2008), 111.

50. Ernestine G.E. van der Wall, "Without Partialities Towards All Men: John Durie on the Dutch Hebraist Adam Boreel," in van den Berg and van der Wall, *Jewish-Christian Relations*, 148.

51. A.K. Offenberg, "Dirk Van Santen and the Keur Bible: New Insights into Jacob Judah (Arye) Leon Templo's Model Temple," *Studia Rosenthaliana* 37 (2004): 403.

52. Shane, "Jacob Judah Leon," 162; Offenberg, "Dirk Van Santen," 407.

53. M.P. De Castro, "To the Reader," in Jacob Jehudah Leon, *An Accurate Description of the Grand & Glorious Temple of Solomon*, trans. M.P. Decastre (London, 1778), iii.

54. Shane, "Jacob Judah Leon," 153–54.

55. Leon, *Afbeeldinghe Vanden Templel*.

56. Shane, "Jacob Judah Leon," 151.

57. Offenberg, "Jacob Jehuda Leon," 107.

58. Leon, translated by Shane, "Jacob Judah Leon," 50.

59. Edwards, "Notes," 54.

60. For a full list of Leon's publications see A.K. Offenberg, "Bibliography of the Works of Jacob Jehudah Leon (Templo)," *Studia Rosenthaliana* 12, July (1978).

61. *Ibid.*, 111–12.

62. Jacob Jehudah Leon, *A Relation of the Most Memorable Thinges in the Tabernacle of Moses and the Temple of Solomon According to Text of Scripture* (Amsterdam, 1675), 16.

63. Leon, *Accurate Description*, 2.

64. Jac Zwart, "Oud-Hollandse Modellen Van De Temple Van Salomo," *Historia Maaudschrift voor Geschiedenis en Kunstgeschiedenis* 4 (1938): 282.

65. De Castro, "To the Reader," ii.

66. Translated by Shane, "Jacob Judah Leon," 155.

67. Johannes Saubertus and Jacob Jehudah Leon, *De Templo Hierosolymitano* (Helmæstadi, 1665).

68. Shane, "Jacob Judah Leon," 156.

69. M. Narkiss, "The Oeuvre of the Jewish Engraver Salom Italia," *Tarbiz: A Quarterly of Jewish Studies* XXVI, no. 1 (1956): vii–viii.

70. Jacob Jehudah Leon, *Tratado de los Cherubim* (Amsterdam, 1654).

71. For example, Leon, *De Templo Hierosolymi*, 38, 39, 41, 43, 45, 54, 57, 62, 63, 89, 92, 93, 102, 103, 122, 123, 149, 154, 157, 184, 188.

72. J.A. Worp, *Rijks Geschiedkundige Publikaten* 32 (1917): 274.

73. Lucien Wolf, "Anglo-Jewish Coat of Arms," *The Jewish Historical Society of England* (1893–94), 156.

74. James Picciotto, *Sketches of Anglo-Jewish History* (London: Trubner, 1875), 43.

75. Leon, *Most Memorable Thinges*, Dedication, n.p.

76. Wolf, "Coat of Arms," 157.

77. Picciotto, *Sketches*, 45.

78. Shane, "Jacob Judah Leon," 153.

79. Lawrence Dermott, *Ahiman Rezon* (London, 1764), xxxiv.

80. Marsha Keith Schuchard, "Dr. Samuel Jacob Falk: A Sabbation Adventurer in the Masonic Underground" in *Jewish Messianism in the Early Modern World*, ed. Matt Goldish and Richard H. Popkin (Dordrecht: Kluwer Academic, 2001), 208.

81. Ryland, "Rabbi Jacab Jehudan Leon," 414.

82. Shane, "Jacob Judah Leon," 158.

83. *Ibid.*, 162.

84. . Robert Hooke, The Dairy of Robert Hooke M.A., M.D., F.R.S, 1672–1680 (London: Taylor & Francis), 179.

85. Wolf, "Coat of Arms," 157; Crawley, "Rabbi Jacob Jehudah Leon.".

86. Wolf, "Coat of Arms," 157.

87. *Ibid.*

88. Dermott, *Ahiman Rezon*, xxxv.

89. Jacob Jehudah Leon, *Retrato Del Tabernaculo De Moseh* (Amsterdam: 1654).

90. Villalpando and Prado, *Ezechielem Explanationes*, chap. 24 and 25 (see chap. 4, n. 50).

91. Leon, *Accurate Description*, title page.

92. "Advertisement," *'s Gravenhaegse Courant*, May 10, 1771: 4.

93. Moses De Castro, "Preface," in Leon, *Accurate Description*, ii.

94. Offenberg, "Dirk Van Santen," 417.

95. Morrison, "Newtonian Conundrum," 96 (see chap. 2, n. 71).

96. Thomas Hunt, "Preface," in *The Chronology of Ancient Kingdoms Amended* (London, 1770), 5.

Chapter 5

1. Jacob Jehudah Leon, *A Relation of the Most Memorable Thinges in the Tabernacle of Moses and the Temple of Solomon* (Amsterdam: 1675), 13.

2. Leon, *Most Memorable Things*, 19.

3. Leon, *Accurate Description*, 1 (see chap. 5, n. 53).

4. *All Its Porches*, A1 (see chap. 1, n. 5).

5. Harrison, *Library of Isaac Newton*, 103 (see chap. 2, n. 74).

6. *All Its Porches*, iv.

7. Leon, *Accurate Description*, 12.

8. *All Its Porches*, 2.

9. *Ibid.*

10. *Ibid.*, A2.

11. *Ibid.*

12. *Ibid.*, 6.

13. *Ibid.*, 24.

14. *Ibid.*, 32.

15. This example is from the Gale database Eighteenth Century Collections Online, sourced from the British Library.

16. Frances A. Yates, *The Art of Memory* (Chicago: University of Chicago Press, 1966).

17. *Ibid.*, 77.

18. *Ibid.*, 174.

19. Paola Casini, "Newton, the Classical Scholia," *History of Science* 22 (1984): 95.

20. Yates, *Art of Memory*, 129–72.

21. Anna Maria Busse Berger, *Medieval Music and the Art of Memory* (Berkeley: University of California Press, 2005); Paolo Rossi, *Logic and the Art of Memory: The Quest for a Universal Language*, trans. Stephen Clucas (Chicago: University of Chicago Press, 2006).

22. Isaac Newton, "The Original of Religions," n.d., Yahuda MS 41, Jewish National and University Library, Jerusalem, 7r.

23. *Ibid.*, 5r.

24. Casini, "Classical Scholia," 8.

25. Dobbs, *Janus Faces of Genius*, 166.

26. Isaac Newton, "Of an Universall Language," *Modern Languages Review* LII, no. 1 (1957).

27. Rossi, *Art of Memory*, 145–75.

28. Francis Bacon, "Advancement of Learning," in *The Works of Francis Bacon*, ed. James Spedding (London: Longman, 1858), 437.

29. Rossi, *Art of Memory*, 145.

30. Bacon, "Advancement of Learning," 435.

31. *Ibid.*, 436.

32. Rene Descartes, "Cogitations Privatae," in *La Vie de Monsieur Descartes*, ed. Adrien Baillet (Paris, 1691), 83; Rossi, *Art of Memory*, 112.

33. Rossi, *Art of Memory*, 113.

34. Harrison, *Library of Isaac Newton*, 93 (see chap. 2, n. 74).

35. Niccolò Guicciardini, *Isaac Newton on Mathematical Certainty and Method* (Cambridge Massachusetts: MIT Press, 2009), 22–23; James E. McGuire and Martin Tamny, *Certain Philosophical Questions: Newton's Trinity Notebook* (Cambridge: Cambridge University Press, 1983), 127–94.

36. McGuire and Tamny, *Newton's Trinity Notebook*, 194.

37. Isaac Newton, "Questiones Quaedam Philosophiae," early 1660s, Cambridge University Library, Cambridge, 75.

38. *Ibid.*, 41.

39. *Ibid.*

40. *Ibid.*

41. Ronald Graham, *Combinatorics: Ancient & Modern* (Oxford: Oxford University Press, 2013).

42. Harrison, *Library of Isaac Newton*, 183–84.

43. Newton, "Incomplete Treatises on Prophecy," Ir (see chap. 2, n. 48).

44. *Ibid.*, Vr.

45. Newton, "The Original of Religions," 1r–7r.

46. Morrison, "Villalpando's Sacred Architecture" (see chap. 2, n. 54).

Chapter 6

1. Isaac Newton, *Observations Upon the Prophecies*, ed. Samuel Horsley (London: Opera omnia, 1785), 254.

2. Daniel 12:4.

3. Revelation 11:19.

4. Newton, *Observations Upon the Prophecies*, 273.

5. Newton, "Growth of Metals and Minerals," 1r (see chap. 2, no. 10).

6. Newton, *Observations Upon the Prophecies*, 16.

7. Newton, "The Original of Religions," 5r (see chap. 6, n. 22).

8. Exodus 25:10.

9. Newton, "The Original of Religions," 5r.

10. *Ibid.*, 6r.

11. Isaac Newton, "A Treatise or Remarks on Solomon's Temple Introduction to the Lexicon of the Prophets, Part Two: About the Appearance of the Jewish Temple," in *Newton's Temple of Solomon and His Reconstruction of Sacred Architecture*, ed. Tessa Morrison (Basel: Birkhauser, 2011), 106.

12. *Ibid.*, 147.

13. Newton believed strongly in the harmony and symmetry of the universe and architecture. The harmony in the universe proved the existence of God and the harmony of architecture was God's invention.

14. Newton, "Sacred Cubit of the Jews," 425 (see chap. 2, n. 65).

15. Newton, "Introduction to the Lexicon," 146.

16. *Ibid.*, 145–6.

17. *Ibid.*, 106.

18. Ezekiel claimed there were twenty cubits of pavement on each side of the Temple. However, this figure contradicts his other figures. Newton makes a complex argument to show that the twenty cubits mentioned by the prophet included the thickness

of the wall of the Temple. This resolved the contradiction. Newton, "Introduction to the Lexicon," 155nh.

19. These fifteen rooms are not consistent, although in Babson MS 434, he also mentioned that there are twelve rooms.

20. Newton, "Introduction to the Lexicon," 148.

21. In his drawing of the temple (see Plate 9) and the brief description that is included in that drawing, he stated there are eight rooms alongside the temple and a further four on the other side of the walkway. In this second plan, there are now a total of fifteen.

22. Newton, "Introduction to the Lexicon," 148.

23. *Ibid.*, 112.

24. *Ibid.*, 141.

25. Newton, "Incomplete Treatises on Prophecy," Vr.

26. Newton, *Observations Upon the Prophecies*, 257.

27. Newton, "Introduction to the Lexicon," 120.

28. *Ibid.*, 144.

29. In fact, this adds up to 98 cubits. Newton has forgotten to write the 2 cubits of the wall between the holy place and the holy of holies, but clearly he has added it in. Newton, "Introduction to the Lexicon," 145.

Conclusion

1. Stephen D. Snobelen, "To Discourse of God: Isaac Newton's Heterodox Theology and His Natural Philosophy" (London: Ashgate, 2004), 39; Jose Faur, "Newton, Maimonides, and Esoteric Knowledge" *Cross Currents* 40, no. 4 (1990), 546.

2. Morrison, "Villalpando's Sacred Architecture" (see chap. 2, n. 54).

3. Stukeley, *Sir Isaac Newton's Life*, 18 (see chap. 4, n. 68).

4. Kelly J. Whitmer, "The Model That Never Moved: The Case of a Virtual Memory Theater and Its Christian Philosophical Argument, 1700–1732," *Science in Context* 23, no. 3 (2010).

5. Edward Edwards, *Lives of the Founders of the British Museum* (London: Routledge, 1996), 195.

6. Susan Pearce, "Introduction" in *Lives of the Founders of the British Museum*, ed. Edward Edwards (London: Routledge, 1996), xiv.

7. Francis Bacon, *The Letters and the Life of Francis Bacon*, Vol. I, ed. James Spedding (London: Longman, Green, Longman and Roberts, 1861), 335.

8. Arthur MacGregor, "The Cabinet of Curiosities in Seventeenth Century Britiain" in *The Origins of Museums: The Cabinet of Curiosities in Sixteenth and Seventeenth-Century Europe*, eds. Oliver Impey and Arthur MacGregor (London: House of Stratus, 2001), 205.

9. Leon, *Accurate Description*, A (see chap. 5, n. 53).

10. *All Its Porches,* Preface, n.p. (see chap. 1, n. 5).

11. Morrison, *Newton's Temple of Solomon*, 102 (see chap. 1, n. 9).

12. For example, Newton, *Prophecies of Daniel* (see chap. 2, n. 44); Newton, "Untitled Treatise on Revelation" (see chap. 1, n. 28).

Bibliography

Ackerman, James A. *The Architecture of Michelangelo*. London: A. Zwemmer, 1966.

"Advertisement." *Daily Courant* London, Tuesday, December 8, Issue 7222 (1724): 2.

"Advertisement." *Daily Courant* London, Monday, December 28, Issue 7238 (1724): 3.

"Advertisement." *Daily Journal* London, Tuesday December 8, Issue 1212 (1724): 2.

"Advertisement." *Daily Journal* London, Tuesday, October 24, Issue 2115 (1727): 2.

"Advertisement. " *Daily Post* London, Wednesday, February 24, Issue 1690 (1725): 2.

"Advertisement." *Daily Post* London, Saturday, April 15, Issue 2359 (1727): 1.

"Advertisement." *London Journal* London, Saturday, August 29, Issue CCLXVI (1724): 2.

"Advertisement." *Mist's Weekly Journal* London, Saturday, August 6, Issue 67 (1726): 2.

"Advertisement." *Gravenhaegse Courant*, May 10 (1771): 4.

Alberti, Leon Battista. *On the Art of Building in Ten Books*. Cambridge, MA: The MIT Press, 1988.

Almond, Philip C. "Henry More and the Apocalypse." *Journal of the History of Ideas* 54, no. 2 (1993): 189–200.

Bacon, Francis. "Advancement of Learning." In *The Works of Francis Bacon*, edited by James Spedding, 275–498. London: Longman and Co., 1858.

_____. *The Letters and the Life of Francis Bacon*. Edited by James Spedding. vol I. London: Longman, Green, Longman and Roberts, 1861.

_____. "New Atlantis." In *Francis Bacon: The Major Work*, edited by Brian Vickers, 457–91. Oxford: Oxford University Press, 2002.

Bede. *The Ecclesiastical History of the English People*. Translated by Judith McClure and Roger Collins. Oxford: Oxford University Press, 1994.

_____. *On the Tabernacle*. Translated by Arthur G. Holder. Liverpool: Liverpool University Press, 1994.

_____. *On the Temple*. Translated by Sean Connolly. Edited by Jennifer O'Reilly. Liverpool: Liverpool University Press, 1995.

Benedict, Barbara M. *Curiosity: A Cultural History of Early Modern Inquiry*. Chicago: The University of Chicago Press, 2001.

Berger, Anna Maria Busse. *Medieval Music and the Art of Memory*. Berkeley: University of California Press, 2005.

Bishop of Rochester. "An Account of Want Related to the Publishing of Sir Isaac Newton's Chronology of Ancient Kingdoms Amended." In *The Chronology of Ancient Kingdoms Amended*. London: 1770.

Black, Jeremy. *Eighteenth Century Britian 1688–1783*. London: Palgrave, 2001.

Bloom, Harold. *William Blake*. London: Chelsea House Publishers, 2006.

Brewster, David. *Memoirs of the Life, Writings, and Discoveries of Sir Isaac Newton*. Vol. 1. Edinburgh: Thomas Constable and Co., 1855.

Briggs, Martin S. "Architectural Models I." *The Burlington Magazine for Connoisseurs* 54, no. 313 (1929): 174–75, 178–81, 183.

______. "Architectural Models II." *The Burlington Magazine for Connoisseurs* 54, no. 314 (1929): 245–47 and 50–52.

Buelow, George J. "Opera in Hamburg 300 Years Ago." *The Musical Times* 119, no. 1619 (1978): 26–28.

Bull, George Anthony. *Michelangelo: A Biography*. London: St. Martin's Press, 1998.

Cahn, Walter. "Architecture and Exegesis: Richard of St.-Victor's Ezekiel Commentary and Its Illustrations." *The Art Bulletin* 76, no. 1 (1994): 53–68.

Cajori, Florian. "Sir Isaac Newton's Early Study of the Apocalypse." *Popular Astronomy* XXXIV, no. 2 (1926): 75–78.

Calvin, John. *Institutes of the Christian Religion*. Translated by Henry Beveridge. Grand Rapids: W.M.B. Eerdman Publishing Company, 1957.

Campbell, Ian. "The New St. Peter's: Basilica or Temple?" *Oxford Art Journal* 4, no. 1 (1981): 3–8.

Cappel, Louis. "Chronologia Sacra." In *Biblia Sacra Polyglotta*, edited by Brian Walton, 1–39. London: 1657.

Carruthers, Mary. *The Craft of Thought: Mediation, Rhetoric, and the Imaging of Images, 400–1200*. Cambridge: Cambridge University Press, 2000.

Casini, Paola. "Newton, the Classical Scholia." *History of Science* 22 (1984): 1–57.

Chetwode Crawley, W.J. "Rabbi Jacob Jehudah Leon." *Ars Quatuor Coronatorum* 12 (1899): 150–63.

Clanchy, M.T. *Abelard: A Medieval Life*. Oxford: Blackwell, 1999.

"Classified Ads." *Daily Courant* London, Tuesday, February 2, Issue 9149 (1731): 2.

"Classified Advertisement." *Daily Courant* London, Thursday, November 12, Issue 9080 (1730): 2.

"Classified Advertisements." *Daily Journal* London, Friday, January 31, Issue 2517 (1729): 2.

"Classified Advertisement." *Daily Post* London, Friday, August 9, Issue 2772 (1728): 1.

"Classified Advertisement." *Daily Post* London, Tuesday, December 24, Issue 2887 (1728): 2.

"Classified Advertisements." *Daily Post* London, Monday, April 12, Issue 3608 (1731): 2.

Conduitt, John. "Drafts of Various Sections of Conduitt's Memoir." Unpublished manuscript, Cambridge: King's College, ca. 1728.

Conhen, I. Bernard, and Richard S. Westfall, eds. *Newton*. New York: W.W. Norton, 1995.

Crosby, Sumner McKnight. *The Royal Abbey of Saint-Denis: From Its Beginnings to the Death of Suger, 475–1151*. New Haven: Yale University Press, 1987.

Curl, James Stevens. *The Art and Architecture of Freemasonry*. London: B.T. Batsford, 1991.

De Castro, M.P. "To the Reader," in Jacob Jehudah Leon, *An Accurate Description of the Grand & Glorious Temple of Solomon*, translated by M. P. De Castro. London: 1778.

Dermott, Lawrence. *Ahiman Rezon*. London: 1764.

Descartes, Rene. "Cogitations Privatae." In *La Vie de Monsieur Descartes*, edited by Adrien Baillet, 81–86. Paris: 1691.

Dobbs, Betty Jo Teeter. *The Janus Faces of Genius*. Cambridge: Cambridge University Press, 2002.

______. "Newton's Commentary on the Emerald Tablet of Hermes Trismegistus." In *Its Scientific and Theological Significance, in Hermeticism and Renaissance: Intellectual History and the Occult in Early Modern Europe*, edited by Ingrid Merkel and Allen G. Debus. London: Associated University Presses, 1988.

Downes, Kerry. *The Architecture of Wren*. Over Wallop, Hampshire: Granada Publishing, 1988.

Edwards, Edward. *Lives of the Founders of the British Museum*. London: Routledge. 1996.
Edwards, Lewis. "Notes." *Ars Quatuor Coronatorum* 73, no. 1961 (1961): 52–54.
Ettlinger, L. D. *The Sistine Chapel before Michelangelo: Religious Imagery and Papal Primacy*. Oxford: The Clarendon Press, 1965.
Fara, Patricia. *Newton: The Making of Genius*. London: Picador, 2002.
Faur, Josè. "Newton, Maimonides, and Esoteric Knowledge." *Cross Currents* 40, no. 4 (1990): 526–538.
Fontes da Costa, Palmira. *Singular and the Making of Knowledge at the Royal Society of London in the Eighteenth Century*. Newcastle upon Tyne: Cambridge Scholars Publishing, 2013.
"For the Public Advertiser." *Public Advertiser* London, Wednesday April 19, Issue 16196 (1786): 3.
Gage, John. "Blake's Newton." *Journal of the Warburg and Courtauld Institutes* 34 (1971): 372–77.
Gjertsen, Derek. *The Newton Handbook*. London: Routledge and Kegan Paul, 1986.
Gleick, James. *Isaac Newton*. London: Fourth Estate, 2003.
Guasti, Cesare. ed. *Santa Maria Del Fiore: La Construzione*. Firenze: M. Ricci, 1887.
Guicciardini, Niccolò. *Isaac Newton on Mathematical Certainty and Method*. Cambridge, MA: MIT Press, 2009.
Hall, A. Rupert. *Isaac Newton: Adventurer in Thought*. Cambridge: Cambridge University Press, 1992.
Harrison, John. *The Library of Isaac Newton*. Cambridge: Cambridge University Press, 1978.
Hart, Vaughan. *Art and Magic in the Court of the Stuarts*. London: Routledge, 1994.
Herrmann, Wolfgang. "Unknown Designs for the Temple of Jerusalem." In *Essays in the History of Architecture*, edited by Douglas Fraser, Howard Hibbard and Milton J. Lewine. Bath: Pitman Press, 1969.
Houston, Chloë. *The Renaissance Utopia: Dialogue, Travel and the Ideal Society*. Farnham: Ashgate, 2014.
Hunt, Thomas. "Preface." In *The Chronology of Ancient Kingdoms Amended*. London: 1754.
Ignatius of Loyola. *Personal Writings: Reminiscences, Spiritual Diary, Selected Letters Including the Text of "the Spiritual Exercises."* Translated by Joseph A. Munitiz and Philip Endean. London: Penguin, 1996.
Inwood, Stephen. *The Man Who Knew Too Much*. London: Pan Books, 2002
Jedin, Hubert. *Crisis and Closure of the Council of Trent*. London: Sheed and Ward, 1967.
Jue, Jeffrey K. *Heaven Upon Earth: Joseph Mede (1586–1638) and the Legacy of Millenarianism*. Dordrecht: Springer, 2006.
Korey, Michael. "The Temple of Solomon and the Jewish Cabinet in the Dresden Zwinger: A Search for Their Historical Traces." In *Fragments of Memory*, edited by Michael Korey and Thomas Ketelsen, 12–25. Dresden: Deutscher Kunstverlag, 2010.
Kruft, Hanno-Walter. *A History of Architectural Theory: From Vitruvius to the Present*. New York Princeton Architectural Press, 1994.
Kubrin, David. "Newton and the Cyclical Cosmos: Providence and the Mechanical Philosophy." *Journal of the History of Ideas* 28, no. 3 (1967): 325–46.
Lee, Samuel. *Orbis Miraculum, or, the Temple of Solomon, Pourtrayed by Scripture-Light Wherein All Its Famous Buildings, the Pompous Worship of the Jewes, with Its Attending Rites and Ceremonies, the Several Officers Employed in That Work, with Their Ample Revenues, and the Spiritual Mysteries of the Gospel Railed under All, Are Treated of at Large*. London: Printed by John Streater for Abell Roper, 1659.
Leon, Jacob Jehudah. *An Accurate Description of the Grand and Glorious Temple of Solomon*. Translated by M.P. Decastre. London: 1778.
_______. *Afbeeldinghe Vanden Templel Salomonis*. Amsterdam: 1642.

_____. *De Templo Hierosolymi*. Translated by Johanne Saubertus. London: 1665.

_____. "Faksimile Eines Kolorierten Stich Des Zeltheiligtums." Amsterdam: 1647.

_____. *A Relation of the Most Memorable Thinges in the Tabernacle of Moses and the Temple of Solomon According to Text of Scripture*. Amsterdam: 1675.

_____. *Retrato Del Tabernaculo De Moseh*. Amsterdam: 1654.

_____. *Retrato Del Templo De Selomoh*. Amsterdam: 1642.

_____. *Tratado De Los Cherubim*. Amsterdam: 1654.

Leon, Jacob Jehudah, and Johanne Saubertus. *De Templo Hierosolymitano*. Helmæstadi: 1665.

Lewittes, Mendell, ed. *The Code of Maimonides (Mishneh Tornh)*: *Book Eight, the Book of Temple Service*. New Haven: Yale University Press, 1957.

Logan, F. Donald. *A History of the Church in the Middle Ages*. London: Routledge, 2002.

Lomas, Robert. *The Invisible College: The Royal Society, Freemasonry and the Birth of Modern Science*. London: Headline Book Publishing, 2002.

MacGregor, Arthur. "The Cabinet of Curiosities in Seventeenth Century Britiain." In *The Origins of Museums: The Cabinet of Curiosities in Sixteenth and Seventeenth-Century Europe*, edited by Oliver Impey and Arthur MacGregor, 201–15. London: House of Stratus, 2001.

Mamiani, Maurizio. "Newton on Prophecy and the Apocalypse." In *The Cambridge Companion to Newton*, edited by I. Bernard Cohen and George E. Smith. Cambridge: Cambridge University Press, 2002.

Manuel, Frank E. *Isaac Newton: Historian*. Cambridge: Cambridge University Press, 1963.

_____. *A Portrait of Isaac Newton*. Cambridge, MA: The Belknap Press of Harvard University Press, 1968.

McGuire, James E., and Martin Tamny. *Certain Philosophical Questions: Newton's Trinity Notebook*. Cambridge: Cambridge University Press, 1983.

McNally, Robert E. *The Council of Trent, the "Spiritual Exercises," and the Catholic Reform*. Philadelphia: Fortress Press, 1970.

Mede, Joseph. *Clavis Apocalyptica or a Prophetical Key*. London, 1651.

Millon, Henry A., and Vittorio Magnago Lampugnani. *The Renaissance from Brunelleschi to Michelangelo: The Representation of Architecture*. London: Thames and Hudson, 1994.

Morrison, Tessa. "Bede and the Temple of Solomon." *The Journal of the Australian Early Medieval Association* 3 (2007).

_____. "The Body, the Temple and the Newtonian Conundrum." *Nexus: Architecture and Mathematics* 12, no. 2 (2010): 342–52.

_____. *Isaac Newton's Temple of Solomon and His Reconstruction of Sacred Architecture*. Basel: Birkhauser, 2011.

_____. *The Origins of Architecture: An English Sixteenth to Eighteenth Century Perspective*. Champaign, IL: Common Ground, 2014.

_____. "The Paradox of the Divine Architecture in Dante's '*La Divina Commedia*.'" *International Journal of Humanities* 8, no. 2 (2010): 295–310.

_____. "Planning to Welcome the Pilgrims of the Middle Ages." *The Journal of the Australian Early Medieval Association* 5 (2009): 147–64.

_____. "Villalpando's Sacred Architecture in the Light of Isaac Newton's Commentary." In *Nexus VII, Architecture and Mathematics*, edited by Kim Williams, 79–91. Turin: Kim Williams Books, 2008.

Morrison, Tessa, and Michael Ostwald. "Shifting Dimensions: The Architectural Model in History." In *Homo Faber: Modelling Architecture*, edited by Mark Bury, Michael Ostwald, Peter Downton and Andrea Mina, 142–57. Melbourne: SIAL, Melbourne Museum and Archadia Press, 2007.

Murrin, Michael. "Newton's Apocalypse." In *Newton and Religion: Context, Nature, and Influence*, edited by James E. Force and Richard H. Popkin. Dordrecht: Kluwer Academic Publishers, 1999.

Narkiss, M. "The Oeuvre of the Jewish Engraver Salom Italia." *Tarbiz: A Quarterly of Jewish Studies* XXVI, no. 1 (1956): v–viii.

Newton, Isaac. "Appendix A—of Natures Obvious Laws & Processes in Vegetation." In *The Janus Faces of Genius*, edited by B.J.T. Dobbs. Cambridge: Cambridge University Press, 2002.

______. *The Chronology of Ancient Kingdoms Amended*. London: Histories and Mysteries of Man, 1988.

______. "Commentarium." In *The Janus Faces of Genius*, edited by B.J.T. Dobbs. Cambridge: Cambridge University Press, 2002.

______. "A Dissertation Upon the Sacred Cubit of the Jews." In *Miscellaneous Works of John Greaves Professor of Geometry at Oxford*. Londres: 1737.

______. "Drafts Concerning Solomon's Temple and the Sacred Cubit." In *Yahuda Ms 2*. Unpublished manuscript, Jerusalem: National Library of Israel, ca. 1680.

______. "Extract from 'the Original of Religions.'" In *Yahuda Ms 41*. Unpublished manuscript, Jerusalem: National Library of Israel, undated.

______. *Fair Copies of the 'Short Chronicle" and "Chronology of Ancient Kingdoms Amended."* Unpublished manuscript, Cambridge: Cambridge University Library. Additional Ms 3988, undated.

______. "Fragments on the Kingdoms of the European Tribes, the Temple and the History of Jewish and Christian Churches." In *Yahuda Ms 28*. Unpublished manuscript, Jerusalem: National Library of Israel, ca. 1675.

______. "Introduction to the Lexicon of the Prophets, Part Two: About the Appearance of the Jewish Temple." In *Isaac Newton's Temple of Solomon and His Reconstruction of Sacred Architecture*, edited by Tessa Morrison, 105–56. Basel: Birkhauser, 2011.

______. "Irenicum." In *Keynes Ms 3*. Unpublished manuscript, Cambridge: King's College, undated.

______. *Miscellaneous Notes and Extracts on the Temple, the Fathers, Prophecy, Church History, Doctrinal Issues, Etc.* Unpublished manuscript, Jerusalem: National Library of Israel, undated.

______. *Notes from Buxtorf.* Unpublished manuscript, Jerusalem: National Library of Israel, undated.

______. *Notes on Villalpando*. Unpublished manuscript, Jerusalem: National Library of Israel, undated.

______. *Observations on the Prophecies of Daniel and the Apocalypse of St. John*. Lewiston: The Edwin Mellen Press, 1999.

______. *Observations Upon the Prophecies*. Edited by Samuel Horsley. London: Opera omnia, 1785.

______. "Of an Universall Language " *Modern Languages Review* LII, no. 1 (1957): 7–18.

______. "The Original of Religions." In *Yahuda Ms 41*. Unpublished manuscript, Jerusalem: Jewish National and University Library, undated.

______. *Questiones Quaedam Philosophiae*. Unpublished manuscript, Cambridge: Cambridge University Library, early 1660s.

______. *The Seven Chapters*. Cambridge: Unpublished manuscript, Cambridge: King's College, late ca. 1680s.

______. *Translation and Transcription of the 'Tabula Smaragdina' of Hermes Trismegistus*. Unpublished manuscript, Cambridge: King's College, ca. 1680–1690.

______. "Treatise on Revelation (Section 2)." In *Yahuda Ms 9.2*. Unpublished manuscript, Jerusalem: National Library of Israel, undated.

______. "A Treatise or Remarks on Solomon's Temple Introduction to the Lexicon of the Prophets, Part Two: About the Appearance (Form) of the Jewish Temple." In *Babson College Ms 434*. Unpublished manuscript, Wellesley, Massachusetts: ca. mid–1680.

______. "Two Incomplete Treatises on Prophecy." In *Keynes Ms 5*. Unpublished manuscript, Cambridge: King's College Library, undated (ca. 1680s).

______. "Two Incomplete Treatises on the Vegetative Growth of Metals and Minerals." In *NMAHRB Ms 1007 B*. Unpublished manuscript, Washington: Dibner Library, Smithsonian Institute, 1670–1675.

Offenberg, A. K. "Bibliography of the Works of Jacob Jehudah Leon (Templo)." *Studia Rosenthaliana* 12, July (1978): 111–32.

______. "Dirk Van Santen and the Keur Bible: New Insights into Jacob Judah (Arye) Leon Templo's Model Temple." *Studia Rosenthaliana* 37 (2004): 401–21.

______. "Jacob Jehuda Leon (1602–1675) and His Model of the Temple." In *Jewish-Christian Relations in the Seventeenth Century*, edited by J. van den Berg and Ernestine G. E. van der Wall, 95–115. Dordrecht: Kluwer Academic Publishers, 1988.

______. "Jacob Judah Leon Templo's Broadsheet of His Model of the Temple." In *Bibliotheca: Treasures of Jewish Booklore*, edited by A. K. Offenberg, Emile G. J. Schrijver and F. J. Hoogewoud, 32–33. Amsterdam: Amsterdam University Press, 1994.

Osborne, Thomas (Bookseller). *A Catalogue of a Choice and Valuable Collection of Books: Being the Libraries of a Late Eminent Serjeant at Law, and of Dr. Edmund Halley, Late Astronomer Royal ... Which Will Begin to Be Sold, the Price Marked in Each Book, at T. Osborne's Shop ... On Thursday the Twentieth of May ... Where Is Also to Be Sold as It Was Sent from the Holy Land, as a Present to the Said Late Doctor, a Most Curious and Compleat Model of the Whole Temple of Christ's Sepulchre at Jerusalem...* London: 1742.

Panofsky, Erwin. *Abbot Suger*. Princeton: Princeton University Press, 1948.

Pearce, Susan. "Introduction." In *Lives of the Founders of the British Museum*, edited by Edward Edwards, i–xxxiii. London: Routledge, 1996.

Perrault, Claude. *Ordonnance Des Cinq Espèces De Colonnes*. Paris: 1683.

Philo. "On the Life of Moses." In *The Works of Philo*, edited by C. D. Yonge, 459–517. Peabody: Hendrickson Publishers, 2004.

Picciotto, James. *Sketches of Anglo-Jewish History*. London: Trubner and Co., 1875.

Plato. *Plato's Republic*. Translated by G. M. A. Grube. Indianapolis: Hackett Publishing Company, 1974.

Popkin, Richard H., and David S. Katz. "The Prefaces by Menasseh Ben Israel and Jacob Judah Leon Templo to the Vocalised Mishnah (1646)." In *Jewish-Christian Relations in the Seventeenth Century*, edited by J. van den Berg and Ernestine G.E. van der Wall, 151–53. Dordrecht: Kluwer Academic Publishers, 1988.

Porter, Roy. *Enlightenment: Britain and the Creation of the Modern World*. London: Penguin, 2000.

Principle, Lawrence M. *The Aspiring Adept: Robert Boyle and His Alchemical Quest*. Princeton, NJ: Princeton University Press, 1998.

Ptolemy. *The Almagest*. Translated by R. Catesby Taliaferro. Chicago: Encyclopaedia Britannica, 1955.

Purkiss, Dianne. *The English Civil War: Papists, Gentlewomen, Soldiers, and Witchfinders in the Birth of Modern Britain*. New York: Basic Books, 2006.

Purver, Margery. *The Royal Society: Concept and Creation*. London: Routledge, 2013.

Ramírez, Juan Antonio, Rene Taylor, Andre Corboz, Robert Jan van Pelt, and Antonio Martínez Ripoll, eds. *Dios Arquitecto*. Madrid: Ediciones Siruela, 1991.

Rosenau, Helen. "Jacob Judah Leon Templo's Contribution to Architectural Imagery." *Journal of Jewish Studies* XXIII, no. 1 (1972): 72–81.

______. *Vision of the Temple: The Image of the Temple of Jerusalem in Judaism and Christianity.* London: Oresko Books Ltd., 1979.

Rossi, Paolo. *Logic and the Art of Memory: The Quest for a Universal Language.* Translated by Stephen Clucas. Chicago: University of Chicago Press, 2006.

Rykwert, Joseph. "Theory as Rhetoric: Leon Battista Alberti in Theory and in Practice." In *Paper Palaces: The Rise of the Renaissance*, edited by Vaughan Hart and Peter Hicks, 33–50. New Haven: Yale University Press, 1998.

Ryland, Harry. "Rabbi Jacab Jehudan Leon." *Freemason*, no. 22 July (1882): 414.

______. "Schott's Model of Solomon's Temple." *Ars Quatuor Coronatorum* 13 (1900): 24–25.

Sakellarakis, J. A. *Herakleion Museum.* Athens: Ekdotike Athenon, 2001.

Saubertus, Johanne, and Jacob Jehudah Leon. *De Templo Hierosolymitano.* Helmæstadi, 1665.

Schuchard, Marsha Keith. "Dr. Samuel Jacob Falk: A Sabbation Adventurer in the Masonic Underground." In *Jewish Messianism in the Early Modern World*, edited by Matt Goldish and Richard H. Popkin, 203–26. Dordrecht: Kluwer Academic Publishers, 2001.

______. *Restoring the Temple of Vision.* Leiden: Brill, 2002.

Schwartz, Gary. "The Temple Mount in the Lowlands." In *The Dutch Intersection: The Jews and the Netherlands in Modern History*, edited by Yosef Kaplan, 111–22. Leiden: Brill, 2008.

Shalev, Zur. "Sacred Geography, Antiquarianism and Visual Erudition: Benito Arias Montano and the Maps in the Antwerp Polyglot Bible." *Imago Mundi* 55 (2003): 56–80.

Shane, Al L. "Jacob Judah Leon of Amsterdam (1602–1675) and His Models of the Temple of Solomon and the Tabernacle." *Ars Quatuor Coronatorum* 96 (1983): 145–69.

Snobelen, Stephen D. "To Discourse of God: Isaac Newton's Heterodox Theology and His Natural Philosophy." In *Science and Dissent in England, 1688–1945*, edited by Paul Wood, 39–65. London: Ashgate, 2004.

Stillman, Robert E. *The New Philosophy and Universal Languages in Seventeenth Century England.* London: Associated University Presses, 1995.

Strong, Roy. *Britannia Triumphans: Inigo Jones, Rubens and Whitehall Palace.* Hampshire: Thames and Hudson, 1980.

Stukeley, William. "The Creation, Music of the Spheres K[ing] S[olomon's] Temple Microco[sm] and Macrocosm Compared &C." In *FM Ms 1130 Stu (2).* London: Freemasons Library, 1721–24.

______. *The Family Memoirs of the Rev William Stukeley Md and the Antiquarians and Other Correspondence of William Stukeley, Roger and Samuel Gales Etc.* Edinburgh: William Blackwood, 1883.

______. *Memoirs of Sir Isaac Newton's Life.* London: Taylor and Francis, 1936.

The Temple of Solomon with All Its Porches, Walls, Gates, Halls, Chambers, Holy Vessels, the Altar of Burnt-Offering, the Molten-Sea, Golden-Candlesticks, Shew-Bread Tables, Altar of Incense, the Ark of the Covenant, with the Mercy-Seat, the Cherubims Etc London, 1725.

Thomson, James. *The Works of Mr James Thomson.* London, 1802.

"To Be Sold at Auction." *Public Advertiser* London, Wednesday, October 26, Issue 14063 (1774): 3.

"To Be Sold by Auction.' *Gazetteer and New Daily Advertiser* London, Thursday, April 27 (1769): 3.

Trismegist, Hermes. "Tabula Saragdina." In *The Janus Faces of Genius*, edited by B.J.T. Dobbs. Cambridge: Cambridge University Press, 2002.

Turner, Harold W. *From Temple to Meeting House. The Phenomenology and Theology of Places of Worship*. New York: Mouton Publishers, 1979.

van der Wall, Ernestine G. E. "Without Partialities Towards All Men: John Durie on the Dutch Hebraist Adam Boreel." In *Jewish-Christian Relations in the Seventeenth Century*, edited by J. van den Berg and Ernestine G.E. van der Wall, 145–49. Dordrecht: Kluwer Academic Publishers, 1988.

van Rooden, Peter. "The Jews and Religious Toleration in the Dutch Republic." In *Calvinism and Religious Toleration in the Dutch Golden Age*, edited by Ronnie Pochia Hsia and Henk van Nierop, 132–47. Cambridge: Cambridge University Press, 2001.

______. *Theology, Biblical Scholarship and Rabbinical Studies in the Seventeenth Century*. Leiden: Brill, 1989.

Vasari, Giorgio. *Lives of the Most Eminent Painters, Sculptors and Architects*. Translated by Gaston du C. de Vere. New York: Harry N. Abrams, 1979.

Villalpando, Juan Bautista, and Hieronymus Prado. *Ezechielem Explanationes Et Apparatus Urbis Hierosolymitani Commentariis Et Imaginibus Illustratus*: Romae, 1604.

Vitruvius. *The Ten Books on Architecture*. Translated by Morris Hicky Morgan. New York: Dover Publications, 1960.

von Simson, Otto. *The Gothic Cathedral: Origins of Gothic Architecture and the Medieval Concept of Order*. Princeton: Princeton University Press, 1984.

Wallace, Ronald S. *Calvin, Geneva and the Reformation*. Edinburgh: Scottish Academic Press, 1988.

Westfall, Richard S. *The Life of Isaac Newton*. Cambridge: Cambridge University Press, 1993.

______. *Never at Rest: A Biography of Isaac Newton*. Cambridge: Cambridge University Press, 1980.

Whiston, William. "A Collection of Authentick Records Belonging to the Old and New Testament." London: The British Library, 1727.

______. *Memoirs of the Life and Writings of Mr William Whiston*. London: 1749.

______. "To Caleb Dánvers." *Country Journal or the Craftsman*. London, Saturday, January 17, Issue 185 (1930).

White, Michael. *Isaac Newton: The Last Sorcerer*. London: Fourth Estate, 1998.

Whitmer, Kelly J. "The Model That Never Moved: The Case of a Virtual Memory Theater and Its Christian Philosophical Argument, 1700–1732." *Science in Context* 23, no. 3 (2010): 1–39.

Williams, J. *The Illustrated Beatus: A Corpus of the Illustrations of the Commentary on the Apocalypse*. London: Harvey, 1998.

Wilton-Ely, John. "The Architectural Model " *Architectural Review* 104 (1967): 27–32.

______. "The Architectural Model: English Baroque." *Apollo* 88 (1968): 250–59.

______. "The Architectural Models of Sir John Soane: A Catalogue." *Architectural History* 12 (1969): 5–38.

Wishnitzer, R. "Maimonides' Drawing of the Temple." *Journal of Jewish Art* 1 (1974): 16–27.

Wittkower, Rudolf. *Architectural Principles in the Age of Humanism*. London: Academy Editions, 1988.

Wolf, Lucien "Anglo-Jewish Coat of Arms." *The Jewish Historical Society of England* (1893/4): 153–69.

Worp, J. A. *Rijks Geschiedkundige Publikaten* 32 (1917): 274–75.

Wotton, Henry. *The Elements of Architecture*. Amsterdam: Da Capo Press, 1979.

Wren, Christopher. *Life and Works of Sir Christopher Wren. From the Parentalia or Memoirs by His Son Christopher*. London: 1750.

______. *Parentalia: Memoirs of the Family of the Wrens*. Londres: 1750.

Wromald, Francis. "The Throne of Solomon and St. Edward's Chair." In *De Artibus Opuscula XI: Essays in Honor of Erwin Panofsky*, edited by Millard Meiss, 51–69. New York: New York University Press, 1961.

Yates, Frances A. *The Art of Memory*. Chicago: The University of Chicago Press, 1966.

______. *Giordano Bruno and the Hermetic Tradition* London: Routledge, 2002.

______. *Theatre of the World*. London: Routledge and Kegan Paul, 1969.

Zwart, Jac. "Oud-Hollandse Modellen Van De Temple Van Salomo." *Historia Maandschrift voor Geschiedenis en Kunstgeschiedenis* 4 (1938): 277–82, 307–10, 81–85.

Index

www.ingramcontent.com/pod-product-compliance
Ingram Content Group UK Ltd.
Pitfield, Milton Keynes, MK11 3LW, UK
UKHW041842150726
7214IPUK00015B/111